ENRICO ACERBI

THE AUSTRIAN
1805-1809 vol

GRENZER, LANDWEHR & ELITE FORCES

KAISERLICHE-KÖNIGLICHE HEER

SOLDIERS&WEAPONS 030

THE AUTHOR

Dr.Enrico Acerbi born in Valdagno (Vicenza - Italy) on 13.8.1952; graduated in Medicine, expert in Toxicology, worked as Blood Transfusionist in local Hospital, now retired and living in Valdagno (Vicenza), partner of the War Museum of Rovereto, member of the Napoleonic Association of Italy and historiographer of the Great War. Enrico Acerbi developed historical Research during the '90s. For five years he collaborated with the Center for Great War Studies at Asiago. He also collaborated with the "Montane Community" of Arsiero as Teacher at the so called Popular University (historical training courses on the First World War) and with the Montane Community Agno-Chiampo (reconstruction of the fortifications made in the Great War). Partner of the Italian War Museum of Rovereto and founding member of the Great War Historical Research Group of Valdagno, currently entrusted to the study of Napoleonic history in Veneto and Italy. Graphic illustrator of articles on Napoleonic history. He has already published several history subjects.

NOTE EDITORIALI

Tutto il contenuto dei nostri libri, in qualsiasi forma prodotti (cartacei, elettronici o altro) quando non diversamente specificato è copyright soldiershop.com. I diritti di traduzione, riproduzione, memorizzazione con qualsiasi mezzo, digitale, fotografico, fotocopie ecc. Sono riservati per tutti i Paesi. Nessuna delle immagini presenti nei nostri libri può essere riprodotta senza il permesso scritto di soldiershop.com. L'Editore rimane a disposizione degli eventuali aventi diritto per tutte le fonti iconografiche dubbie o non identificate. I marchi Soldiershop Publishing, Bookmoon, Museum s e relative collane sono di proprietà di soldiershop.com o Luca Cristini Editore; di conseguenza qualsiasi uso esterno non è consentito.

PUBLISHING'S NOTES

None of unpublished images or text of our book may be reproduced in any format without the expressed written permission of Soldiershop.com when not indicate as marked with license creative commons 3.0 or 4.0. Soldiershop Publishing has made every reasonable effort to locate, contact and acknowledge rights holders and to correctly apply terms and conditions to Content. In the event that any Content infringes your rights or the rights of any third parties, or Content is not properly identified or acknowledged we would like to hear from you so we may make any necessary alterations. In this event contact: info@soldiershop.com. Our trademark: Soldiershop Publishing @, The names of our series & brand: Museum book, Bookmoon, Soldiers&Weapons, Battlefield, War in colour, Historical Biographies, Darwin's view, Fabula, Altrastoria, Italia Storica Ebook, Witness To History, Soldiers, Weapons & Uniforms, Storia etc. are herein @ by Soldiershop.com.

LICENSES COMMONS

This book may utilize part of material marked with license creative commons 3.0 or 4.0 (CC BY 4.0), (CC BY-ND 4.0), (CC BY-SA 4.0) or (CCo 1.0). Or derived from publication 70 years old or more and recolored from us. We give appropriate attribution credit and indicate if change were made in the acknowledgements field.
All our books utilize only fonts licensed under the SIL Open Font License or other free use license.

ACKNOWLEDGMENT

I would particularly like to thank Robert Burnham of http://www.napoleon-series.org and all the friends, who participate in this very interesting website; above all Mr. Robert Ouvrard and Mr. Leopold Kudma. Thanks also to István Nagy for having send me part of his interesting works and articles (also if reading them in Hungarian language it had been an hard task to perform). Many thanks also to Prof. Vladimir Brnardić of Zagreb for having provided considerable assistance with the Croatian sources. Finally thanks to "The 1809 International Research Society" for the Certificate of Honour they gave to m for this work about the "Kaiserlich-königlich Armée". Naturally, a special thanks to Soldiershop for giving me this beautiful opportunity.

ISBN: 9788893273701   1st edition September 2018

Title: Soldiers&Weapons 030 - **The Austrian army 1805-1809 - vol. 2 - Grenzer, landwehr & elite forces**
by Enrico Acerbi
Editor: Luca Cristini Editore, for the brand: Soldiershop. Cover & Art Design: Luca S. Cristini.

In cover: Landwehr, grenzer and border troops 1805-1809 (Ottendeld artwork)

PREFACE

Can we shed some light on the evolution of the Austrian infantry Uniforms of the Military Border? Csákó is an ancient hungarian word which means "tall hat". (Dr. Ida Bobula tells it came from a Sumerian root through Medians, Dacians etc.) It was the Hussar hat. In 1792 the "Grenzer", who went also in Italy, were so equipped:

Grenz-Scharfschütze (and probably Gyulai Freikorps)
- Casquet like infantry (the Austrian called the pre-1798 hat, Kasket, while the after 1798 was called Helmet) .. Kasket was not a Csako.
- white coat, cutting and facing like regular infantry, small "Börtchen" and lapels attached to straps, white trousers with hungarian lining.

Grenzinfanterist:
- Filzmütze (this was the official name for the Klobuk, a Csako .. tall hat) with small black-yellow pompons.
- white coat (but those from Slavonia had dark brown hunting suites) cut as hungarian coats, [mit verschiedenfärbiger Aufschlagfarbe, Schößenklappen nicht egalisiert], white trousers with hungarian lines, [Verschnürung in] facing colours, later black-yellow. "Riemzeug" white.

Grenzartillerist
- like Scharfschütze (not Klobuks)
- coat same of Scharfschütze but with regimental facings
- white trousers with hungarian lines
- Tornister sack with a lace embroidered with a small gun
- Hungarian sabre

All had Home-uniforms with dark brown coats and trousers. Home uniforms had to be woven with local fabrics. It was decided to adopt the black color. Unfortunately, the colour did not hold the washing procedure and tended to fade into a dark brown color that, over the years became the official one of the "Grenzer" jackets.

Note: not everyone knows that the official coat colour of the later regular "k.k. artilleristen" wasn't Brown but "Rehfarben" a sort of reddish brown similar to the fox fur.

It was in December 23, 1795, that Gränzberichtigung was written. In it:

Von der Mondir=und Uniformirung (sic) The Grenzer must wear the Aerarial=Montur. In the Grenz Service this consists in: 1 Csako, 1 Mantel, 1 black coat von Haustuch (a sort of square apron in an extremely hard-wearing quality with side-sewn tie-bands), ... as said the repeated washing of those coats maybe did cause the black hue fading to the known dark brown, 1 white corsage (Leibel), 1 pair of white trousers and a pair of Bundschuh (traditional historic leather shoes tied with a long strap).

source: Johann Christian von Engel, Staatskunde und Geschichte von Dalmatien, Croatien un Slawonien, J.J. Gebauer, 1798

Die Adjustierungsvorschrift v.J. 1798 told that the men equiped with Klobuks could retain the same hats; that in absence of leather sacks (Tornistern) they can carry linen (Leinen) knapsacks. This probably generated a bit confusion.

The initial sign of a change came in 1805. The coats became the same of regular infantry but with a dark brown hue. The Klobuk got a Sonnen- und Nackenschirm (front and back screen) .. And this was a true Csako!

In a "Montursentwurf für ein ausmarschierendes Grenzbataillon v.J. 1805"was written:

Klobuk with Rose, coat with Facings and "Leibel", cravat, including buckle, Hungarian blue pants, heavy mantle (Rockelor), underwear, Hungarian shoes, calfskin backpacks, cartridge-box and belt, bayonet including belt "Überschwungriemen", belts for pants and "Flienten", battery cover, camp cap (Holzmütze) and mittens.

(source Johann Karger, Die Entwicklung der Adjustierung, Rüstung und Bewaffnung der österreichisch-ungarischen Armee 1700-1809, LTR-Verlag, 1998

Artillerymen, however, did receive corsican hats, not Csakos. So I think is difficult to state what was the hat of Grenz artillery unless considering the 1795 term Czako equal to Klobuk.

Enrico Acerbi

CONTENTS :

The Grenzer corps .... Pag. 05
The Austrian Landwehr in 1809 .... Pag. 41
The Hungarian Insurrectio as in 1809 .... Pag. 81
The lost districts .... Pag. 93
The Austrian feldjager battalion 1809 .... Pag. 97
The Austrian order of battle 1809 .... Pag. 107

▲ Archdukes Karl of Austria in battle I, by P.J.Krafft

THE GRENZER CORPS
MILITARY BORDER SYSTEM AND DISTRICTS

INTRODUCTION TO THE MILITARY BORDER SYSTEM

After 1699 the Border of the Habsburg Empire was definitely stabilized on the rivers Sava and the Danube. A conflict between military and church authorities broke out on the issue of organization of the newly conquered regions. The bishops and Court Chamber tried to turn as many peasants as possible into serfdom, while the Generals tended to have them all in military service for the new parts of the Border. The status of the Border Guard was favoured among the population, and it was very difficult to distinguish the guardsmen from the contributors. It was done in 1703, although incompletely, so that the chaos of the disposition of population continued during whole first half of the eighteenth century, until the reforms of Maria Theresa in 1740s.

During the first half of the eighteenth century the disposition of the population, as well as the division between the paor (serfs) and military men was completely chaotic. Bandits and uprisings spread all over the area. The Border was organized no sooner than the middle of the century, when the reforms were issued by Maria Theresa. During the "War for Austrian Succession" (1741-1748) the Border troops were to be used in European battlefields, so that the standardization and unification of the Border were initiated. In 1743 the Empress dissolved the Kriegsrat in Graz, and in 1748 the maintenance of the Border was transferred to the state budget, and the administration handed over to the Hofkriegsrat. The forming of regiments was ended until 1750.19 In 1754 the reforms were rounded up with new administrative and court regulations, named Militaer-Grenz-Rechten.

The border was divided into 11 regiments. The Upper Border consisted of four: the regiments of Lika, Otocac, Ogulin and Slunj. The Banal Border was divided into two regiments: the first and the second Banal regiment. The Lower Border, i.e., the Border of Slavonia, consisted of five regiments: the regiments of Križevci, Gjurgevci, Gradiška, Brod and Petrovaradin.

Thus, in the era of Enlightened Absolutism, the process of reconstruction of the Military Border was completed and it became subordinated directly to the Court as a corpus separatum and the ruler's instrument. Thus, the constant conflict with the estates was originated. Since the estates did not want to bear costs for the defence any

RECRUITMENT
MILITÄR GRENZE
AND
HUNGARIAN DISTRICTS
CROATIA-SLAVONIA AND SERBIA
1805-1809

▲ Austro-Hungarian Landwehr, grenzer and border troops 1805-1809 about. From Ottenfeld artwork

longer, and the Court could not do it, the military fief for the support of the communal household was established. Thus, the fief became the basis and the main source of the communal household economic independence. Beside the military fief, the basis of the military organization was the **zadruga** (joint family household) and regiment organization. Some convulsions occurred when županije (comitats) were divided from the Border. That, however, brought stabilization of population and more favourable economic conditions.

To the end of the Border history (until 1873), no significant changes in the Border organization occurred. Its importance was decreasing; it was incapable to adapt to the demands of the time, both in military and economic respect. In 1787, Joseph II attempted to share the power between the military and civilian authorities in the regiments. This corresponded to his ideas about the functioning of a modern state, but after his death this experiment, as well as most of his reforms, failed. The last attempt to modernize the Border - the reforms of Archduke Karl - occurred at the beginning of the next century, in 1803, but it was also a failure. The frontiersmen supported themselves by tilling the soil, without any time spare to learn new military skills.

Military Border Territories (Militär Grenze) 1809. An year to be forgotten

In 1809 every one of the 17 regiments had 2 battalions with a strength of around 2966 (among them were 44 artillerymen and 240 snipers or scharfschützen). Every regiment had one Reserve (third) battalion (Kader) of 1437 men and the 13 regular Grenzregiments had also a Landwehr (or Insurrectio) battalion of 675 men (i.e. the Warasdin brigade of the Insurrectio had a strength of 10000 men). In order to avoid gaps from desertions, the Landwehr coys had to be made with 200 men (instead of the 180 men regular companies). The Reserve and Landwehr battalion were organized after the August 20, 1808 Order of the Grenze-commander in chief, archduke Louis of Austria. The third or Reserve battalions had 1171 men (six coys of 180 men) while the Landwehr (IV battalions) had 1291 men (six coys of 200).

The Szekler Hussars had 8 squadrons and the Tchaikjsten battalion had 1000 men in field. All the Grenzer's manpower was, so, around 100.000 men.

The staff and company organization of the grenz regiments were as follows:

Regimental Staff before the 1809 French rule:

1	Oberst (Colonel)	6	Cadets
1	Oberstleutnant (Lieutenant Colonel)	9	Quartermaster sergeants
2	Major (Majors)	1	Regimental Auditor
1	Catholic Chaplain (Croatians)	1	Regimental Accountant
		1	Regimental Adjutant
		1	Provost
1	Regimental Surgeon	6	Assistant Surgeons
2	Battalion Adjutants	2	Senior Surgeons
6	Domestics or Servants	1	Regimental Drummer
6	Standard bearers	8	musicians

Companies (battalions):

8	Hauptleute (Captains)	18	Sergeant-majors
4	Capitanlieutenants	12	Fourierschützen (Batmen)
12	Oberlieutenants (Senior lieutenants)	24	Drummers
12	Unterlieutenants (Junior lieutenants)	144	Corporals
12	Fähnrichs (Cadets)	24	Carpenters
36	Domestics or Servants	50	Artillerists
2,160	Fusiliers (battalion)		
2,516	Total		

In the year of Wagram they were so distributed:
Regular Army

the 2 batt. of Grenzregiment n. 9 Petrovaradin (Peterwardein) under the III Corps.
the 2 batt. of Grenzregiment n. 12 Deutsch-Banater of Pancsova under the IV Corps.
the 2 batt. of Grenzregiment n. 13 Wallachisch-Illyrisches (Karansebes) under the IV Corps
the 2 batt. of Grenzregiment n. 7 Brod an der Sava under the V Corps
the 2 batt. of Grenzregiment n. 8 Nova Gradiska under the V Corps
the 2 batt. of Grenzregiment n. 5 Varazdin (Kreuzer) under the VI Corps
the 2 batt. of Grenzregiment n. 6 Varazdin (St.Georger) under the VI Corps

the 2 batt. of Grenzregiment n. 14 Szekler under the VII Corps in Poland.
the 2 batt. of Grenzregiment n. 15 Siebenbürgisches-Romänen (Transylvania) under the VII Corps
the 8 sqns. of the Szekler Hussars under the VII Corps
the 2 batt. of Grenzregiment n. 10 or First Banal (Glina) under the VIII corps
the 2 batt. of Grenzregiment n. 11 or second Banal (Petrinja) under the VIII Corps
the 2 batt. of Grenzregiment n. 3 Ogulin under the IX corps
the 2 batt. of Grenzregiment n. 4 Szluin under the IX Corps
the 2 batt. of Grenzregiment n. 2 Otoschatz (Otočac) under the IX Corps

GrenzCorps general Stojčević (with one sqn. of Hohenzollern Chevau-légers)
the 2 batt. of Grenzregiment n. 1 Lika
the 4 Reserve batt. of Grenzregiment n. 1-2-3-4
the 4 combined Landwehr batt.
one sqn. of Carlstädter Serezaner
120 Serezaner infantry

Note the numbers of the manpower had few differences, during the peace periods and during wartime, because the Military Border territory was considered as "always in war-alarm land". These were the definitive 1809 numbers:

Grenz battalions	Peace time		Wartime		Wartime	Reserve batt.		Landwehr
	staff	manpower	staff	manpower	reg. manpower	Land duty	War duty	Manpower
Croatia and Slavonia	37	1286	16	1308	2677	1406	1439	1406
Banat	37	1286	16	1308	2677	1406	1439	1406
Transylvania	42	1130	?	1164	2387		775 w. 50 artillery	
Szekler Hussars			51	1299 (1237 horses)		Res. esc.	180 (171 horses)	
Czajkisten				1289 with the staff and 139 artillerymen			376 Reserve div.	316 Landes div.

RANKS IN GRENZ CROATIAN-SLAVONIAN UNITS

FRANCUSKI (French)	AUSTRIJSKI (Austrian)	HRVATSKI – POVIJESNI (Croatian)
marechal	Feldmarschall	maršal
colonel général		general pukovnik
général en chef	Feldzeugmeister	general armije
général de division	Feldmarschall-leutenant	general divizije /podmaršal
général de brigade	General-major	brigadni general
adjudant commandant		brigadir
colonel	Obrist/Oberst	pukovnik
colonel-major	Obristleutenant/Oberstleutenant	potpukovnik
colonel en second		
lieutenant colonel		
major		
chef de bataillon	Major/Oberstwachtmeister	major, četnik
capitaine	Hauptmann	kapetan, stotnik, satnik
lieutenant	Oberleutenant	natporučnik
sous lieutenant	Fähnrich	potporučnik/zastavnik
adjudant major		časnički namjesnik
sergent major	Feldwebel	feldbaba, stražmeštar
sergent	Corporal	kaplar
caporal fourrier	Fourier	opskrbatt.ik, končar
caporal	Gefreiter	kaplar
table courtesy of: Dr. Vladimir BRNARDIĆ (Zagreb)		

Grenzer uniforms

With the "kaiserliche Entschliessung" of August 18, 1808 the former difference between Home and Field uniforms was abandoned. Difference from Home and War uniform disapperaed but still remained differences between campaign uniforms and camp uniforms. Campaign uniforms were received by the central Government without fee, while camp uniforms had to be home made, with a little compensation from the regimental cash.

In fact, earlier during the war, while going outside the Military Border, Grenzers were obliged to carry Battalion white "Montur", which they got from the military warehouse or from military suppliers. Domestic and peacetime uniforms were brown and were worn during service in areas within the Military Border. The new regulations had eliminated differences in color between the two uniforms, so that both were brown. The only difference between them was what actually they intended for peacetime uniform: old ones or made within the home cooperatives. The color brown began to become the distinguishing hue of the Grenzers, easy to note among the white infantry. The main reason which led to the adoption of this new colour, was the depot large availability of the former old Home uniforms.

As another reason for the introduction of brown colours we must tell about the fact that were introduced, for Grenzers, in 1805, the black belts worn over the jacket. It also mentioned the fact that the soldiers in the white uniform had chiefly a great disadvantage during the reconnoissances of the enemies.

According to Article 2. of the 1808 regulations, in the robes were comprised: shako (čakov), linen camp-cap (Foragiermütze), the croat national neck tie, the black "Halsbindel" , two pairs of lower and upper underwear, two shirts, a white "Weste", the dark brown military jacket (jakna) (Waffenrock – same colours for Unter and Ober officers), the work "jakna" (Kittel), an overcoat, required only in war (Mantel), tight blue pants "à la hongroise", heavy shoes with laces (Schnürschuhe) and bag of bread. NCOs in addition of the aforementioned things had to have leather gloves and the saber (Porte d'Épée). Auditore, Rechnungsführern and Verwaltung officers had same uniforms but without shako (they wore the "Dreispitz" hat, tricorne). The selection of the Uniform magazine and the tissues quality were left to the Grenzer regiments choice. This determined a bit of confusion.

Note: with the 1807-1808 reform the Grenzer battalions had to change the old white jackets with the new brown ones, comprehensive of black shoulder belts. In 1809 few units had assumed the new ordinance uniform and among them coexisted regiments dressed in different way. Moreover the regimental facings, at least regarding some colours, had a bad impact on the new brown background. Insofar, in the following years, some regiments changed also their own historical facings. This table regards facings:

Regiment	n.	buttons	old facing	new colour	year of change
Carlstädt-Liccaner (Lika)	1	GOLD	violet	Emperor Yellow	1807-1808
Carlstädt-Otoschatzer (Otočac)	2	Silver	violet	Emperor Yellow	1807-1808
Carlstädt-Oguliner (Ogulin)	3	GOLD	Orange	Orange	1807-1808
Carlstädt-Szluiner (Szluin)	4	Silver	Orange	Orange	1807-1808
Warasdiner-Kreuzer	5	GOLD	Crab	Crab	brown jacket-1814
Warasdiner-St. Georger	6	Silver	Crab	Crab	brown jacket-1811
Slavonian-Brod	7	Silver	gris-de-lin	pale red	1807-1808
Slavonian-Nowa Gradiska	8	GOLD	gris-de-lin	pale red	1807-1808
Slavonian-Peterwardein	9	GOLD	pike-grey	light pike grey	1807-1808
1st Banal - Glina	10	GOLD	carmine	crimson	1807-1808
2nd Banal - Petrinja	11	Silver	carmine	crimson	1807-1808
Deutsch-Banater	12	Silver	dark brown	light blue	1810
Wallachisch-Illyrische	13	Silver	pike-grey	light pike grey	1810
1st Szekler	14	GOLD	rose	rose	1810
2nd Szekler	15	Silver	rose	rose	1810
1st Walachische	16	GOLD	poplar green	poplar green	brown jacket-1813
2nd Walachische	17	Silver	poplar green	poplar green	brown jacket-1813
Titler (Czajkist batt.)	18	Silver			

The 1809 Campaign

Croatians - Regiments of the Carlstädt croatian area (Carlstädter Generalat)
Military Border Regiment n. 1 Licca
Lička graničarska pukovnija br. 1 - Grenzregiment n. 1 Lika (Liccaner)
Organized in 1746 – disbanded in 1873

Depot Kader HQ	Gospić (Gospich)
Commander oberst	marquis Josef Belcredi
Oberstleutnant	Andrej Ivanković von Streitenberg
Majors	Josef Rukavina von Liebstadt
1810 Staff	None. Under French rule.

History: Licca regiment aws formed in 1746. as the first of eleven Border Regiment of the Croatian and Slavonia territories. Since 1764 the regiment was divided into 4 battalions, each battalion had 4 company. That year changed the internal structure of the regiment (reduced the number of soldiers). The regiment then had three battalions, 2 had 6 companies (satnje), and the third (depot) 4 companies.

Facts: HQ Command of the Border Regiment was the highest military, administrative and judicial authority of the territory. Companies (Satnje) were the lowest military, territorial and command-administrative units of the regiment. A company was led and operated by a Captain (Satnik) and they have also administrative officers and clerks. The regiment was divided into 12 companies: Zrmanja n. 1, Srb n. 2, Donji Lapac n. 3, Bruvno n. 4, Udbina n. 5, Podlapac– Zvonigrad n. 6 (Krbava), Gračac n. 7, Lovinac n. 8, Medak n. 9 (Lika), Kaniža n. 10, Smiljan n. 11, Osik n. 12. Each Company had its recruiting villages. The administrative system was based on house numbers on which they numbered soldiers, for the control of conscripts (male population of 20 - 60 years). The headquarters of the company was not a military headquarter, they were regional administrative regiments' offices, such as forestry and land office.

The regiment was subordinated to the united General Command of Karlovač-Ban-Varaždin under a superior HQ at Karlovač / Zagreb (Agram), subordinater to the Royal Military Council in Vienna, and, from the 1848 directly to the Zagreb general Command (General Command for Croatia) and to the Ministry of War.

Baron Filip Vukasović (Vukassovich) returned to its regiment, in year 1794, becaming the commander of the Liccaner.

1809: (2 regular batt., one Reserve or third batt.)

Recruitment District: southeastern area of the Carlstädter Generalat, the former county of Licca and Corbavia (Lika-Krbava). Reserve battalion in Dalmatia.

- Before Aspern.: 3 Batt. with the Brig. Stojchevich - Stojčević, Div. Knesevich, detached from the Inner Austria army. The so called Grenzcorps of general Stojchevich - Stojčević was formed by the 1st and 2nd Liccaner battalions, the four Reserve battalions of the Carlstädt area (R1 to R4), four combined croatian Landwehr battalions, one squadron of mounted scouts (Seressaner or Serezaner) and 120 Serezaner infantry (with a Sqn. of Hohenzollern Chevaulégers). Around 6000 men (10000 with the Landwehr). Only 2/3 of the Landwehr was (home) armed, many without uniforms and mantles, many without shoes. With impracticable roads till April 20, they also remained without food and supplies. In that day Stojchevich - Stojčević began to march with his Grenzer (but with all the Landwehr units) and with the 7th, 8th and 9th companies of the Liccaner contingents of recruitment (Gračac). During the night (April 26-27) they entered Dalmatia. They marched in two columns (the first led by Oguliner major Slivarich-Slivarić, the second under the Otochaner major Novich - Nović) across the Velebit against the left flank of the Marmont's troops. During the French counterattack at Klavibrod one Liccaner batt. (major Kapcherment) defended the bridge of that town. The two Liccaner line battalions then occupied the center of the division and defended the deployment during a French encircling attempt. On May the Liccaner people defended their villages against the pillaging attempts of the Turks, supporting the French operations.

On May 16 marmont did attack. It seemed the objective should have been the Klavibrod bridge, but it was a fake. The French drove directly towards the Kitaberg hills (Pliševica hills), where a Landwehr comp. of Licca was entrenched. The opponent column led by general Masséna broke the line forcing the Liccaner commander, colonel Rebrovich, to take the leadership, having lost the communications with Stojcevich. Rebrovich with the main column and the guns withdrew till Zrmanja, the Kitaberg detachment (captain Gerstorf) covered the main column retreat. One Liccaner comp. was cut off; captain Hrabovsly retreated inside the Bosnian territory, gathered other seven Grenzer comp. in rout along the Border and, forcing marches, reached Gospić on May 19.

In the Kitaberg clash the Grenzers lost 700 men dead or missing and 300 wounded.

May 21-22 (days of Aspern) Battle of Bilaj (Gospić)

Rebrović placed most of his troops, five infantry battalions (the 2 Licca operational battalions, a Dalmatian Freikorps, 1 Otočac reserve battalion) and the artillery in the center on left bank of Lika river at the Bilaj bridge; to secure his right flank on the line Ribnik-Citluk-south of Divoselo he placed the reserve battalion, 2 Licca land detachments and local Landwehr defenders; left flank was secured at Barleta, north of the Jadova stream with nine detachments and Otočac Landwehr. Against the bulk of the Border Observation corps, protected by the unfordable Lika river, Marmont placed his skirmishers (voltigeurs) while moving the Clausel and Montrichard divisions in direction of Barleta-Ostrovica-Budak, so threatening the left flank of the Border corps and the road Gospić- Otočac, its main communication line.

Noting the French move, Rebrović moved his center across the Bilaj brigde and then, splitting it in three col-

▲ Grenzer infantry 1800-1805 about. From Ottenfeld artwork

umns, moved forward in order to capture the surrounding hills, from which he planned to attack the French left flank. However the crossing of Lika river took a long time and Marmont had enough time to turn bache the Montrichard division in order to attack Bilaj. In an hasty combat the French seized the central hill in front of Bilaj, engaging parts of Clausel division in battle, and pushed back Austrian Grenzers across the Lika river. According to French sources, the counterattackers had around 200 dead and 800 wounded, including 3 generals, but captured around 2000 Grenzers. According to Austrians sources, the Grenzers lost 64 dead, around 500 wounded and 500 captured. In the meantime the French 8th Light Regiment (division Clausel) crossed the Jadova stream at Barleta and pushed back the weak Grenzer flank detachment, when captain Hrabovski, who was in command of the Austrian flank, managed to hold the advancing French south of Ostrovica, with the help of two Banal reserve battalions, just arrived from reserve.

On the following day, May 22, Rebrović reinforced his left flank at Ostrovica, so allowing Hrabovski to deploy 4 regular and 2-3 irregular militia battalions beside the Landwehr. At the same time Marmont moved, across the Jadova, his 5th, 23rd and 81st regiments, with all his artillery, beginning the final assault. The positions south of Ostrovica were bitterly held by Grenzers and seized till the nightfall, despite of heavy casualties. Under the cover of the darkness, the Austrian corps withdrew towards Karlovać. French entered Gospić and marched northwards through Otočac and Senj.

Battle of Bilaj (Gospić) austrian Order of Battle

1 --- two field Liccaner battalions (Lika I and Lika II) colonel Rebrović - Rebrovich

2 ---- four Reserve battalions of the Carlstädt regiments (Lika III, Ogulin III, Otočac III under major Nović, Szluin III)

3 --- other four Combined Landwehr battalions (from recruitment areas of Carlstädt - Varazdin and Ban) (Landwehr I – II – III and IV) –They had names such as Combined Carlstadter-Banal Landesbataillon etc.

4 --- 1 squadron chevaulégers Hohenzollern of the 1st Major-division Lachowsky

5 --- 1 Combined squadron of Serezaner (Eclaireurs à cheval) Rittmeister Lonçar

6 ---- 120 Serezaner infantry.

7 --- A bunch of Dalmatian volunteers. (Guides)

8 --- when the Corps was split in 2 lines in order to defend one of the Barleta bridges (on the Jadava) and the other near Ribnik (bridge on the Lika). Under the first "Treff" colonel Rebrović sent his 700 armed peasants in the mountains (milice from Liccaner and Otochaner people).

Here the corps was reinforced with 2 Reserve battalions of the Banal regiments Glina and Petrinja (III battalions), from the brig. Stojčević (Stojchevich).

- between Aspern and Wagram: 2 Batt. in the Brig. Rebrovich, Kolonne Zach, IX Corps, 1 Batt. with Brig. Stojchevich - Stojčević, detached from the Inner Austria army. Many Liccaner units were made prisoners or marched in the mountains beginning their "kleine krieg" as partisans. In July the austrian general Peter Knezevich made a second attempt to invade Dalmatia. He advanced with the Liccaner reserve battalion, three comp. of the Liccaner Landwehr and one Serezaner Sqn. (a total of 4200 men). The expeditionary force, which aimed for Zara (Zadar), had two lucky combats at Benkovac (July 23) and Zemonica (July 25). At Benkovac the main "conquest" of the Liccaner was the capture of 110 oxen. Then 1st Lieutenant Gobosac and captain Čorić (both Liccaner) formed two small units (Streifabteilungen) harassing the inner French lines of communication.

Military Border Regiment n. 2 Otočac
Otočka graničarska pukovnija br. 2 - Grenzregiment n. 2 Otoschatz
Organized in 1746 – disbanded in 1873

Depot Kader HQ	Otočac (Otoschatz)
Commander oberst	Josef von Soretti (Soreth)
Oberstleutnant	Josef Schmidt
Majors	chevalier Peter Vukassovich
	Jacob Rukavina von Liebstadt
1810 Staff	None. Under French rule

History: like the n° 1. It was the second Border regiment formed.
Facts: the regiment was divided into 12 Companies: Kosinj n. 1, Klanac n. 2, Perušić n. 3, Bunić n. 4, Zavalje n. 5, Korenica n. 6, Vrhovine n. 7, Škare n. 8, Sinac n. 9, Otočac n. 10, Brlog n. 11, Sv. Juraj n. 12.
Organization and subordinations: same as the n. 1 Licca.

Recruitment District: upper area of the Carlstädter Generalat and part of the Coast area.
Kapitanate: Zengg, Bründl, Otocac.
1809. (2 regular batt., one Reserve or third batt. led by major Nović). Inner Austria army.
- before Aspern: it began the campaign with 2 Batt. in the Brig. Kalnássy, Div. Wolfskehl, IX Corps – 3rd Batt. with Brig. Stojchevich, Div. Knesevich, Inner Austria army in Dalmatia, with the combined Landwehr batt.; at Sacile, left flank, fought the detachment of colonel Gyurkovich with 3 comp. Otoschaner. The 1st and the 2nd batt. (the remaining 9 comp.) were in the vanguard of the IX Corps. On May 2 they fought at Tavernolo and Ponte di Brenta. At the Piave battle (May 8) they were in the brig. Marziani (not Gavassini), IX Corps. There the 2nd Otoschaner batt. was sent ahead in order to help the Brig. Kalnássy at bay. (For the reserve battalion see campaign in Dalmatia under rgt. n.1).
- between Aspern and Wagram: 1 batt. and 2/3 were in Carniola with Brig. Gavassini, division Zach, Corps Ignaz Gyulai und Knesevich, the III reserve batt. at the Graz battle, was employed to help the Brig. Munkácsy. At St.Leonhard they were with the Brig. Kalnássy.
The Landwehr combined batt. was always in Dalmatia.

Military Border Regiment n. 3 Ogulin
Ogulinska graničarska pukovnija br. 3 - Grenzregiment n. 3 Ogulin
Organized in 1746

Depot Kader HQ	Ogulin
Commander oberst	Ignaz Csivich von Rohr (Čivić)
Oberstleutnant	Ignaz Csivich (promoted)
Majors	Cirill Rodich
	Carl Pauer von Traut
1810 Staff	None. Under French rule

History: like the n° 1. It was the third Border regiment formed.
Facts: the regiment was divided into 12 Companies: Krivi put n. 1, Brinje n. 2, Jezerane n. 3, Modruš n. 4, Oštarije n. 5, Ogulin n. 6, Drežnik n. 7, Plaški n. 8, Rakovica n. 9, Primišlje n. 10, Tounj n. 11, Dubrave n. 12.
Recruit. Dist.: Northwestern area of the Carlstädter Generalat and a small part of the Coast. Kapitanate Tersich, Thuin, Ogulin.
1809 (2 regular batt., one Reserve or third batt.) Inner Austria army.
It began the war with the Brig. Kalnássy, Div. Görupp, IX Corps. At the battle of Fontanafredda it was with brig. Marziani, IX Corps and attacked the French on the banks of Livenza stream. The reserve battalion with Brig. Stoichevich, Div. Knesevich in Dalmatia. During the night (April 26-27) they entered Dalmatia. They marched in two columns (the first led by Oguliner major Slivarich-Slivarić, the second under the Otochaner major Novich - Nović) across the Velebit against the left flank of the Marmont's troops. The first attack was not successful, then the battalion followed the fate of the Corps Stojcevich (see 1gt. 11.1).
They advanced with the Frimont vanguard under their colonel Čivić, fording the streams Guà and Chiampo, after Vicenza. During the retreat they formed the army rearguard fighting at Olmo (May 2). On May 8 (Piave battle) they were in the brig. Gavassini and three days after they fought at San Michele. The two Ogulin comp. Modruš and Jezerane, with the regiment's artillery, defended the fortress of Malborghetto under the Staff officers Cesar and Vučetić (and the Engineer fortress commander Hensel). Then retreated fighting at Tarvis.
- between Aspern and Wagram: the two line battalions marched with the FML Franz von Jellačić division, Brigade GM Gajoli, VIII Corps being at Raab without fights.
– they ended the war in the Brig. De Vaux, Div. Colloredo, VIII Corps.

Military Border Regiment n. 4 Szluin
Slunjska graničarska pukovnija br. 4 - Grenzregiment n. 4 Szluin
Organized in 1746 – disbanded in 1873

Depot Kader HQ	Szluin or Slunj (croatian)
Commander oberst	baron Josef Ställ von Holstein
	Ferdinand von Fellner
Oberstleutnant	Gregor Miljanić (Myllianich)
Majors	Michail von Sivković
	count Georg Branković
1810 Staff	None. Under French rule

History: like the nº 1. It was the fourth Border regiment raised.
Facts: the regiment was divided into 12 Companies: Slunj n. 1, Vališ selo n. 2, Krstinja br.3, Vojnić n. 4, Veljun n. 5, Krnjak n. 6, Perjasica n. 7, Barilović n. 8, Vukmanić n. 9, Švarča n. 10, Kostanjevac n. 11, .Kalje n. 12.
Recruit. Distr.: northeastern area of the Carlstädter Generalat, Kapitanate Barilovich, Stain, Sichelburg .
1809: (2 regular batt., one Reserve or third batt.) Inner Austria army.
- before Aspern: it began with the Brig. Kalnássy, Div. Görupp, IX Corps. At Sacile they were in the vanguard Div. Frimont, Brig. Kleinmayer, IX Corps. After the retreat they fought at the Piave with heavy losses having two comp. detached in the Belluno valley. On May 9 a detachment under major Dumontet, with the two battalions, covered the brig. Kálnassy retreat. The Pojer comp. defended the Predil fortress under Engineer commander Hermann. Of this comp. it survived only a Feldwebel. Other 4 comp. were sent in Croatia to support the insurrection.
- between Aspern and Wagram: 1 Batt. was at Raab with the Brig. oberst Siegenfeld, Div. FZM Davidovich. Another batt. was with Brig. Gavassini at Graz and after that battle under the brig. Kalnássy, IX Corps at the combat of St.Leonhard. Laibach (Ljubliana) and Leoben were defended by detachments of Szluiner Landwehr (major Dumontet at Laibach). In summer and till the end of the war the two line battalions gathered under the Brig. Bianchi, detached in Preßburg (Bratislava).

Warasdiner (reg. of Varaždin counties - Croatia)
The Generalat (Generalship) of Varaždin was the first territory to experiment the reform of Prince Joseph Friedrich of Saxony-Hildburghausen. There was organized the first structural regiment and there the first uniforms were assigned to the "Grenzers".
The first regular formations of Varaždin participated in the War of Austrian Succession (1740 -1748). They distinguished further in the battle of Chotusitz, 1742, and Kesselsdorf, 1745, and in other smaller clashes. In 1757 they also tried to imprison Friedrich II (Frederick the Great) without succeeding.
The Grenzers penetrated in his room and they looted it also bringing some flags (this fact, many years later was blamed by Adolf Hitler to Ante Pavelic, leader Ustascia, referring it as a deceitful and reprehensible action).
Historically the regiments of Varaždin were two:
Varaždinsko križevačke krajiške pješačke pukovnije br. 5
or regiment Kreuzer of Warasdin (Kreuzer or Kürüz in Hungarian it was the territory of recruitment and it made reference to the crusaders flags anti Islam).
Varaždinsko-đurđevačke krajiške pješačke pukovnije br. 5
or regiment of Gjurgevatz or St. George (Warasdiner Sankt Georger Regiment).
Such organization was actually maintained till 1809, with the exception of the period of the French Revolutionary Wars (1793 -1798). The courage and abnegation of the departments of Varaždin are evident in the awards of the regiment: gold medal in 1790 and in 1809 as well as 41 silver medals to the single formations.

Military Border Regiment n. 5 Kreuzer
Varaždinsko-križevačka graničarska pukovnija br. 5 - Grenzregiment n. 5 Varazdin (Kreuzer)
Organized in 1746 – disbanded in 1871

Depot Kader HQ	Bjelovar
Commander oberst	Franz Anthony (is a surname!!) von Siegenfeld
	Theodor von Russo
Oberstleutnant	count Josef Preising - Theodor von Ruszo
Majors	Theodor von Russo
	Andrej Čorić (Andreas Chorich)
1810 Staff	Theodor von Russo – baron Alois Bernjaković
Oberstleutnant	Andreas Benezek

History: After the native reforms of the generalship of Varaždin in 1745 the general Hildburghausen divided the territory in two areas of recruitment (1749) copying the structure of the old police units of Varaždin. In 1756 it took the name by its owner or Inhaber, the colonel Leylersberg, then returning to be the regiment of Varaždin. From 1769 the unit had the number 64 of the Austrian infantry order of battle and with the 1798 reform it received the official denomination of: National Border regiment n.5.
Facts: the regiment was divided into 12 Companies: 1. (satnija) Vukovje, 2. Garešnica, 3. Hercegovec, 4. Berek, 5. Ivanska, 6. Čazma, 7. Farkaševac, 8. Gudovec, 9. Criž, 10. Kloštar, 11. Mali Ivanič or Sveti Ivan, 12. Vojakovec.
Recruit. Distr.: western part of the Warasdiner Generalat, Kapitanate Kopreinitz and Creuz (Kürüz).

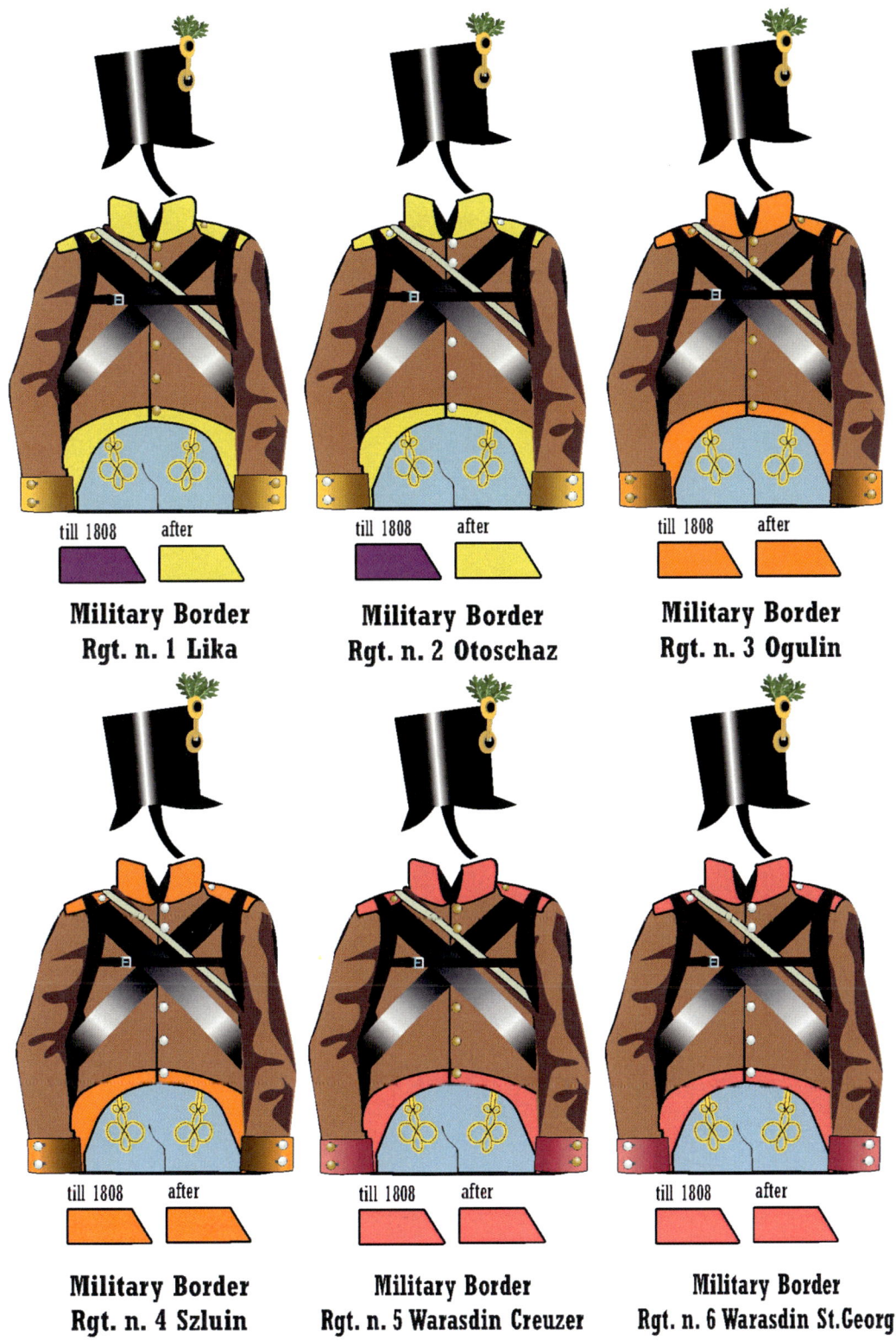

▲ Military Border regiments nr. 1, 2, 3, 4, 5 & 6

1809 (2 regular batt., one Reserve or third batt.). The reserve batt. was with the Brig. Szörenyi in Pest, Div. Lippa under Alvinczy. The Landesbattalion (Landwehr) gave companies to the combined units in Dalmatia and was with Brig. Khevenhüller, Reserve Corps Zach.
- before Aspern: two line battalions were under the VI Corps FML baron Johann von Hiller early with Brig. Provenchères, Div. Jellacich, seizing the Bavaria capital city, Munich.
From May 1 till 20, the two line battalions (Brig. Legisfeld, Div. Jellachich) defended pass Lueg near Salzburg.
- before Wagram: the gathered three battalions were in reserve with Division FML Jellacich, Brigade GM Lutz at the time of the Raab battle..

Military Border Regiment n. 6 St. Georger
Varaždinsko-đurđevačka graničarska pukovnija br. 6 - Grenzregiment n.6 Varazdin (Sankt Georger)
Organized in 1749 – disbanded in 1871

Depot Kader HQ	Bjelovar
Commander oberst	Andreas von Roditzky
Oberstleutnant	Mihail von Mihaljevic (Mihalievitz)
Majors	Niclas Czaar
	Mihail Mihajlović von Schlachtfeld (Michailovich)
1810 Staff	Andreas von Roditzky
Oberstleutnant	Niclas Czaar – Cirill Rodich (Oguliner)

History: after the 1745 Generalat's reform the delegate general Hildburghausen organized, in 1749, the Varaždinsko-đurđevačka krajiška pješačka pukovnija or St. George regiment. Its first commander and Inhaber, from 1749, was the "pukovnik", then general (General-Feld-Wachtmeister) Nicolaus Freiherr von Kengyel. In the year 1754 its owner was the general (GFWM) Sigmund Benvenuto count Petazzi, and after a couple of years, in 1756, the general Joseph Philipp count Guicciardi. With the 1769 Reform the regiment assumed the number 65 of the Austrian army. In 1798 it had the name of National Border regiment n. 6 recruiting in the areas of the Varazdin generalship, and especially in the territories of Đurđevac and Ivanić. The HQ was actually in Đurđevac till 1758 and then it was transferred to Bjelovar.
Facts: the regiment was divided into 12 Companies: Grubišno Polje n. 1, Kovačica n. 2, Severin n. 3, Rača br, 4, Đurđevac - Sv.Juraj n. 5, Pitomača n. 6, Trojstvo n. 7, Virje n. 8, Novigrad n. 9, Peteranec n. 10, Sokolovec n. 11, Kapela n. 12.
Recruit. Distr.: eastern area of the Warasdiner Generalats, Kapitanate Ivanich and St. George.
1809 (2 regular batt., one Reserve or third batt.) the reserve batt. originally with the Brig. Szörenyi in Pest, Div. Lippa under Alvinczy.
- before Aspern: the two line battalions were with the Avantgarde Nordmann (II Wing) advancing from Ach till the river Salza. Div. Vincent, VI Corps. On April 21, at Moosburg, one batt. tried to stop the advance of Masséna. During the battle of Abensberg two companies were in the detachment of major von Scheibler, VI Corps, and the remaining units with Nordmann. During the folowing retreat (battle of Landshut) with Nordmann rearguard (left wing) remained only 4 companies, the others detached or missing. At Neumarkt they were the avantgarde (Nordmann) of the 3rd column (left wing). The same unit (again in the left wing) was also at Ebelsberg. Before Aspern the avant-garde Nordmann was part of the Div. Kottulinsky, VI Corps.
- at Aspern: they passed in the right army wing with the 1st Column FML Hiller, Brig. Nordmann, Div. Kottulinsky, VI Corps, but also acting as an independent brigade. The two battalions had no more than 544 men in total.
- at Wagram: the VI Corps was under count FZM Klenau (interim commander for FML baron Hiller) and the two line battalions in the Div. Vincent, Brig. August Vécsey.
- after Wagram: a remaining battalion was in the Brigade GM count Wallmoden-Gimborn, Div. Vincent, VI Corps at Wolframitzkirchen – not participating at the Znaim battle.

The Serežani (Seressaner)
Serežani wore folk costumes, or a kind of folk uniforms because the clothes had not officially been prescribed. However, basically there was a sort of uniformity of appearance in suits called "serežanskih way", which differed only in details. The suits were made within home cooperatives. Material for making clothes consisted of wool, flax and hemp, mastered by women in order to obtain cloth and linen. To create "serežani" suits the Generalat gave an annual cash fund. The suits consisted of: robe or cloak, hats, shirts, vests, short jackets, belts to carry weapons, pants, socks and shoes or "nazuvaka".

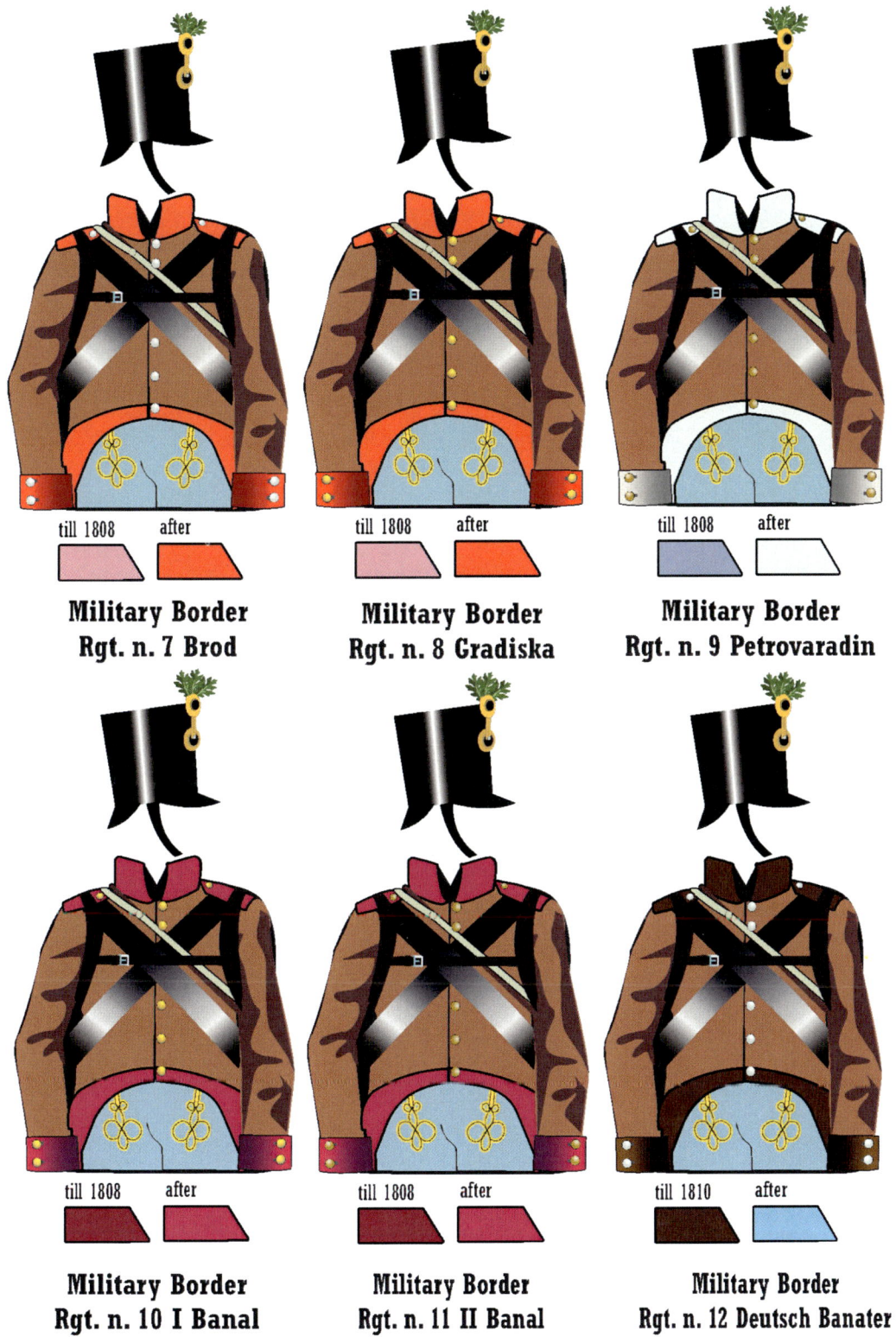

▲ Military Border regiments nr. 7, 8, 9, 10, 11 & 12

Serežani wore clothes in shades of red, green, blue, white, brown and black. The mantle, or cloak was usually brown or dark red, made of homespun, and sometimes decorated with a stylized application of felt and trimmings. It consisted of a jacket with a collar and a hood, and the "zakopčavala", laces under the throat. According to the cloak, from which the Military Border guards had been known up to that time anywhere in war, it caused them some nicknames, such as "Crvenohaljetci" or "Crveni kapucini", red caps, which were pronounced with fear. Bag shaped hat, with an extended lateral part, was also made of red cloth or baize. Hats were sometimes wrapped in striped scarf or towel. In winter, was worn a fur with a red bag Kalpaka.

Slavonians

Slavonia (Croatian: Slavonija, Hungarian: Szlavónia, Latin: Sclavonia) is a geographical and historical region in eastern Croatia. It is a fertile agricultural and forested lowland bounded, in part, by the Drava river in the north, the Sava river in the south, and the Danube river in the east.

The Slavonian Military Frontier or Slavonian Krajina was part of the Habsburg Military Frontier. It was formed out of territories the Habsburgs conquered from the Ottoman Empire and included southern parts of Slavonia and Syrmia; today the area it covered is mostly in eastern Croatia, with its easternmost parts in Vojvodina, Serbia. During history borders of Slavonian Krajina has been changed few times. Shortly after creation in the 1500s Slavonian Krajina bordered the Ottoman Empire to the east, the Kingdom of Croatia (part of the Habsburg Empire) and Croatian Krajina to the west, and the Kingdom of Hungary, also part of the Habsburg Empire, to the north. After the Treaty of Karlowitz, the expanded Slavonian Krajina bordered the Kingdom of Croatia, Croatian Military Frontier to the west, the Kingdom of Hungary to the north, the Banat Military Frontier to the east and the Ottoman province of Bosnia to the south.

Slavonski military district was one of the last areas of the Military Border, where the reorganization was implemented in regular regiments. In 1747 it was abolished the old structure of the Sava, Danube and Srijemski border and the whole area converted into three large districts with seats in Gradiska, Brod and Petrovaradin. This was the beginning of the establishing of regular regiments, which Vice Marshal von Engelshofen began in 1750. He wanted to form three regiments with two battalions of five Companies. Each regiment was supposed to count 5600 soldiers, and the entire military district was to raise 16,800 infantry men. The Slavonian Krajina was divided between three districts, named after cities in the area: Gradiška, Brod, and Petrovaradin; however, the regimental seat of the Brod regiment was in Vinkovci.

However, after the original organization it followed an utter reorganization by FML count Serbelloni, who, in 1752-1753, gave the final shape of the regiments. Each regiment had four battalions with four companies of 240 troops and two battalions of 120 elite soldiers - grenadiers. Later, in 1769, the grenadiers were replaced with the "oštrostrijelcima" (Sharpshooters).

In 1776, the rural population of the Slavonian military frontier was 177,212. The number of Roman Catholic men was 43,635 and 33,970 were Orthodox. The number of inhabitants of cities was 11,353, and that giving a total of 188,565 inhabitants.

In Brod and Gradiška regiments Catholics outnumbered the Orthodox, and in Petrovaradin regiment the Orthodox were more numerous. The 1790 population census recorded 388,000 Serbs and 325,000 Croats, while the religious structure was 52.1% Catholic and 46.8% Orthodox.

The courage and sacrifice of Slavonian Frontiersmen are witnessed by the 5 gold and 94 silver medals for bravery gained, from 1790 till 1809, by members of some units of Slavonski Generalat.

The Brooder - Military Border regiment n. 7 Brod

Brodska krajiška pješačka pukovnija br. 7 - Grenzregiment n. 7 - Brod an der Sava

The city of Slavonski Brod, Croatia, which was an important strategic and traffic center controlling the border crossing towards Turkey and connecting main commercial trails at the time, in the period between 1715-1780 Austria built the large imperial and royal border Fortress of Brod on the Sava River, which along with the fortified baroque towns of Slavonia, namely Osijek and Stara Gradiška, belongs to the great defense system on the border towards the Turkish Empire, designed by the prince Eugene of Savoy in the first half of the 18 century.

It was constructed by peasants of the Military Border under forced labor more specifically 634 a day, who also gave 53 horse-drawn carts daily for the transport of material. The regular star-like form of the fortress was determined by the flat-country. It was built of rammed earth, bricks, wood and partially stone, and designed for the accommodation of 4.000 soldiers, mostly infantry and 150 cannons. From 1747 the new regulations of Slavonian

Krajina had its eighth of the eleven Border Regiment in Croatian and Slavonia territories. Till 1764 the regiment was divided into 4 battalions, each battalion had 4 companies. That year changed the internal structure of the regiment (reduced the number of soldiers). The regiment had then three battalions, 2 had 6, and the third (depot) 4 companies. This organization was common to all Slavonian units.
Organized in 1747 – disbanded in 1873

Depot Kader HQ	Vinkovci
Commander oberst	count Hugo Eltz
	Gabriel von Milletich (Miletić)
Oberstleutnant	Gabriel von Milletich (Miletić)
Majors	Jakob von Filipović (Philippovich)
	Jepht. von Rasković
1810 Staff	Gabriel von Milletich (Miletić)
Oberstleutnant	Jakub von Pavlić (Paulich)

History: The first owner (Inhaber) of the regiment in 1750 was artillery General Friedrich Sigmund Gaisruck, while, from 1754 to 1765, he was replaced with artillery general Anton Ignaz-Mercy Argenteau.
Facts. The regiment was divided into 12 Companies: 1. Podvin, 2. Trnjane, 3. Garčin, 4. Andrijevci, 5. Sikirevci, 6. Babina Greda, 7. Ivankovo, 8. Cerna, 9. Vinkovci, 10. Nijemci, 11. Županja and 12. Drenovci. Each Company had its villages, for example the Vinkovačka Company n. 9 had under its command the villages of Laze, Mirkovci, old and new Jankovci Orolik, Zadar, Vinkovci and Slakovci.
Recruiting District: Kapitanate Brčka, Illok.
1809: (2 regular batt., one Reserve or third batt.).
- in Bavaria, before Aspern: it began the campaign with the "reconnaissance" Brigade GM baron Josef Mesko de Felsö-Kubinyi (Mesko Brig.), Division FML Emmanuel von Schustekh, V Corps archduke Louis. During the Abensberg battle the two line battalions advanced with the Division FML prince Henri XV Reuss-Plauen Column, 8 companies detached under FML von Schustekh, 4 comp. with Mesko. The Schustekh Detachment had an hard battle at Kloster Rohr. At Neumarkt they (Brig. Mesko) were the 2nd avant-garde column. After the bloody battle of Ebelsberg (May 8 a third of Batt. in the Avant-garde Nordmann, VI Corps) with FML von Schustekh remained two weak comp. (142 men). They were sent with the Détachement GM von Scheibler (watching the main road Schärding – Linz)
- at Aspern: with the Avant-garde Brigade GM Armand von Nordmann, VI Corps . At the Raab battle was present a Combined Landwehr batt. of Brod and Gradiska (detachment GM Ettingshausen).
- at Wagram: they went with the St.Georger in the Div. Vincent (VI Corps), Brig. August Vécsey.
- after Wagram: the two comp. with Brig. Wallmoden, Div. Vincent, VI Corps.

The Gradiskaner – Military Border regiment n. 8 Nova Gradiska
Gradiška krajiška pješačka pukovnija br. 8. - Grenzregiment n. 8 Nova Gradiska
Organized in 1750 – disbanded in 1873

Depot Kader HQ	Gradiška
Commander oberst	Carl von Greth
	Theodor Milutinovich von Milovsky (Milutinović)
Oberstleutnant	Matias Rebrović (Rebrovich)
Majors	Theodor von Pavić
	Ivan Mihić (Johann Mihich)
1810 Staff	Theodor Milutinovich von Milovsky
Oberstleutnant	Josef Taza

History: the city of Nova Gradiška was founded in 1748. It had been founded because of Vojna krajina (Soldatensiedlung der Grenzgarnison Nr. 8) and was first named as Friedrichsdorf. With the army in the newly established village Friedrichsdorf did come the civilian population, especially craftsmen and merchants. Their arrival precipitated the declaration of Nova Gradiska as "free army Municipality". Since then, its residents were not subject to more Border commitment, and had population rapidly growing . In the village there are more traders and craftsmen, and they appear and the first craft associations. First tradesmen come in Nova Gradiska were: one Meisch, immigrant from Austria, maybe the first civilian resident, with him came the baker and blacksmith named Frank Gansnek. The traders came from neighboring Cernik, who was part of the county Požega. Accord-

ing to some information about Nova Gradiska in 1762 the military had 39 military, 70 civil town houses and 11 "bolti" - big stores. On 1776 was performed the first census in the city: of 366 residents, 70 were craftsmen.
Reforming the defences along the Sava River FML Engleshofen formed in 1747 the Slavonia and Krajina Gradiska regiment. In 1753 the regiment was reorganized and named Gradiska Krajina Infantry Regiment, and in 1769 had the serial number 67. From an utter reform it received the serial number 8. The regiment was raised with part of the border territory along the Sava river, which belonged to the former "Kapitanat" Kobas. Regiment command initially was in Bogoševcima and later in the town of Gradiška.
Facts. The regiment was divided into 12 Companies: 1. Lipovljani, 2. Novska, 3. Rajič, 4. Čaglić, 5. Okučani, 6. Mašić, 7. Rešetari, 8. Petrovo Selo, 9. Nova Kapela, 10. Oriovac, 11. Stupnik and 12. Sibinj.
Recruit. Dist.: central area of the Sava river (Kapitanat Kobas).
1809: (2 regular batt., one Reserve or third batt.).
- before Aspern: the two line batt. began the campaign in the Avant-garde Brigade GM count Josef Radetzky, Div. Schustekh, V Corps archduke Louis. On April 16 the Scharfschützen (sharpshooters) of the Rgt. took position among the Landshut houses. By 2 PM GM Radetzky launched his attack against the bridges, defended by the Bavarians, with a column of two Gradiskaner comp., 30 sharpshooters, 30 pioneers and a wing of hussars led by 1st Lieutenant Tkalčević. Staff captain baron Simbschen led other 4 comp. of the regiment, widening the occupation of the town of Seligenthal. Finally colonel von Greth led his 10 companies against the flank of the bavarian general Deroi and won the battle.
After the unlucky battle of Abensberg the two batt. remained with Radetzky in rearguard tasks. During the second Landshut battle they were in the 1st Rearguard Brig. Radetzky (left wing), fighting also at Neumarkt and in the retreat beyond the river Isar. At Ebelsberg they were in the rearguard under Division GM baron Carl Vincent, Brig. Radetzky, distinguishing themselves in that bloody day at Kleinmünchen and Blindenmarkt. The sharpshooter comp. of Čvetić stopped the advance of the Po and Corsican Tirailleurs at the bridge.
Before Aspern they were deployed: one battalion with Radetzky rearguard at Gaspoltshofen, Div. Schustekh; the other with Brigade GM chevalier Adrian Joseph Reinwaldt von Waldegg at Schwanenstadt. (on May 10 at Krems bridge). They went not to Aspern and Wagram.
- after Wagram: they were reached by the third reserve batt. in the V Corps FML prince Reuss-Plauen, Div. Weissenwolff, Brig. GM count Klebelsberg, deploying behind the town of Znaim.

Serbo-slavonians of Syrmia
The majority of the Serbian population in Croatia and Slavonia were included into the organization of the Military Border. After the Lower Slavonia had been liberated from the Ottomans, the new parts of the Border were formed in 1701 and 1702: on the Sava, the Danube, and the Theiss-Maros military districts.
The whole area between the Kupa and the Una was also re-conquered in this war. The Banal Border was enlarged and dominated by the ruler, while a great part of it was subordinated to the Bishop of Zagreb and the Kaptol. The Emperor gave land to the population to use it only for acquiring soldiers in return, with the Croatian Ban as a commander. The Croatian Council (the Sabor) took part in re-conquering the areas between the Kupa and the Una. At that time, Croatian help was needed by Vienna for the uprising in Hungary (the insurrection of Rakoczy 1703-1711), so that the Ban was appointed a commander by the Court. Since 1703 the Banal Border has been subjugated to the Hofkriegsrat (War Council) in Vienna. All the hinterland was assigned to the Hofkammer and županije (counties).
The Serbs were not assigned privileges as a political community, but as a religious one,and so their position depended on the position of the church in general. The on-coming era of enlightened absolutism meant decline of the influence of the church in favour of the state. Therefore, the legal position of the Serbs based on privileges was getting weaker.
Later the "Wallachian privileges" disappeared, the frontiersmen were exposed to severe regulations, while those in the Provintial were reduced to the peasant status. Within the Border the Serbs could reach higher military positions, while in the Provintial they could not participate in the "županija" political bodies.
During the First Serbian Uprising (1804-1813) the Serbs from both sides of the Border were bound together in the joint attempt to overthrow the Ottoman rule over Serbia, so that for the first time in the history of the Serbs in Habsburg Monarchy the question of their loyalty to the Emperor was set. Then (1809) came the French rule in the Balkans.

The Peterwardeiner – Military Border regiment n. 9 Petrovaradin (Peterwardein)
Petrovaradinska krajiška pješačka pukovnija br. 9 - Grenzregiment n.9 Peterwardein
Organized in 1748 – disbanded in 1873

Depot Kader HQ	Mitrovica (Petrovaradin)
Commander oberst	Ignaz von Leuthner
Oberstleutnant	baron Josef Ställ von Holstein
Majors	Maximilian Radovanović
	Bernard Gollubičić (Gollubicsich)
1810 Staff	Ignaz von Leuthner - Ignaz Čivić von Rohr (Csivich)
Oberstleutnant	Vinzenz Landt

History: Petrovaradin Fortress (Hungarian: Péterváradi vár, German: Peterwardein) is a fortress near Novi Sad, Serbia. It is located in the province of Vojvodina, on the right bank of the Danube river. The cornerstone of the present-day southern part of the fortress was laid on October 18, 1692, by Charles Eugène de Croÿ. Petrovaradin Fortress has many underground tunnels as well (16 km of underground countermine system). The first larger fortifications were created with the arrival of the Romans who built the fortress (Cusum) which was a part of the fortified borders (Limes) along the Danube. The turning point in the history of the area came in 1235 when King Bela IV of Hungary brought a group of the Order of Cistercians from France. This order of monks built the monastery Belakut upon the remains of the Roman fortress of Cusum. The walls of this monastery were built between 1247 and 1252 and represent the fortifications at this site during the Middle Ages.

Syrmia - Sremska Mitrovica. After the final expulsion of Turks from Srem, Mitrovica came, under the provisions of the Peace Treaty of Pozarevac in 1718. under the Austrian rule. Until the year 1745, it formed a part of estates of the counts Colloredo and Pejačevic and afterwards it belonged to the Military Border of Srem as the seat of the headquarters of the regiment of Petrovaradin and of the Srem brigade for some time also as a free commune of the Military Border. Its Serbian population was formed for the most part of immigrants from Serbia an Bosnia and the Catholic population consisted of Croats from the surroundings of Dubica and of Germans coming from various parts of the German Empire, firstly from the province of Hesse. When it had been proclaimed a Border community, in 1765, it opened still wider the doors to immigrants, particularly artisans and tradespeople (Aromuns); therefore its population was constantly increasing and its economy, chiefly the trade, in permanent progress.

Facts: it recruited the Satnje at: 1. Morović, 2. Adaševci, 3. Lačarak, 4. Mitrovica, 5. Hrtkovci, 6. Kupinovo, 7. Surčin, 8. Simanovci, 9. Golubinci. 10. Stara Pazova, 11. Stari Banovci and 12. Beška.

Recruit. Distr.: Lower basin of the Sava, Danube and serbian Border.

1809 (2 regular batt., one Reserve or third batt.).

- before Aspern: they began the campaign in the III Corps Hohenzollern, Avant-garde Div. baron Philipp Vukassovich, Brigade GM prince Moritz Liechtenstein. At the battle of Teugen-Hausen only the first battalion remained with Liechtenstein at Bachel, while the 2nd batt. was with Brig. Pfanzelter under the colonel Leuthner and engaged the enemy inside the Teugen forest. The regiment gathered on the Waldspitz, while 3 comp. under major Golubovich covered the flank. At Abensberg the two line batt. still in different brigades received the central ram of the French attack and withdrew northwards. At Eggmühl they were 1 batt. and half again with Div. Vukassovich, III Corps, Brig. Moritz Liechtenstein.

After the retreat in Bohemia they were assigned to the Div. marquis Hannibal Sommariva, III Corps Kollowrath (defence of Bohemia), the 1st batt. with the detachment colonel von Leuthner, the 2nd with the detachment major Emerich Zaborsky de Zabora and fought the battle of Urfahr-Linz. The two battalions were successively attached to the Division marquis Hannibal Sommariva, Brigade GM comte Carl Crenneville. They did not participate at Aspern and Wagram.

Territories of the Ban (Croatian Supreme commander), Banal Croatia (Banal Generalät)

After the wars against the Turks there was also the necessity to organize the border (or Cordon) with the Ottoman empire and particularly the border between the Kupa and the Sava rivers, the so-called Banal Grenz (Banska). On the military model of the Slavonia, then the Croatian Ban Count Karol Batthiányi raised, in 1750, two infantry regiments drawn by the areas of Petrinja and the Banal Border, along with a regiment of Grenzer cavalry.

The first regiment Banal was recruited west in the area of Glina, the second regiment came from the east or the areas of Petrinja and Dubička. The structure of every regiment was on four battalions with four companies (satnije) of 240 soldiers, with two more companies of 120 selected soldiers or grenadiers. After the 1769 reform, the grenadiers were replaced by the sharpshooters (Scharfschützen), every regiment counted 4080 among soldiers, noncommissioned officers and officers. The two regiments began to have the name of their owner, the Ban of Croatia, serving in their ranks, above all, officers drawn by the local nobility. They were directly placed side by side the other Croatian regiments and submitted to the command of the Croatian Council of war. The courage of the Banal Grenzers is manifest by the award gained from 1790 till 1809: 3 gold and 12 silver medals.

The title of ban persisted in Croatia after 1527 when the country became part of the Habsburg Monarchy, and continued all the way until 1918. Between the most distinguished bans in Croatian history were the two Erdödys: Toma Erdödy, great warrior and statesman in one person, and Ivan Erdödy, whom Croatia owes much for protecting her rights against the Hungarian nobility, his mostly known words in Latin are "Regnum regno non praescribit leges", "a kingdom may not impose laws to a(nother) kingdom".

The Croatian Ban of the napoleonic Era were Franjo Balassa de Gyarmat 1785–1790, count Ivan Erdödy 1790 - March 30, 1806, FML Ignaz Gyulai von Máros-Nemethy und Nádaska 1806–1831, commander of the IX Corps in 1809.

The Banal Border was always very vulnerable. Areas of Glina and Petrinja were ruled mainly by the Catholic Church and the military skills were poor. Who decided to do the soldier (defenders against Turks) had some privileges, but the social texture was various. For example a misunderstandings about the status of Petrinja lasted until 1753. The "Petrinjski" soldiers since 1689 enjoyed of the bishop's possessions along Mošćenice stream, and of the estates received from the Bishop of Zagreb, who gave them as own and for which they were not obliged to pay any tax. Furthermore, the paid German army was dissolved in Petrinja and remained only lightly armed and poorly trained unpaid soldiers, the Border (Krajina) Guards, which would have not been able to successfully remove a stronger enemy like Turks.

In 1753 Petrinja was committed for the "Banska Krajina" when they began to build the Petrinja fortress and forming the settlements of Petrinja and Glina. Starting from the first house built outside the fort, soon Petrinja has five hundred Catholic houses. In 1765 Petrinja was proclaimed a military district and its magistrates left the place to the military officers.

Banal Military Border Regiment n. 10 or First Banal of Glina

Prva banska krajiška pješačka pukovnija br. 10 – Banal Grenzregiment n. 1 (Banalisten) - Owner: Banus FML Ignaz Gyulai von Maros Németh.

Organized in 1745 – disbanded in 1873

Depot Kader HQ	Glina
Commander oberst	Markus von Boxich (Božić)
	baron Alois von Bernjaković
Oberstleutnant	baron Alois von Bernjaković
Majors	Franz Einkhemer
	Mihail von Ljubibratić (Liubibratich)
1810 Staff	None. Under French rule

History: 1st regiment born in 1749, but it was officially recognized only in the 1750. The Croatian Ban, of the time, count Karol Batthiányi, organized it in the territories of Banal border. In the reforms of the Austrian army of 1769 the regiment had the number 69, and in the 1798 following reform it got the new denomination of "Regiment of infantry of the National Military Border" with the new number 10. After 1809, when Austria surrendered at Schönbrunn, the 1st regiment Banal Grenz was given by the Austrians to the service of France.

Facts: it recruited the Satnje at: 1. Čemernica , 2. Vranovina , 3. Glina, 4. Maja , 5. Klasnić, 6. Maligradec , 7. Kraljevčane , 8. Gora, 9. Stankovac , 10. Bović , 11. Lasinja e 12. Vrginmost.

Recruit.Dist.: Banal territory (southern part) (Kapitanat Glina)

1809 (2 regular batt., one Reserve or third batt.). Reservedivision : with Stojčević, in Dalmatia, detached from the Inner Austria army, with the Landwehr (combined Carlstädter-Varasdiner-Banal Landesbataillon). The III reserve batt. was at the battle of Gospić.

The two line battalions entered the campaign with VIII Corps (marquis Chasteler) then Albert Gyulai, with the 2nd Division FML Frimont, Brig. GM von Wetzel. The II batt. under the colonel von Božić fought at Pordenone - Rorai Grande. At Sacile 10 comp. of the avant-garde von Wetzel were the vanguard of the VIII corps, while 2 comp. were sent along the Tolmezzo road. After the retreat they were at the Piave battle with Brig. GM Gajoli, Div. and VIII Corps Albert Gyulai.

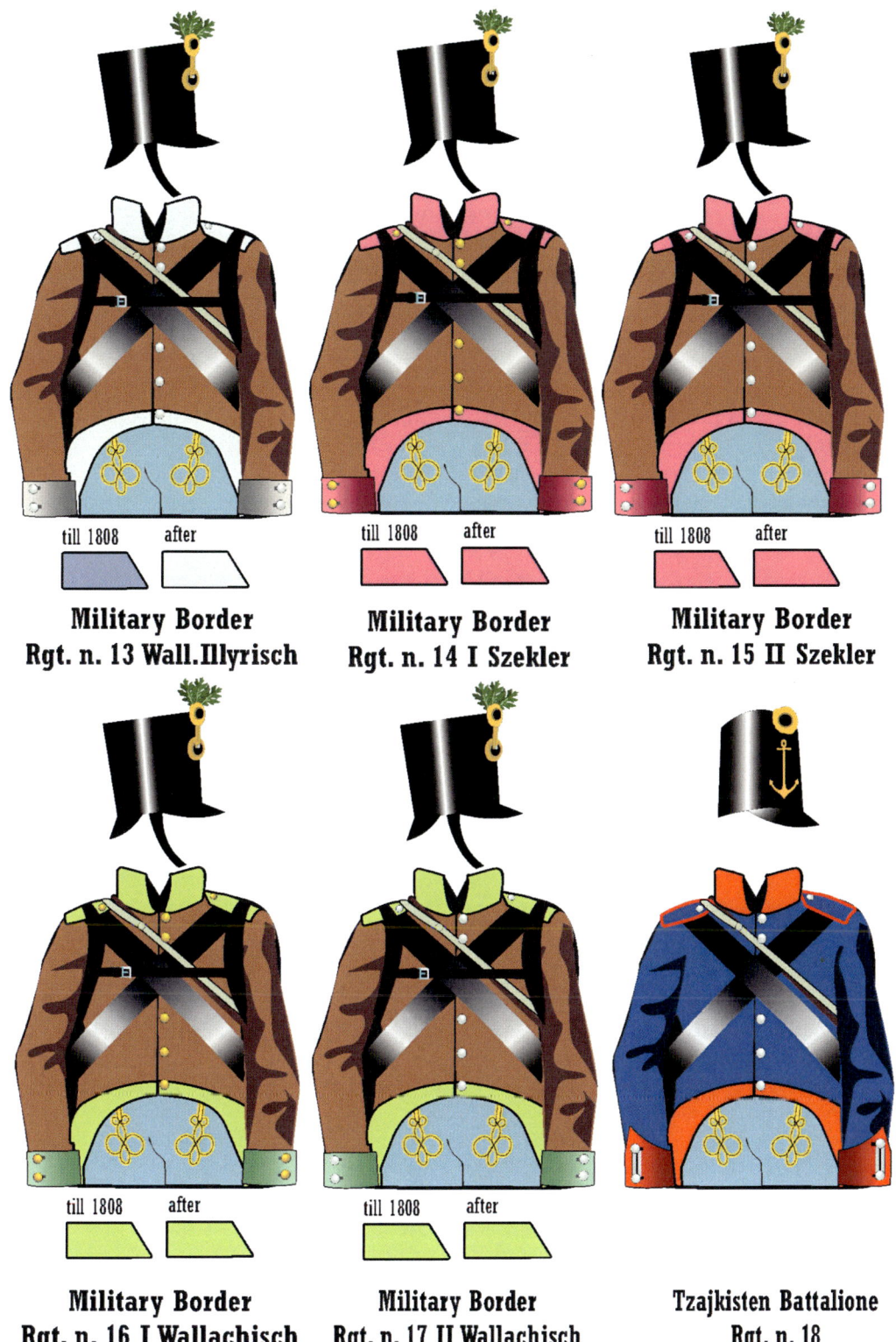

▲ Military Border regiments nr. 13, 14, 15, 16, 17 & 18

- between Aspern and Wagram: the 1st batt. was at Raab with Div. FML Franz Jellačić, Brigade GM Sebottendorf.
- at Wagram: in reserve with the Division FML Jellacich, Brigade GM Lutz, was major Benjaković with a combined (remnants) Banal batt. (Glina) and the 2nd Banal (Petrinja) led by major Vasquez.

Banal Military Border Regiment n. 11 or Second Banal of Petrinja
Druga banska krajiška pješačka pukovnija br. 11 – Banal Grenzregiment n. 2 (Banalisten) Owner: Banus FML Ignaz Gyulai von Maros Németh.
Organized in 1745 – disbanded in 1873

Depot Kader HQ	Petrinja
Commander oberst	marquis Vincenz (Vicente) Vasquez
Oberstleutnant	Jakub von Pavlić – Tomas Rukavina
Majors	Maximilian von Wnorowsky
	Josef Gramatica
1810 Staff	None. Under French rule.

History: as previous one
Facts: its companies were recruited at: 1. Rujevac, 2. Dvor, 3. Divuš - Zrin, 4. Umetić - Mecenčanim, 5. Jabukovac, 6. Petrinja - Siska, 7. Graduš, 8. Drljače - Sunj, 9. Staz - Hrastovac, 10. Majura - Kostajnica, 11. Dubica e 12. Jasenovac.
Recruit.Dist.: Banal territory (nothern and western part) (Kapitanat Petrinja)
1809 (2 regular batt., one Reserve or third batt.). Reservedivision : with Stojčević, in Dalmatia, detached from the Inner Austria army, with the Landwehr (combined Carlstädter-Varasdiner-Banal Landesbataillon). The III reserve batt. was at the battle of Gospić.
The two line battalions entered the campaign with VIII Corps (marquis Chasteler) then Albert Gyulai, with the 2nd Division FML Frimont, Brig. GM. Freiherr von Schmiedt. On April 11 one battalion fought at Venzone. At Pordenone they were in the right wing of the VIII Corps in the Brig. GM Gajoli (but in effects they were still part of the first column GM Schmiedt, while the third column GM von Wetzel had 4 comp. of Banalisten. Gajoli took the command of one batt. only during the Porzia's attack, battle of Sacile). At Sacile one batt. was in the detachment of Oberstlieutenant Volkmann (cover and support of the right army flank). The 1st battalion fought at Ronche. At the end of the battleday Gajoli and Volkmann reunited the regiment marching to Sacile.
After the retreat the two battalions (Brig. Schmiedt) covered the left flank. On May 4 near Bassano they were attacked and repulsed, being later sent to the Tirol's units. 1 batt. was with the Brigade GM baron Franz Philipp Fenner von Fenneberg, 4 comp. with Brigade GM baron Peter Ignaz Marschal von Perclat.
- between Aspern and Wagram: also with the Brig. Buol, detached from Corps Chasteler. after ending the campaign with Brig. Bianchi, Div. Frimont . At the Graz clash the main Corps (left Mur bank) FML Gyulai - FML Knezevich comprised the Brigade Munkácsy with the III batt. reserve Banal and the Landwehr batt. provincial Banal.
- at Wagram: in reserve with the Division FML Jellacich, Brigade GM Lutz, the 2nd Banal (Petrinja) led by major Vasquez. Some sources refer the two battalions, which had been at Graz, with the Brig. De Best, Div. Jellachich, Inner Austria army (rearguard). Later were with theBrig. Pásztory, Inner Austria army.

Banat (one german - one Romanian)
The term "banat" or "banate" designated a frontier province led by a military governor or ban. In the 17th century, parts of the Banat were incorporated into the Habsburg Monarchy of Austria. In 1716, Prince Eugene of Savoy took the last parts of the Banat from the Ottomans. It received the title of the Banat of Temeswar after the Treaty of Passarowitz (1718), and remained a separate province in the Habsburg Monarchy under military administration until 1751, when Empress Maria Theresa of Austria introduced a civil administration. The Banat of Temeswar province was abolished in 1778. The southern part of the Banat region remained within the Military Frontier (Banat Krajina) until the Frontier was abolished in 1871.
Maria Theresa also took a great interest in the Banat; she colonized the region with large numbers of German peasants, encouraged the exploitation of the mineral wealth of the country, and generally developed the measures introduced by Mercy d'Argenteau. German settlers arrived from Swabia, Alsace and Bavaria, as well as people from Austria. Many settlements in the eastern Banat thus were mostly German-inhabited. The ethnic Germans in the Banat region became known as the Danube Swabians, or Donauschwaben. Some of them, coming from French-speaking or linguistically mixed communes in Lorraine, maintained the French language for several generations, and developed a specific ethnic identity, later labelled as Banat French, Français du Banat. Hungarians were not allowed to settle in the Banat during this colonization period.

In 1779, the Banat region was incorporated back into Habsburg Kingdom of Hungary, and the three counties Torontál, Temes and Krassó were created.

According to 1774 data, the population of the Banat of Temeswar numbered 375,740 people and was composed of:
* 220,000 (58.55%) Romanians
* 100,000 (26.61%) Serbs and Greeks
* 53,000 (14.11%) Germans
* 2,400 (0.64%) Hungarians and Bulgarians
* 340 (0.09%) Jews

The Military Border region or the Banat Krajina was divided into Serbian (Illyrian), German (Volksdeutscher) and Romanian (Vlach) sections. This part of the Military Frontier bordered the Principality of Serbia to the south, Voivodship of Serbia and Tamiš Banat to the north, Transylvania and Wallachia to the east, and the Slavonian Military Frontier to the west. The Banat Krajina also included the south-eastern part of Bačka region, known as Šajkaška.

Banat Military Border Regiment n. 12 or German Banater
Grenzregiment n. 12 Deutsch-Banater of Pancsova
Organized in 1742 – disbanded in 1881

Depot Kader HQ	Pancsova (Pančevo in Serbian)
Commander oberst	Georg von Ringelshaim
	Bonaventura Mihanović - Franz von Hordinsnky
Oberstleutnant	Franz von Hordinsnky
Majors	Johann Kljunović von Kampfberg
	Anton Kengyel - Ludwig Schwind
1810 Staff	Franz von Hordinsnky
Oberstleutnant	Anton Kengyel - Ludwig Schwind

History: the Military Border territory was organized in 1718, but only with the Maria Theresia Reform of 1750, Austria did a unambiguous division between the civil Temescher Banat and the militarized area.

In 1751, the northern parts of the province were placed under civil administration, while the southern parts (including Pančevo) were included into Military Frontier (Banat Krajina). During this time the Habsburg administration encouraged massive immigration of German settlers to develop the land. Soon the town of Pančevo was divided into two municipalities: one Serb, one "German". According to the 1767 data, the population of the Serb municipality numbered 424 families, while the population of the German municipality numbered 132 families. According to the 1787 data, the population of the city was composed of 3,506 Orthodox Christians and 2,005 Roman Catholics. The city was briefly restored to Ottoman administration from 1787 to 1788. In 1794, Serb and German municipality were joined into one.

Facts: The 12th Grenz District (Kapitanat) had 12 compagnies with barracks (Standorten) at:

1. Company Alibunar Alibunar, Karlsdorf (Banatski Karlovac), Ilandja, Lokve (Sv. Mihajlo), Seleusch
2. Company Glogon (Glogonj) Glogonj, Bortscha, Debeljatscha, Apfeldorf (Jabuka), Franzfeld (Kacarevo), Kovatschica, Sefkerin
3. Company Grebenaz Grebenaz, Dubowatz, Zagajica, Kajtasovo, Oresac, Parta
4. Company Isbischte Isbischte, Nikolinci, Ulma
5. Company Jarkowatz Jarkowatz, Margitica (Banatska Dubica), Dobritza, Ludwigsdorf (Padina), Samosch, Usdin
6. Company Kubin (Kovin) Kubin (Kovin), Gaj, Deliblato, Ostrowa, Ploschitz (Plocica)
7. Company Neudorf (Banatsko Novo Selo) Neudorf (Banatsko Novo Selo), Petersdorf Vladimirovac, Zrepaja (Crepaja)
8. Company Homolitz (Omoljica) Homolitz (Omoljica), Bawanischte, Brestowatz
9. Company Oppowa (Opovo) Oppowa (Opovo), Baranda, Sakula
10. Company Perles Perles, Idwor, Farkasdin, Tschenta
11. Company Startschowa (Starcevo) Startschowa (Starcevo), Dolowo
12. Company Tomaschewatz Tomaschewatz, Botosch, Orlowat

Recruitment District: Leopoldova, Teissaufwärts till Keresztár (below Szegedin)

1st batt.: oberst Bonaventura Mihanovich

2nd batt.: major Nestor.

1809 (2 regular batt., one Reserve or third batt.)
before Aspern: it began the campaign with IV Corps Rosemberg, Div. Sommariva, avant-garde Brig. Stutterheim, with which was in the 2nd Column at Teugen and in the centre at Abensberg, then left wing at Eggmühl. After the retreat in Bohemia it was attached to the autonomous Brigade GM Paul von Radivojevich, formally part of the III Corps (Kollowrath), sent to the Bohemian Border from Eisenstein till Eger. The remnants of the two line batt. were with the detachment of oberst count Wenzel Sporck (commander of the 1st Časlau Landwehr batt.). They remained in Bohemia till the armistice.

Banat Military Border Regiment n. 13 or Valachian Banater
Regimentul de graniţă romano-bănăţean nr. 13 - Grenzregiment n. 13 Wallachisch-Illyrisches (Karansebes)
Organized in 1767 – disbanded in 1881

Depot Kader HQ	Caransebes
Commander oberst	Johann von Peretić
	Mihail von Mihaljević (Mihaljevich) (Warasdiner)
Oberstleutnant	Gottlieb Betzmann
Majors	Johann Gollnbovich
	baron Franz Cerrini – Franz Weinzierl
1810 Staff	Mihail von Mihaljević
Oberstleutnant	Mathias Betzmann - Franz Weinzierl

History: Was founded in 1767. Since its establishment, the regiment had several names: - in 1769: N. 72 Border Regiment. - in 1775: Border Regiment Romanian-Illyrian - in 1798: Wallachian-Illyrian Border Regiment n. 13 - in 1838: Wallachian-Banat Border Regiment n. 13 - in 1849: Rumenian-Banat Border Regiment n. 13. The area had undergone many stages of organization, and ultimately include: Bistra Valley, from village Marga till Caransebes, the Timis-Cerna corridor (with adjacent valleys) from Orsova to the village Sviniţa; the Banatean Krajina till the Almaj valley, from village Prigor to village Lăpuşnicul Mare.

In peacetime the regiment was organized on 12 companies having a variable number of common frontier-guards. The training of the border guards were made as follows:
- recruits for three years in Caransebes
- reservists with training sessions on Sundays and holidays.

Border Watch Service - each military border company (grănicereasca) received a variable number of guard outposts on the border – the soldiers stood eight days in the watching-stations, according to a schedule made by the company commander. Postal service was at Caransebes, Marga, Bistra Valley and the Timis-Cerna corridor (Slatina Teregova, Cornea, and Orsova) - military post was held by couriers on horseback. Health Service - at the regimental military hospital of Caransebes - the regiment had a regimental chief doctor, two main doctors, four secondary doctors and surgeons, 8 physicians - at each company there was a doctor and a nurse.

In the 104 years of the regiment's life, it gave 25 generals, over 200 senior officers, a large number of junior officers and NCOs. Over 40 men were awarded for acts of bravery. The flag of the regiment did have the following medals: 10 gold, 31 silver Class 1 and 36 2nd class silver.

Facts: its companies were recruited at:
Comp. 1 of Dalboşeţ: 1-Dalboşeţ, 2-Sopotul Vechi, 3-Moceriş, 4-Lăpuşnic, 5-Şopotul Nou, 6-Ravensca
Comp. 2 of Bozovici: 1-Bozovici, 2-Prilipeţ, 3-Bania, 4-Gârbovăţ
Comp. 3 of Prigor: 1-Prigor, 2-Putna, 3-Rudăria (Eftimie Murgu), 4-Pătaş, 5-Borlovenii Vechi, 6-Borlovenii Noi (Breazova)
Comp. 4 of Petnic: 1-Petnic, 2-Iablaniţa, 3-Lapuşnicel, 4-Globucraiovei, 5-Mehadica, 6-Pîrvova, 7-Şumiţa
Comp. 5 of Mehadia: 1-Mehadia, 2-Băile Herculane, 3-Valea Bolvaşniţa, 4-Plugova, 5-Globu rău, 6-Pecinisca, 7-Birza
Comp. 6 of Orşova: 1-Orşova, 2-Eşalniţa, 3-Ogradena nouă, 4-Ogradena Veche, 5-Dubova, 6-Plaşeviţa, 7-Eibenthal, 8-Tisovita, 9-Jupalnicul Vechi, 10-Jupalnicul Nou, 11-Tufari, 12-Coramnic, 13-Toplet
Comp. 7 of Cornereva: 1 Cornereva, 2-Bogîltin
Comp. 8 of Cornea: 1-Cornea, 2-Cruşovat, 3-Cuptoare, 4-Cănicea, 5-Domaşnea
Comp. 9 of Teregova: 1-Teregova, 2-Verendin, 3-Luncaviţa, 4-Rusca, 5-Feneş
Comp.10 of Slatina: 1-Slatina Tmiş, 2-Sadova Veche, 3-Sadova Nouă, 4-Ilova, 5-Vârciorova, 6-Vălişoara, 7-Petroşniţa, 8-Bucoşniţa, 9-Goleţ, 10-Armeniş, 11-Weidenthal (Brebu Nou), 12-Wolfsberg (Gărâna)
Comp.11 of Caransebeş: 1-Caransebeş, 2-Caransebeşul Nou, 3-Cicleni, 4-Dalci, 5-Turnu Ruieni, 6-Borlova, 7-Bolvaşniţa, 8-Cârpa (Valea Timişului), 9-Poiana, 10-Buchin, 11-Lindenfeld, 12-Zlagna, 13-Zerveşti
Comp.12 of Ohaba Bistra: 1-Ohaba Bistra (Oţelu Roşu), 2-Obreja, 3-Ciuta, 4-Glimboca, 5-Ciresa, 6-Crâşma (Măgura), 7-Mal, 8-Măru, 9-Marga, 10-Valea Mare (Valea Bistrei), 11-Var, 12-Zăvoi, 13-Voislova, 14-Iaz

Recruit. Distr.: eastern Banat. the Karansebes regiment was partially recruited in the german Banat and had some "grenz" fortresses in its area: Mehadia, Orsova and Bosovich. It recruited from the kapitanate: Weisskirchen (Fejértemplom) siege of a battalion, Schupanek, Teregova, Töplic, Vár, Mezerich or Möserich.

1809 (2 regular batt., one Reserve or third batt.)

before Aspern: The two line batt. began the campaign with the troops detached to the blockade of Passau (Oberhaus fortress) Division FML baron Franz von Dedovich, Brigade GM Paul von Radivojevich, IV Corps Rosenberg. After the retreat the division was ordered to watch the Danube left bank (northern) and the two battalions were in the detached Brig. oberst Grätze, at the Ebelsberg battle and finally sent alog the road Linz - Schärding.
- at Aspern : the Brigade oberst Grätze was in the avant-garde Division FML prince Victor de Rohan (IV Corps or 5th Column Rosenberg). The two batt. had around 1300 men.
- between Aspern and Wagram: 2 Batt. w. Avantgarde Nordmann, II Flügel Hauptarmée
- at Wagram: colonel Grätze led the Banaters in the avant-garde of the left wing, Division Nordmann, Brigade GM baron Peter von Vécsey. After the battle they retreated with the II Corps Hohenzollern, reached Znaim and deployed behind the cavalry reserve (Division FML baron Ulm, Brigade GM Hardegg).

Transylvanian Border (Siebenbürgen)

The Székely military Border

The Széklers or Székels (Hun. Székely, Lat. Siculi), were a Transylvanian people of Ugro-Finnic origins, similar to the Magyars, about 450.000 fellows who colonized the area between Kronstadt (south) and Maros-Vasarhely - Gyergö St Miklos (north). A legend told they were sent there by St. Ladislaus in order to watch the Border against Muslims. The name Szèkel would come from szék (chair – siege or the equivalent of the German word Stuhl of the Transylvanian Saxons). The hungarian Székely, therefore, would only mean "Border sentinel".

The Székely were considered the finest warriors of medieval Transylvania. They were part of the Unio Trium Nationum ("Union of Three Nations") , a coalition of the three Transylvanian Estates, the other two nations being the (also predominantly Hungarian) nobility and the "Saxon" (that is, ethnic German) burghers. These three nations ruled Transylvania, usually in harmony though sometimes in conflict with one another.

Their origin has been much debated; it is, however, now generally accepted that they are true Hungarians (or at least the descendants of a Magyarized Turkic peoples), transplanted there to guard the frontier, their name meaning simply "frontier guards". Their organization was of the Turkic type, and they are probably of Turkic stock. There is historical evidence that the Székely were part of the Avar confederation during the so-called Dark Ages, but this does not mean that they are ethnically Avar. By the 11th century they had adopted the Hungarian language.

The Sun and Moon are the symbols of the Székely, and are used in the coat of arms of Transylvania and on the Romanian national coat of arms. The Sun and Moon symbols represented proto-Hungarian gods. After the Hungarians became Christians in the 11th century, the importance of these icons became purely visual and symbolic. Their original religious significance was lost.

In 1762, Empress Maria Theresa decided to set up border troops on the frontier of Transylvania, based on the Military Frontier system already in place on the Ottoman border area. Mostly Romanians were recruited in the Southern Carpathians (Fogaras area) and Székelys in the Eastern Carpathians. The drafting was organised partly on voluntary, partly on compulsory basis, and resulted in conflicts in many places, especially in Székely Land. The Székelys requested that instead of the imperial officers, they have their own leaders according to the traditions, and that they are not ordered to go in action abroad.

As the negotiations failed with the army, Székelys openly protested and some of the Seats contacted each other to start co-ordinated actions. As the drafting was only partly successful, the chief officer responsible for the recruitment gave up his plans and ordered that the so far distributed weapons are returned by the Székelys. They, however, gave back only part of the equipment and kept the rifles as a compensation for the weapons confiscated after the Rákóczi Uprising.

The next, already violent attempt by the imperial officers to recruit Székely border soldiers culminated in a tragic event, the Mádéfalva Massacre, commemorated until today. In December 1763, the men sought refuge from drafting in the mountains, at Mádéfalva (Romanian: Siculeni), some of them equipped with weapons. On 7 January, 1764, an army unit of 1300 soldiers, with two cannons, attacked the peaceful crowd and massacred hundreds of them. The drafting in Székely Land was quickly and easily completed after these events. Border troops were set up in every Seat except for Udvarhely and Maros Seat.

▲ Slavonian and border irregular Infantry 1798-1805. From Ottenfeld artwork

After the Mádéfalva Massacre, many Székelys crossed the Carpathians and escaped to Moldova. Those who stayed in the Moldavian Voivodate, became one of the subgroups of Csángó people. Others moved to the Bukovina Region and founded their final settlements with the help of General András Hadik. This group retained their traditions and are regarded to as the Székelys of Bukovina.

The Military Frontier Organisation put an end to the autonomy of the Székely Nation in some respects. The self governance of the settlements was seriously hurt by the border guard commanders. They interfered with the election of judges, the local agriculture and schooling, also with the every-day life of the Székely guards. Property transactions or weddings could be done only with the permission of the officers. In local communities, however, many of the traditions were kept, the Székely pride and their strong desire for freedom remained. They organised their own life, set rules for the building of roads and bridges, also for the election of their leaders and jury members. (Most of these issues were decided by landlords in the noble counties.) The ancient system of redistributing common lands was still a practice by the end of the 18th century, but ceased to exist in a couple of decades.

Szekely Military Border Regiment n. 14

Grenzregiment n. 14 Szekler n. 1 Csikszereda Organized in 1762 – disbanded in 1851

Depot Kader HQ	Csíkszereda
Commander oberst	baron Michael Markant von Blankenschwert
	Bonaventura von Roscher
Oberstleutnant	Bonaventura von Roscher
Majors	Stephan Arady de Kajal
	Mathias Betzmann – Johann Földvary
1810 Staff	Bonaventura von Roscher
Oberstleutnant	Stephan Arady de Kajal

History: Miercurea-Ciuc (Hungarian: Csíkszereda, German: Szeklerburg) is the county seat of Harghita County, Romania. It lies in the Székely Land, an ethno-cultural region in eastern Transylvania. The town is situated on the banks of the river Olt, at the foot of the Nagysomlyó Mountain (1033m).

Facts: the companies recruited at:

1. Fel Csik (Plăiesii de Sus); 2. Kozmás (Cozmeni); 3. Csik-Szent-Imre (Sântimbru); 4. Csik-Szent-György (Ciucsângeorgiu); 5. Várdótfalva (Sumuleu Ciuc); 6. Szépviz (Frumoasa); 7. Rákos (Racu); 8. Csik-Szent-Tamás (Tomesti); 9. Újfalu (Suseni); 10. Szent-Miklós (Gheorghieni); 11. Al-Falu (Joseni); 12. Ditró (Ditrău).

1809 (only one combined batt. Recruit. Distr.: areas of Csik, Gyergyö, Part of the counties Maros and Aranyos.
- it began the campaign with the Brig. Branovatzky, Div. Schauroth, VII Corps archduke Ferdinand remaining with the twin Combined Szekler batt. n.2 along the whole campaign in Poland.

Szekely Military Border Regiment n. 15

Grenzregiment n. 15 Siebenbürgisches-Romänen (Transylvania) or 2nd Szekler Kézdivásárhely
Organized in 1762 – disbanded in 1851

Depot Kader HQ	Kézdivásárhely
Commander oberst	Johann von Grammont
	Anton von Divecky
Oberstleutnant	Anton von Divecky
Majors	chevalier Josef Widemann
	Theodor von Kiebel – Angel Kapschermet
1810 Staff	Anton von Divecky
Oberstleutnant	chevalier Josef Widemann

History: Târgu Secuiesc (Hungarian: Kézdivásárhely; German: Szekler Neumarkt; Latin: Neoforum Siculorum) is a city in Covasna county, Transylvania, Romania. The town was first mentioned in 1407 as Torjawasara, meaning in Hungarian "Torja Market". Originally, the Hungarian name Kézdivásárhely was also used in Romanian in the form Chezdi-Osorheiu, but this was altered to Tîrgu Secuiesc (now spelled Târgu Secuiesc).

Facts: it recruited this companies: 1. Bölön (Belin); 2. Barót (Baraolt); 3. Telegdi-Batzon (BăŇani); 4. Sepsi-Szent-György (Sfântu Gheorghe); 5. Uzon (Ozun); 6. Zágon (Zagon); 7. Dálnok (Dalnic); 8. Zabola (Zăbala); 9. Felsö-Tsernaton (Cernatu de Sus); 10. Kézdi-Vásárhely (Târgu Secuiesc); 11. Beretzk (Brezcu); 12. Polyán (Poian).

1809. (only one combined battalion) Recruit. Distr.: areas of counties Háromszék and Údvarhély (Barocz)
- it began the campaign with the Brig. Branovatzky, Div. Schauroth, VII Corps archduke Ferdinand remaining with the twin Combined Szekler batt. n.1 along the whole campaign in Poland.

The Wallachians (Romanians)

The name Wallachia, generally not used by Romanians themselves (but present in some contexts as Valahia or Vlahia), is derived from the ethnonym Valach, a word used originally by Germanic peoples to designate their Romance-speaking neighbours, or foreigners in general, and subsequently taken over by Slavic-speakers to refer to Romanians, with variants such as Vlach, Blach, Bloc, Bloh, Boloh.

In effect the Military Wallachian Border was that of the Transylvania area in which there were no Szekelys. The Transylvania (Romanian: Ardeal; Hungarian: Erdély; German: Siebenbürgen) is a historical region in the central part of Romania, at the time on the Ottoman Border.

The Habsburgs acquired the territory shortly after the Battle of Vienna in 1683. The Habsburgs, however, probably recognized the Hungarian sovereignty over Transylvania (it is not certain), while the Transylvanians recognized the sovereignty of the Habsburg emperor Leopold I (1687), and the region was officially attached to the Habsburg Empire, separated in all but name from Habsburg controlled Hungary and subjected to the direct rule of the emperor's governors. The Kuruc Rebellion (1703-1711) separated Transylvania from the Austrian lands; However, Habsburg sovereignty was again recognized by Transylvania's diet in the Peace of Szatmar (1711), in which the country's privileges were confirmed.

While Royal and Ottoman Hungary were reunited to form the (Habsburg) Kingdom of Hungary, Transylvania was not included, but remained a separate entity. The principality's representative body was the diet; it did not meet between 1761 and 1790. The Austrian authorities, with some success, interfered in the appointment of officials, with the result of Catholics often given preferential treatment.

Transylvania had a capital of it's own - Kolozsvar (Cluj, Klausenburg), a diet of it's own dominated by the Hungarian nobility and the often German representatives of the cities. Although Transylvania granted freedom of religion, a clear distinction was made between Accepted Confessions - Lutheranism, Calvinism, Catholicism - and Tolerated Confessions/Religions (Orthodox Christianity : the Vlachs, and Judaism). The Vlachs (Romanians), which probably formed the population majority, were not represented on Transylvania's diet.

The border regions of Transylvania were placed under military administration (Militärgrenze). Alba Iulia was fortified 1715-1738.

The mission of the establishment of new regiments was given on 5 July 1761 to the austrian cavalry general, Adolf Nicholas Buccow. According to the draft prepared by Buccow, October 13,1761, the Aulic Council decided to disband the frontier guards and their organization, for a good effectiveness and minimum military expenditure along the border of Transylvania, Banat and Bukovina.

General Buccow proposed in this occasion, the establishment of a "border militia" composed of two infantry Romanian regiments, each comprising 3000 troops, two regiments of Szekler infantry, a regiment of Romanian "dragons" (cavalry) and one of Székely "Hussar", each with 1000 riders. Transylvanian border-guard numbers (by these units) was estimated to reach 17000 troops. Border militarization started in 1761 reaching a self-going organization by the year 1766, when Empress Maria Theresa sanctioned a military Status of the border regiments, composed of 84 articles. Apart from guarding the border and to fight under the banner of Habsburg, Romanian border soldiers also had the responsibility of making health cordons (quarantine), to stop entry of cholera patients in the provinces of the Empire, and emigration over the Carpathians mountains of discontented subjects. Of an entire Regiment (3708 soldiers) worked as summer guards a total of 908 border soldiers, while winter guards were reduced to 695. Each company was entrusted to guard a well delimited area of the border. Guarding the border was done in fixed postations, pickets or cordons, but also with patrols in different periods, depending on the importance of the watched route.

Transylvanian Military Border Regiment n. 16 or 1st Wallachian
Grenzregiment n. 16 Siebenbürgisches- 1st Walachen.
Organized in 1762 – disbanded in 1851

Depot Kader HQ	Orlath
Commander oberst	Franz Auftieffern von Eulenburg
	Carl Leibinger
Oberstleutnant	Carl Leibinger
Majors	Michael Sotterius von Landsberg
	Lorenz Pettenek
1810 Staff	Carl Leibinger
Oberstleutnant	??

History: In 1766 the Romanian border regiment based in Orlat was formed under direct supervision of General Ziskovic. The slogan worn by the regimental battle flag from Orlat is almost forgotten, it was "Viribus Unitis" (united powers).

Facts: the 12 companies of the Orlath regiment were:

1. Rakosd (Răcăstia); 2. Hátszeg (Hateg); 3. Zajkány (Zeicani); 4. Kudzsir (Cugir); 5. Sima (Jina); 6. Orláth (Orlat) - Véstény (Veştem) - Felsö-Porumbak (Porumbacu de Sus); 7. Rákovitza (Racovita); 8. Alsó-Vist (Vistea); 9. Vajda-Rétse (Recea); 10. Mardsina (Mărgineni); 11. Ohaba; 12. Dumbravita (Tantari).

Recr.Dist.: near the north part of the Carpathian mts. (districts of the Hunyadi county, expecially in the Hátszeg valley, in the Fogaras district of the free Wallachia (Romanen), borderlands Boern and Puskas from Rotenthurm till the Bodzaer Paß

1809: (only one combined battalion of six comp.)

- before Aspern: - it began with 1 Combined batt. with Brig. Branovatzky, Div. Schauroth, VII Corps archduke Ferdinand. After April 1st the two Wallachian batt. (1st Rgt. and 2nd Rgt. Combined battalions under colonel Auftieffern) were in the autonomous avant-garde brigade GM Mohr with order to advance till Radom. They were at the Raszyn battle and then in Warsaw. The first batt. (major Kreitter) was detached to Radzymin; the 2nd batt. marched with its commander. The two battalions fought at Grochow and then, April 29, crossed the Vistula at Gora defending the bridgehead. After the withdrawal, colonel Auftieffern and the 1st battalion were detached to defend Sandomir and Zamosc. On May 15 the Mohr Brig. with the 2nd batt. attcked the bridgehead of Thorn. On May 18 they abandoned Sandomir.

On May 20 the Poles attacked Zamosc, where stood 3 comp. of the rgt. The regiment there lost 571 men, made prisoners, and the battalion commandr major von Pettenek. Now the 3 remaining comp. of the 1st Batt. were at the Gorcyze clash. On June 15 the 3 comp. returned on the Vistula left bank under Brig. GM Trautenberg and then withdrew till the armistice.

Transylvanian Military Border Regiment n. 17 or 2nd Wallachian

Grenzregiment n. 17 Siebenbürgisches- 2nd Walachen.

Organized in 1762 – disbanded in 1851

Depot Kader HQ	Nasaud (Naszod)
Commander oberst	Franz Grätze
	Ignaz Lenk von Trauenfeld
Oberstleutnant	Franz Grätze - Ignaz Lenk von Trauenfeld
Majors	Peter Mehesi de Kis-Bun
	Johann Kreitter
1810 Staff	Ignaz Lenk von Trauenfeld
Oberstleutnant	Johann Kreitter

Command HQ: till 1786 Orasul Bistrita became the county civil seat of area Bistriţa-Năsăud.

History: Austro-Hungarian Empress, Maria Tereza, assigner to this Border regiment the areas of the Rodna valley, Şieului valley and Someşului valley. The battle flag of the 2nd Regiment of the Nasaud Romanian border wear the slogan "rediviva Romanian Virtus (resurrected Romanian Virtue).

Facts: it recruited these companies: 1. Monor (Monor); 2. Nagy-Falu (Măriselu); 3. Borgó-Prund (Prundu-Bîrgăului); 4. Borgó-Zsoszány (Josenii Bârgăului); 5. Rodna (Rodna); 6. Szinr-Zsorzu (Sângeorz Băi); 7. Folre (Feldru); 8. Rebrisora (Rebrisoara); 9. Naszeud (Năsăud); 10. Tyelts (Telciu); 11. Zagra (Zagra); 12. Makód (Mocod).

1809. (one combined battalion of six comp.) Recr.Dist.: Kolos and Doboka counties, Bistritz and Borgoer Districts in the northeastern Transylvania.

- before Aspern: After April 1st the two combined Wallachian batt. were in the autonomous avant-garde brigade GM Mohr with order to advance till Radom. See above.

The battalion Czajkist (Tschajkist later Titler) boatmen of Danube

Czajkists or Tschaikisten, also called Nassadisten (serbian Šajkaši), were river sailors of the Danube, which had the task to defend (originally) the port of Belgrad and to watch the Border with the Ottoman Turkish Empire. Originally they served under the Kingdom of Hungary and later under the Habsburg, when they obtained the "Grenzer" status (Militärgrenze). During the battle of Peterwardein (1526, close to the battle of Mohács) the Tschaikisten fought the Ottoman Danube Flotilla under the serbian Commander Radič Božić.

The Turkish conquest of Belgrad moved the Danube "Marines" in the area of Petrovaradin, where they rebuilt their flotilla. Many moved also to Slovakia. When Austria consolidated its rule over Hungary and the current serbian region of Vojvodina, it was also created a Tschaikist province, the "Šajkaška" inside the Batschka (Baczka). The so called "Czajkisten Battalion", as part of the Military Border, was raised in 1763. In the beginning, the population of the region was composed entirely of Serbs, which were brave and skilful warriors.

Their military command in 1809 was in Titel, 2217 inhabitants in 1820, 498 of whom were german, placed in the corner between the Danube and the Tisza (Theiss) rivers. In the Militärgrenze time, there they recruited the personnel for the so-called "Tschaikisten" Battalion, the Tschaikisten Distrikt being formed by villages of: Lock - Vilova - Moschorin - Gardonovacz - Unter-Kovill - Ober-Kovill - Unter Sz. Ivany - Josephs-Dorf - Gozpodincze - Kaats - Georgievo - Csurug – Nadaly.

Their name came from their characteristic boats: the "Tschaika" or Nassen (Shajka), a long and narrow rowing boat similar to a small galley, with a single sail, and with one gun (the Şayka-Geschütz, or with the generic Ottoman name of Topçu). During the "Napoleonic" times the battalion was organized as a Pontoons unit. The battalion was under the Oberst-Schiff-Amt (Supreme Naval Bureau) at Wien (GM Josef Schwäger von Hohenbruck). Its "sailors" had to watch the "Schiffämter" (Naval Commands) at : Linz, Scharnstein, Prague, Cracow, Pressburg, Komorn, Pest, Szegedin, Esseg, Peterwardein, Semlin, Temesvar, Pancsova and Sissek.

Staff at Vienna and Klosterneuburg, then Titel.

1809 commander: major-oberstlieutenant Aaron von Stanissavljevich. They were part with the Army of Germany (145 pontoons) and part with the Inner Austria Army.

The danubian navy and pontoons battalion (Czajkisten bataillon) or Titler batt. had the following force:

Line	Econ. Section	Czajkisten Bataillon Staff 6 Companies	Line	Econ. Section	
1	--	Stabs-Offizier (commander)	1	--	Major
--	1	Oekonomie-Hauptmann	--	1	Auditor
--	1	Rechnungsführer	--	1	Grundbuchsführer
1	--	Corps-Feldarzt	3	3	Unter-Ärzte
1	--	Bataillons Adjutant	3	--	K.k. ordinare Cadetten
--	3	Stabsschreiber	3	3	Fouriere
1	--	Bataillons Tambour	4	--	Hautboisten
3	--	Führern	1	--	Profoß
2	--	Fourierschützen	2	--	Halb-invaliden Privatdienern
		Schiffpersonale (Ship personnel)			
	1	Hauptmann-Schiffbaumeister		1	Schiffszimmer-Polier
	12	Civil-Handswerksleute		1	Privatdiener

Line	Econ. Section	Czajkisten Compagnie	Line	Econ. Section	
4	--	Hauptleute	2	--	Capitain-Lieutenante
6	--	Oberlieutenante	6	--	Unterlieutenante
--	3	Oekonomie Oberlieutenante	--	3	Oekonomie Unterlieutenante
6	--	Oberbrückenmeistern	6	6	Tschaikisten Feldwebeln
1	--	Artilleriste Feldwebel	36	12	Tschaikisten Corporalen
4	--	Artilleriste Corporalen	--	6	Compagnie Schreiber
6	--	Fourierschützen	12	--	Tambouren
72	24	Tschaikisten Gefreyten	12	--	Artilleriste Gefreyten
48	--	Zimmerleute	18	--	Halb-invaliden Privatdienern
			--	6	Ganz-invaliden Privatdienern

Notes about the Evolution of the Military Border Troops after 1809 1810 – the "French" Croatians

The Decree of 1 January 1810 began the reorganization of six Grenz regiments along French guidelines. Initially, all the senior officers were replaced with French officers, but this eventually changed. However, the commanding officers were to remain French throughout their short history in the French army.

As there was already an established seniority amongst these regiments, the French decided to retain that seniority and the croatian regiments were renamed as follows:

Old Name	new N.
Liccaner	1
Otochaner	2
Oguliner	3
Szluiner	4
1st Banal	5
2nd Banal	6

▲ Pioneer and pontoonier 1798-1805. From Ottenfeld artwork

Initially each regiment was organized on two battalions, but during 1812, the regiments raised a 3rd and 4th battalion. The strength of a two battalion regiment was 60 officers and 2,680. These men were organized into the standard six company organization of a French light battalion. They had a carabinier, a voltigeur and four chasseurs companies each. The regimental staff consisted of:

1	Colonel	1	Regimental adjudant
1	Colonel-major	1	Regimental surgeon major
2	Chefs de bataillon	2	Battalion surgeon majors
1	Adjudant-major capitaine	1	Teneur des livres (Bookkeeper)
1	Capitaine d'economie	6	Cadets
1	Sous-lieutenant d'economie	3	Fourriers
3	Auditors (Regimental judges)	6	Fourriers d'economie
2	Maitres de comptes Chief accountants)	1	Drum major
6	Porte drapeaux (Flag bearers)	1	Chef de musique
1	Provost	7	Musicians

Each battalion had:

6	Capitaine	36	Sergeants
6	Lieutenant	12	Sergeants d'economie
3	Lieutenants d'economie	48	Corporals
6	Sous-lieutenants	48	Corporals d'economie
6	Sous-lieutenants d'economie	6	Carpenters
6	Ensigns	12	Drummers
6	Sergeant majors	24	Domestics or Servants
6	Sergeant, majors d'economie	1,080	Carabiniers, Voltigeurs and Chasseurs
		1308	Total

The artillery company remained probably retaining a strength of 50 men. In addition, the old formation of the Grenz regiments had a very large staff of non-military personnel, such as priests, schoolmasters, carpenters, masons and foresters. The staff of "extra" personnel for the first four regiments remained high with 97 men, but in the 5th and 6th Regiments this staff consisted of only 19 men.

In order to train these units in the French tactical system was established a military school in Carlstadt, where each regiment had to send six officers and two non-commissioned officers.

As full line units, these regiments never took the field for the French flags. Instead were formed "Provisional" regiments by breaking off single battalions from each regiment and then merging them with other battalions. The 1st Provisional Croatian Regiment was organized on October 26, 1811, by grouping the first battalions of the 1st and 2nd Croatian Regiments.

The 2nd Provisional Regiment was formed on February 25, 1813 with the 1st battalions of the 3rd and 4th Regiments. The 3rd Provisional Regiment was organized on September 21, 1811 with the first battalions of the 5th and 6th Regiments.

"Rassjia" !

The 1st and 3rd Provisional Regiments joined the Grande Armee in its catastrophic invasion of Russia and fought very bravely. The 3rd Provisional Regiment proved itself to be an extremely brave and hard fighting regiment when, at the second battle of Polotsk, it attempted rather unwisely to outperform the 4th Swiss Infantry Regiment.

It appears that a serious rivalry had arisen between these two regiments and that only the battlefield could provide the appropriate arena for showing who was the braver. The only result of this display of bravado was a serious beating for both, when they attempted to engage the entire 1st Russian Corps of Count Wittgenstein by themselves.

As the 3rd Provisional Regiment began to withdraw towards France, it was engaged at Berezina. Here it lost two officers killed and 18 wounded. It appears it was an hard fighting unit, with so many officers "hors de combat".

Though details of their actions are scarce, the 1st Provisional Regiment was awarded with 6 Crosses of the Legion d'honneur (on 18 October by Napoleon). It fought at Malo-Jaroslavetz and lost a chef de bataillon and one captain killed outright, and 3 captains and 8 lieutenants mortally wounded. It was obviously in the bulky of the fighting. When the 1st Provisional Regiment returned from Russia it had only 22 officers and 31 non-commissioned officers. The campaign was slightly kinder for the 3rd Provisional Regiment and it returned with 16 officers and 141 non-commissioned officers and men. These men were absorbed into their original parent units and the provisional regiments were never raised again.

The 2nd Provisional Regiment, raised in 1813, was sent to Germany where it became part of the garrison of Glogau. When the city was besieged they were shut in and remained there until the city capitulated. The regiment was returned to the Austrians who promptly disbanded it.

It seems also they have been raised a 4th Provisional Regiment in August 1813. It appeared to have fought with Eugene, but its fate is currently unknown. When the Croatian provinces were returned to Austria, it was disbanded what remained of the former Croatian regiments.

The "other Grenzers" after 1809

After the reduction in consequence of the lost war of 1809, 11 Border Regiments remained with the K.K. army:
- Warasdin-Kreuzer Nr. 5 - Warasdin-St. Georger Nr. 6
- Brooder Nr. 7 - Gradiskaner Nr. 8 - Peterwardeiner Nr. 9
- Deutsch-Banater Nr. 12 - Wallachisch-Illyrische Nr. 13
- 1. Siebenbürgisches Szekler Nr. 14 - 2. Siebenbürgisches Szekler Nr. 15
- 1 Wallachische Nr. 16 - 2 Wallacisceh Nr. 17

The peacetime force of one austrian regiment of the 2 Croatian and 3 Slavonian Grenzinfanterie was fixed (by the Hofkriegsrat on August 10, 1811), in 12 companies and one administrative section (Ökonomie-Abteilung).

Line	Econ. Section	Croatian-Slavonian Grenzinfanterie Regiment's STAFF	Line	Econ. Section	
1	--	Colonel regiment's commander	1	--	Oberstlieutenant
2	--	Majore	--	1	Oekonomie Hauptmann
1	--	Auditore	--	1	Oekonomie Unterlieutenant
1	--	Regiments Feldarzt	--	1	1ter Rechnungsführer
--	1	Grundbuchsführer	1	--	2ter Rechnungsführer
1	--	Regiments Adjutant	1	--	Ober-Arzt
6	--	K.k. ordinare Cadetten	6	6	Unter-Arzten
3	6	Fourieren	--	5	Stabsschreiber
1	--	Regiments Tambour	8	--	Hautboisten (Hoboisten)
3	--	Führer	1	--	Profoß
4	--	Fourierschützen	3	--	Halb Invaliden Privatdiener
--	6	Ganz (totally) Invaliden Privatdiener			
		TOTALS	43	27	

Line	Econ. Section	Croatian-Slavonian Grenzinfanterie 12 Companies	Line	Econ. Section	
8	--	Hauptleute	4	--	Capitain-lieutenants
12	--	Oberlieutenants	12	--	Unterlieutenants
12	--	Fähnriche	--	6	Oekonomie Oberlieutenant
12	12	Feldwebel	--	6	Oekonomie Unterlieutenant
12	24	Corporalen	--	12	Compagnieschreiber
12	--	Fourierschützen	24	--	Tambours
96	96	Gefreyte	12	--	Zimmerleute
			?		Gemeine Fusilier, Scharfschützen, Artilleristen as stated
--	6	Ganz (totally) Invaliden Privatdiener	3	--	Halb Invaliden Privatdiener

The Wallachisch-Illirische Regiment was formed by 16 companies.

Line	Econ. Section	Valachian-Illyrian Grenzinfanterie Regiment's STAFF	Line	Econ. Section	
1	--	Majore	1	--	Fourierschütz

Line	Econ. Section	Valachian-Illyrian Grenzinfanterie 16 Companies	Line	Econ. Section	
4	--	Hauptleute	4	--	Capitain-lieutenants
4	--	Oberlieutenants	4	--	Unterlieutenants
4	--	Fähnriche	4	--	Fourierschützen
10	--	Privatdiener			
		TOTALS	34		
--	2	Oekonomie Oberlieutenant	--	4	Compagnieschreiber
--	2	Oekonomie Unterlieutenant	--	16	Gefreyte
--	4	Feldwebel	--	8	Corporalen
--	4	Privatdiener			
		TOTALS	40		

The four Border reg. of Transylvania (Siebenbürgischen Grenz-infanterie-regimente) had 12 companies in peacetime.

Line	Econ. Section	Transylvanian Grenzinfanterie Regiment's STAFF	Line	Econ. Section	
1	--	Oberst Commander	2	--	Majoren
1	--	Regiments Caplan	1	--	Regiments Rechnungsführer
1	--	Auditor	1	--	Regiments Adjutant
1	--	Regiments Feld-Arzt	1	--	Regiments Tambour
2	--	Ober-Ärzte	6	--	Unter-Ärzte
6	--	K.k. Cadetten	6	--	Führern
6	--	Fourieren	4	--	Fourierschützen
8	--	Hautboisten	1	--	Profoß
5	--	Privatdienern			
		Total Staff	54		
Line	Econ. Section	Transylvania Grenzinfanterie 12 Companies	Line	Econ. Section	
8	--	Hauptleute	4	--	Capitain-lieutenants
12	--	Oberlieutenants	12	--	Unterlieutenants
12	--	Feldwebeln	72	--	Corporalen
96	--	Gefreyten	12	--	Fourierschützen
24	--	Tambouren	12	--	Zimmerleute
24	--	Privatdienern			

The Grenz Regiments recruited in their territories, each company or squadron in ist own province (Canton). In autumn 1813 some of the old (disbanded) Grenzerbataillone were reorganized

Notes

1   From Ranka Gašic, "History of the Serbs in Croatia, Slavonia and Dalmatia from the Sixteenth to the Eighteenth Century", Ph.Diss., univ.of Belgrade.

2   To enhance economy in the Border, the so-called "military communities" were formed: the cities within the Border, in which crafts and trade were developed. The first military communities, formed in 1748, were Petrovaradin, Zemun and Sremski Karlovci. In 1779 the Communitaeten-Regulativ was issued.

3   Sources: Direktion des k. und k. Kriegsarchives. Befreiungskrieg 1813 und 1814. Einzeldarstellung der entscheidenden Kriegsereignisse. II. Band Österreichs entscheidendes Machtaufgebot 1813. (pp. 1, 132f)
Schwicker J.H., Geschichte der Österreichischen Militärgrenze, Prochaska, Teschen, Wien 1833.

4   As for Schwicker (see sources) each regiment had a staff of 48 officers/NCOs (plus 30 administrative officers/NCOs), 2570 "gemeine" and 198 administrative soldiers. The Tschajkisten had 26 off/NCOs (17 administratives) and a force of 1287 men (plus 77 administratives). Note the Siebenbürgisches regiments (Transylvanian) had no administrative unit (no officers/NCOs and so on).

5   The croatian particular habit to wear a black tie originated the italian term "cravatta" (French : cravate; from "croata, croate")

6   **Generalate** were military regions with the rank of territorial divisions (brigades). They were split into **Kapitanate**, smaller regions equivalent to a territorial battalion (regiment) recruitment area.

7   Source: http://www.vojska.net.

8   **Varaždinsko križevačke krajiške pješačke pukovnije br. 5** or Kreuzer regiment of Warasdin (Varaždin) where Kreuzer or Kürüz in hungarian was the name of the recruitment district (Crusaders) remembering the St. Stephan's Crosses on the anti-islamic flags. The regiment recruited in its own zone of the Generalat or in the Kapitanate of Koprivnice and Križevac. While the first siege of the staff was probably Križevac, it was transferred to Bjelovar since1758.

9   **Varaždinsko-đurđevačke krajiške pješačke pukovnije br. 6** or Gjurgevatz regiment, also St. George's regiment (Warasdiner Sankt Georger). Till 1758 its staff was at Đurđevac, then was transferred to Bjelovar. The recruitment companies (Satnije) were: 1. Grubišno Polje, 2. Kovačica, 3. Severin, 4. Rača, 5. Đurđevac, 6. Pitomača, 7. Trojstvo, 8. Virje, 9. Novigrad, 10. Peteranec, 11. Sokolovec, 12. Kapela

10   Nazuvaka were Turkish knitted slippers.

11   **Gradiška krajiška pješačka pukovnija br. 8**. The regimental staff has its barracks at Bogoševcima, and then at Gradiška (current Nowa Gradiska).

12   The Danube, Theiss and Maros borders did not belong to the territories of the Kingdom of Croatia and Slavonia, but to Hungary. However, within the defence system they were all the part of the border on the Sava. The

▲ Austrian various grenzer soldiers

borders of Theiss and Maros were demilitarized in 1749-1750, which brought about the migration of the Serbs from that territory to Russia. See: A Fori_kovic, Seobe Srba u Rusiju tokom 18.veka, Istorija srpskog naroda IV-1, Beograd 1986 (Immigration of the Serbs to Russia during the eighteenth century; The History of the Serbs IV-19.

13   The Serbs fought to preserve their border privileges, according to which they were free soldiers who recognized the autority of the Emperor and his Generals only. In no way would they agree to be serfs of the lords whose abandoned lands they inhabitated. They wanted to be the free owners of the soil they tilled and to preserve their Orthodox faith. During the seventeenth century the Croatian and Slavonian estates fought a constant battle against the commanders of the Borders for the status of the "Wallachians". They wanted to turn them into serfs they needed to work on their estates, and the Bishop of Zagreb demanded that they pay taxes for the Catholic church. The frontiersman appealed to Generals, usually with success, because they were irreplaceable in the defence.

14   Provintial (provincial) were the territories not in the Military Border, ruled by lords of feudal like estates. The "županije" were the counties of the Croatian-Slavonian lands.

15   **Peterwardein** a royal free town and fortress of Hungary in the county of Syrmia, Croatia-Slavonia; situated on a promontory formed by a loop of the Danube. It was connected with Neusatz (today Novi Sad) on the opposite bank by a boat-bridge and a ferry. The fortifications consisted of the upper fortress, on a lofty serpentine rock rising abruptly from the plain on three sides, and of the lower fortress at the northern base of the rock. The two fortresses could have accommodated a garrison of 10,000 men. The Petrovaradinska krajiška pješačka pukovnija br. 9 had not its siege at Peterwardein, while at Mitrovica (today Sremska Mitrovica and ancient Syrmium).

16   The word ban means "lord, master; ruler". The Slavic word is probably borrowed from late Thracian *ban meaning "master (of a house)" (cf. Albanian bánë, banésé - "house", Romanian ban - nobility rank, Bănie, Banat - "region under the rule of bans"). Another assumption for the origin of the ban was a borrowing from a Turkic language, from the Avar word bajan meaning "ruler of the horde", South Slavic ban is a result of the contraction from the earlier form bojan. The long form is directly attested in 10th-century Constantine Porphyrogenitus' book De Administrando Imperio, in a chapter dedicated to Croats and the organisation of their state, describing how their ban "has under his rule Krbava, Lika and Gacka".

17   **Prva banska krajiška pješačka pukovnija br. 10**. Was one of the austrian regiments which went under the French rule, in 1809, after the Treaty of Schönbrunn. It recruited in the south-western area of the Banal territory, in the Kapitanat of Glina, where was the staff. The commands of its Satnija were at:
1. Čemernica , 2. Vranovina , 3. Glina, 4. Maja , 5. Klasnić, 6. Maligradec , 7. Kraljevčane , 8. Gora, 9. Stankovac , 10. Bović , 11. Lasinja e 12. Vrginmost.

18   **Druga banska krajiška pješačka pukovnija br. 11**. In 1809 it followed the destiny of its „brother" n° 10. The regiment recruited in the northern and western areas of the Petrinja Kapitanat.

19   The Karansebes regiment was partially recruited in the german Banat and had some "grenz" fortresses in its area: Mehadia, Orsova and Bosovich. It recruited from the kapitanate: Weisskirchen (Fejértemplom) siege of a battalion, Schupanek, Teregova, Töplic, Vár, Mezerich or Möserich.

20   The hungarian area (later County) Háromszék means "three seats". The Háromszék region was a combination of three settlements (seats) of the Székely: Kézdiszék, Orbaiszék and Sepsiszék. Háromszék county was formed in 1876, when the administrative structure of Transylvania was changed.

21   For the 8 sqns. of the Szekler Hussars or 11th Hussars Regiment under oberst baron Martin von Rakowsky, see after under the hungarian Hussars part.

22   Csik (Csik-Szereda, Csik-Somlyo, Szépvisz, Bánkfalva) - Gyergyö (Gyergyö-Szt.Miklos, Nagy-Kászon) - Maros (Marosvásarhély, Illyefalva, Jobágyfalva, Abod, Sellye, Szovata) - Aranyos (Felvincz, Kövend)

23   Údvarhély (Székely- Údvarhély, Bözöd, Fartzád, Bardocz, Bögöz, Homorod-Almás, Szitás-Keresztur, Oláhfalva, Pakatfalva) Háromszék (Kézdivásarhély, Alsö-Csernaton, Szt.Lelék, Zabola, Zágon, Zálány, Étfalva, Fekete-ügy, Sepsi-Szt.Ivány)

24   " Ces Wallaques aiment le vin et l'eau-de-vie avec passion. Ces deux vices ne dérangent pas moins leur fortune que leur santé. Du reste, la dance est pour les filles Wallaques ce que 1'amour de la boisson est pour les hommes, et les un.et les autres s'adonnent avec excès aux plaisirs qu'ils aiment. "

25   Fogaras (Alsó-Árpás, Fogaras, Törcsvár-Zernest, Sárkány) – Hunyad (Petrozsényi, Szászváros, Hátszeg, Puj) – Szeben (Orlath-Keresztény, Nagyszeben, Szászeben, Szerdahely). Siege of staff at Orlath.

26   Bestercze (Naszod, Uj-Radna, Bestercze (Bistritz), Borgó Bestercze, N.Sajé) -Szolnok-Doboka (Szamosújvár,

Dés, Bethlen, Csákigorbó, Kápolnokmonostor, Kékes, Magyarlápos, Nagyilonda) - Kolosz (Tekes, Mocs, Mezőörményes) - Maros (Szászregen, Toplicza). The regimental siege was at Naszod.

27 The Tschaikist battalion was in effect a medieval naval force, protecting the riverine borders in the Slavonian and Syrmian frontier areas against smuggling and the spread of the bubonic plague. The unit remained on the military establishment of the Military Border after 1747, and redeployed to Titel in the area between the Danube and Theiss rivers in 1763. In 1764, the battalion establishment was increased from two to four companies. The Tschaikist battalion operated light rowed and sailed gunboats, imperial Freikriegsschiffe, armed with one heavy and several smaller guns. Tschaika gunboats (slavic for "lapwing"), were similar in construction to the Nassadist flatbottomed gunboats built in Hungary. They proved much more suitable for riverine warfare on the Danube and its navigable tributaries, than the large 40- to 64-gun ships of the Danube Flotilla which were lost by grounding without exception. Komorn Fortress in Hungary became the key strongpoint, naval shipyard and repair facility of the Tschaikist battalion.

28 Datas until beginning of 1813.

▲ Austrian soldiers of grenzer regiment nr. 17

▲ Austrian Landwehr 1809. From R.Knotel artwork

THE AUSTRIAN LANDWEHR

"… eine bloss zur Vertheidigung des Vaterländischen Bodens abzweckende…" "To be aimed only on the defence of the Fatherland"   K.K. Patent of June 8, 1808

The farsighted and innovative Austrian Archduke Charles developed the idea of a territorial reserve, whose basic concept intended a kind of militia system with purely defensive character. Were to be considered 3 essential motives in order to this provision:

1— the extensive exhaustion of the military potential of the Austrian lands, considering the positive experiences with armed citizen's contingents (Volksaufgeboten) in Tirol and Salzburg in 1800 and 1805;

2— the success of the French people's armies in the Coalition Wars, absolutely astonishing for expert military leaders coming from the school of the 17th Century;

3-- as the perhaps most essential factors even were to put the low expected costs, especially for the short training time and the State arming, also for clothing and the other equipment, however, provided by the countryland and partially from the Landwehr men themselves.

On June 9th, 1808 an Imperial Patent for the people did the organizing of the Landwehr institute. The Emperor Franz said in it:

"We have opened, in our Patent, Our beloved matter with the intention of an institution connected to the reserve establishment, namely for the defence of the Monarchy with such means which grant the possibility to Us to facilitate the finances of the State by decreasing those of the active Army.

In just this intention We think for good to organize a territorial Force (Landwehr) aimed only on the defence of the Fatherland…. For its execution We have appointed authorized persons, already known for their proficiency, their zeal and their devotion to Us and to the government, namely for Styria, Carinthia, Krain, Trieste and Salzburg: our esteemed Brother Imperial Highness Archduke John; our Court Commissioner Count Saurau: for Bohemia, Moravia and Silesia… ".

Archduke John did come on June 22, 1808, at Salzburg with Count Franz von Saurau in order to start the organizatione of the Landwehr. At the time they had to raise 4 battalions, the Staff Officers of which could have been retired military officers of the former Bishopric or Electoral Principate (of Salzburg), who had decided to be a volunteer in the new project. Only 4 officers and 1 Corporal for each Landwehr company had to come from the K.K. regular Army.

After this first examples, since 1808, in the German Hereditary lands (Germany, Outer and Inner Austria, Bohemia, Moravia, Silesia, Tirol), they raised this Militia, organized with men fit to combat in each imperial province. I t was estimated that Austria would raise 180000 Landwehr and Hungary 50000, but such numbers were never attained; the Hungarian Diet refused to sanction it, and it was thought dangerous to raise it in Galicia, whose Poles were believed disaffected. In Bohemia, this force, (how it will be stated by Hofkriegsrat Notification of June 13, 1811), had to be of about 50000 men.

Landwehr based its organisation upon the new concept of Reserve duty or Service which could lead towards a true national army, rather than towards another kind of Militia. It stated that:

1 – Every man in the age of military service, from then was also required to fulfill the Reserve duty; this modified also the previous way of recruiting people;

2 – After having recognized their military fitness, citizens did receive one certificate, signed by military and political authority, with which he, where it would be necessary, had to identify themselves.

But who could enlist with the Landwehr? The service in the Landwehr was allowed to:
- Residents temporarily free from service duty (i.e. religious, jobs exemptions);
- Residents, who had been legally dismissed as veterans after a full duty period and had not yet served for a total period of 20 years, provided they wanted not to become Capitulanten; [i]
- fit for service retired Capitulanten;
- Häusler (namely inhabitants who had only house but not fields to cultivate. Also poors, contrary of the well-off people);
- common Conscripts assigned to the category of various jobs (vermischten Beschäftigung)
- common Conscripts with minor phisical defects;
- who was signed in the Register of the less suitable subjects for the Conscription.

The Landwehr soldiers' service was compulsory for all men aged between 18 and 45, unless they belonged to exempt categories or were army reservists. Initially they had to train themselves on every Sunday and holiday, while monthly they were gathered in larger units, coming from the nearby villages, and sent to the battalion manoeuvres, which did not have to last more than three hours. Later this system was changed and they had to instruct themselves with the weapons in short periods of 14 days, under the military Rule (generally half of the total force trained itself in Spring, the others in Autumn, or in periods stated by the territorial regiment command). When employed in these training camps, the militias were supplied by the provinces. The trainings periods was recorded by the Districts-Commissariate (which maintained the Landwehr's lists) and signed in the personal Folios (Karten). These were managed directly by the Kreis-Hauptmanns or the Bataillons-Commandanten. In the case of a War call-to-arms the Landwehr men had to:
- gather themselves in their battalions;
- give their oath to the national flag;
- follow the orders of their General-Commandant.

The Landwehr generally wore a grey jacket (Rock) with red facings (later various colours), had a cartridge-box (Patronentasche) with 36 cartridges, bayonet, and hats (every land battalions could have personal hats). Every battalion had also to form a special section of snipers (Scharf-schützen) generally armed with the best rifles and with the Jägerstutzen (see also Feldjäger battalions and Tirol's Schützen).

The Model in the figure is a Waadtland Swiss type, used in all lands of Alps, for hunting. This weapon allowed a secure fire result up to 300 paces, while the common infantry muskets cannot go over a 100 paces. Landwehr firearms depended upon availability; muskets of 1754, 1774 or 1784 pattern were used, with hunting rifles, cavalry carbines, even Crespi breech loaders and air rifles among the Jägers.

In practice, shortage of equipment resulted in wide variations. Though officers and NCOs usually wore regulation dress, other ranks were permitted different uniform providing all members of a company were dressed alike. In 1808 civilian dress was adapted (sometimes simply by adding a cockade to the hat!), the only issue items being the coat and the leather equipment.

The Landwehr was proportioned to the width of the Circle (Kreis) in which it could be raised one or more battalions. Each battalion (800 men) had 4 companies; each company (200 men) had 4 platoons (Züge); each platoon (50 men) had 2 Squads or Korporalschäften of 25 men each.[ii] The companies were led by an Hauptmann and 3 other officers.

In each province the Landwehr was split in two parts (Abtheilungen), the first formed by the best fit men, the second by the less fit to comBns. In this second section of that new regional armies it could be found what more resembled to the old Landmiliz or to the Town-Guards (Bürgereinheiten). It was the first draft of the nineteenth-century K.K. Landwehr (national army), in competition with the K.u.K. (gemeinsame) Heer (imperial army), while the second military choices went to form what in the future will be the K.K. Landsturm.

Therefore, in this second Corps, were also the men aged from 45 till 50 years, the family fathers (Hausväter) and all who owned a firearm (till the age of 50 years); provided, all the above mentioned, they were not completely fit for the Landwehr duty. This early prototype of Landsturm had the task to provide to the order and discipline of the inner land, to defend the inner ways of communications and villages, to garrison the fortresses and towns, to escort prisoners and other military services. The 2nd Class Landwehr had less difficult duties, often ordered directly by provinces. These civil governments provided also to the soldiers uniforms and equipments. During war-time these forces were led by former Officers in retirement, recalled on duty.

The Supreme Patent Act (Allerhöchstes Patent) of June 9, 1808, stated also that the towns, villages, in which was no military unit (regular or Landwehr) had to form (with armed citizens), during wartimes, Security patrols (Sichereitswachen) and had to give men for transports duties to the army.

After the defeat of 1809 Napoleon demanded the deactivation of the Landwehr; but registers were kept, and in 1811 it was decreed that when re-formed, they would form the fourth battalions of each Line regiment.

Lantveři National Army of Bohemia 1809

In Bohemia on October 31, 1808, the local Parliament (Landtag) convened in the Prague Castle, granted the sum of 1.509.000 fl. to cover the expense for the Landwehr equipments.

The Bohemian Landwehr wore "Hungarian" type uniforms of a brown "Spencer"-style jacket with red facings and braid, a round hat with black and yellow pompon, Hungarian breeches, high boots and black equipment. Otherwise those uniforms, perhaps, were those of the 1800 Archduke Charles volunteers. See after for some detail.

Other sources quoted the Prague Student Corps wore similar dress plus a bicorn with a red-tipped white feather. The Prague city Landwehr had long, singlebreasted brown coats with green collar, cuffs and piping; white breeches, black (white ?) gaiters and equipment, and a shako with brass badge and black and yellow pompon. [iii]

Two Words upon Uniforms

In the Web and in the interesting site www.primaplana.cz has appeared a notable historical article of Karel Sáček and Karl Bag, which tries to make light on the type of military uniform worn by the Bohemian Landwehr in 1809. The article has, unfortunately, the defect to be written in Czech language, not comprehensible to all. I tried to make here a summary of what was written there.

A man dressed in a knee-long coat and Corsican hat on his head is probably the first image that will strike you, speaking about the Landwehr, years 1808-1810. Right a man so dressed was immortalized by painter Johann Peter Krafft in 1813 in his famous "Farewell of the Territorial" (in Czech: zeměbrance from země = Land and branec = recruit) painting, which became a symbol of the modern Austrian patriotism (the image is not provided for copyright rights). The subject, in effects, is wearing the same uniform as the Landwehr men on the front page of another quoted publication on the matter: the book "Landwehr Anno Neun".

However these uniforms applied to the Landwehr battalions formed in Vienna, Lower Austria and other neighborhoods. Their numerous options are set as in the synthesis of the book "Das Heer unter dem Doppeladler", where, in addition, authors even wrote a warning label: "In fact, Landwehr uniforms were very dissimilar in different regions." [iv]

How, then, looked the Landwehr from the Czech lands? The absence of detailed description of their uniforms (or yet to be discovered), forces to refer briefly to the regulation in force in Lower and Upper Austria,

"The service coat must be such that a man could wear it in winter over the other clothes in the summer only over a shirt. It should have two pockets. The Landwehr long coat extends up to the knees, so that the trousers colour may not be uniform. The man receives his own rounded hat (Runden-Hut), in which front is attached a brass plaque, where one can read to the provincial and district number of the battalion. The Landwehr training team should walk with their own clothes as jackets, but together homogeneous for weaponry. This weaponry belongs to a little bag (Sack) for 36 rounds, which is worn on a black lacquered wide strap, two and a quarter inches over the right shoulder strap of the bayonet, as for the infantry. Men wear the bags over the right shoulder.

The men were armed by the Central Government with rifles and bayonets, which had weapons for every local security group, watched in a safe place. For the officer corps, however, and also for men was issued a special "Landwehr uniform", adapted to the national costumes of each Crown's region, usually not homogeneously prescribed. This uniform consisted, by the main part, of a long overcoat, in different colours, with a single series of white buttons, with a rigid hat having a brim bent up on one side and a brass plate on which were embossed the letters LW (Land Wehr), then region and number of the battalion.

Each man was to be provided with one cartridge bag for 36-40 rounds, sack for bread and the suspension strap (belt) for a bayonet. Equipment and military clothing were provided by the Regional Administration."

In relation to the Moravia-Silesia Landwehr battalions, however, this booklet provided only: "They were wearing a gray coat with blue facings." [v]

Otakar Frankenberger, with reference to primary sources collected in Prague, limited himself to stating that "Landwehr of Czech lands wore a gray coat, blue epaulettes, trilby hat with rosette shaped pins and brush." At the same time he added that: "There was a proposal under which each Region should have a different colour of the facings. The buttons should be for Czech (white) and for Moravian Landwehr (yellow)". [vi]

According to other sources, Moravia decided that: "the uniform had to be a gray coat with red facings and a round hat with a brass plate ... at least every battalion had to have the same wearing." [vii]

According to Dave Hollins' Czech, Moravian and Silesian simulated uniforms of Landwehr battalions and Lower Austrian peasant hats, their facings was to be officially light blue, but many units used to copy the same colour as the ordinary infantry regiment linked to the District (so the Saaz Landwehr battalion loaded Orange "County" facings as did the Erbach Infantry Regiment No. 42). In Moravia, probably, they wore more Landwehr black "peasant hats", because of the large presence of farmers. [viii]

Excerpts for Landwehr equipments were recorded in eastern Bohemia: "The train group attended the exercises in their own clothes, but each one should have had a strange high hat with brass letters and badges and the same cartridge sacks, all were available in Prague: a badge for 21 kr., an hat for 2 zl. 24 kr." [ix]

▲ Austrian Infantry Landwehr uniforms regiments

Another, although very bizarre, source describing the equipment is a Landwehr mocking song, that was sang by regular army soldiers of Frelich Infantry Regiment No. 28:
"Lantveři (Landwehr) with linen trousers, back too much "tanestry" / rifles are old, "pagnety" red, on their heads pig wool hats.
Those are the words, by honour, run Brethren, Jesus Maria!" [x]

So far written sources. More attention must be paid to iconographic sources. Among them it occupies a privileged position a series of 13 Landwehr images of the Imperial Countries, which Josef Eder issued at Vienna in 1810. [xi]
Three of those images relate to the Bohemian lands. As for the "Czech Landwehr of the Royal Capital city of Prague" it must be told that this may not be the right guide for recreating the appearance and the idea of Landwehr uniforms in the Czech lands. The intention was to distinguish that units as much as possible, as in the case of the Student Volunteer battalion, which had to be different from the Archduke Charles Legion of 1800 – The red epaulet on the officer's right shoulder is probably a symbolic reference for continuing that tradition.
In Moravian and Silesian Duchy Landwehr, the gold metal letters in the hats look different than the above-illustrated Prague Landwehr - in this case, it can be also clearly recognized the letter "M" referring probably to the Moravian territory.
They have classical Landwehr coats and equipment. However the hat is decorated with letters LW. Why? Rigid hats, round hats, etc
... these features suggest only that the so-called typical Corsican hat did not predominate on Bohemian territory. This is confirmed by other contemporary illustrations of Czech Landwehr, camped, on June 23, 1809 at Dresden. [xii] This iconographic source derived from a collection published by Peter Hofschrörer and Dave Hollins and shows seven captured soldiers with the cylinder-shaped hat having bents reversed on both sides.
The Bohemian hat of the "Dresden camp" is similar to that immortalized by Eder in 1810 for Moravians. This is the same type, that was widespread among Czech Archduke Charles Legion volunteers already since 1800. [xiii]
The cylindrical hat with a bent brim, then, was probably the most typical element for the Czech Landwehr in 1809 and distinguished them from other countries. This just let's add that officers who were assigned to the Landwehr from the army, have the right to retain their original former uniform.
General Count Kinsky, in whose brigade were included three Landwehr battalions of the Loket region and two from Saaz and Rakovnik, indicated the actual state of the Landwehr's equipment in a report to the FML Sommariva (early May 1809): "The bad state of uniforms and lack of shoes is the cause of many diseases among the units. The 2nd Königgrätz Battalion had to be again completely withdrawn, due to bad arming, from the South Bohemian border and replaced by the 4th Chrudim battalion." [xiv]
This may suggest that the Landwehr, like in a common volunteer battalion, should have to be equipped with different uniforms, based on the regular infantry-style. Maybe this manifestation was captured by Josef Eder and was confirmed by several other sources.
The third image "Moravian Landwehr (?) A volunteer corps" illustrated a "Moravian Landwehr" with a typical Jäger clothing - here the author obviously made a mistake in the description. In 1809 in Moravia no volunteer Jäger formation emerged, which could be incorporated into the Feldjäger corps; those uniforms are likely to be perhaps accredited to the Prague volunteers (Watterich) battalion, or to the Feldjäger or to the the Lobkovitz Kinsky formation.
In order to end this short trip among the Czech Landwehr uniforms ther is a rather "hot and picquant" note related to the Legion troops of Archduke Charles, left by FML Klenau in his report dated March 24, 1809:
"The Landwehr men serving in the legion, as well as the new recruited ones, do not wear underwear (kleinen Montur) under the coat. Therefore I consider it necessary to allocate shirts and underwear (Gati) to the men, in order, at least, to partially hide their nudities. This deficiency results from poverty and from the fact that the majority, when Legion was rallied, took with him only one shirt, which is by now completely worn". [xv]

Joking with Landwehr in 1809 [xvi]

War preparations continued in Prague so zealously that, on October 31, 1808, Czech Lords resolved to give the State Council cash of 1.509.000 zl. for the newly established army, the Landwehr, and, in addition, to provide a further 4.000.000 zl. contribution to be spending by the war fund.
Over the winter, certain of the pending war, all became tense and eager to setting up the Land's defense, Landwehr, which were quickly dressed in uniform and trained to the field service of war.
The hurry and the rush of training territorials inspired confidence in the regular troops, by their supposed

military superiority, and they became jealous, so they laughted at their old land-soldiers upon the meaning of the letters LW (which meant Land Wehr), saying the letters meant "Lauf weg !", in German "Run away !" and questioned about their fitness and the various antics uttered by this new army. Also even there were composed skittish songs about Territorials. So sang soldiers of the regiment Vogelsang in Prague:

"Not far from Vienna in a village small and fine - Flagbearer Landwehry at the waist carrying a swine ....."

And perhaps they would have even more teased Territorials, when an abrupt spring called to arms people from Prague up to the field, against Napoleon. Therefore, on May 1st, 1809, after the Territorials, volunteers and students got the 1800 flags and went from Prague to the Klattau region, occupying the Bohemian border. That year the month of May was, in Bohemia, same as "Month of War", so that even during the feast of St.John Nepomucene in Prague, instead of wandering devout pilgrims, walked brilliant fellows singing war songs and ballads against the detested Napoleon, pro the celebrated Archduke Charles and laughing at the Territorials ... For the security and the safety of Prague had been discarded the palisades and the city was fortified with trenches with embankments around, where several thousand people worked for a day pay of 30 kr.

Since 1808, in the German hereditary lands (Germany, outer and inner Austria, Bohemia, Moravia, Silesia, Tirol), had been raised a special militia, organized with men fit to combat in each imperial province. This force, as for the Hofkriegsrat Notification of June 13, 1811, had to be of about 50000 men. The service in the Landwehr was allowed to:

- residents temporarily free from service duty (exemptions);
- residents, who had been legally dismissed as veterans after a full duty and had not yet served for a total period of 20 years, provided they wanted not to become Capitulanten; [9]
- fit for service retired Capitulanten;
- Häusler (namely inhabitants who had only house but not fields to cultivate. Also poor, contrary of the well-off people);
- common Conscripts assigned to the category of various Jobs (vermischten Beschäftigung)
- common Conscripts with minor phisical defects;
- who was signed in the Register of the less suitable subjects of the Conscription.

The Landwehr soldiers period of duty was from 18 y.o. men till the age of 45. Initially they had to train themselves on every Sunday and holiday, while monthly they were gathered in larger units, coming from the nearby villages, and sent to the Battalion manoeuvres, which did not have to last more than three hours. Later this system was changed and they had to train with the weapons in short periods of 14 days, under the military Rule (generally half of the total force trainded itself in Spring, the others in Autumn, or in periods stated by the territorial regiment command). When employed in these training camps, the militians were supplied by the provinces. The trainings periods was recorded by the Districts-Commissariate (which maintained the Landwehr's lists) and signed in the personal Folios (Karten). These were managed directly by the Kreis-Hauptmanns or the Bataillons-Commandanten. In the case of a War call-to-arms the Landwehr men had to:

- gather themselves in their Battalions;
- give their oath to the national flag;
- follow the orders of their General-Commandant.

The Landwehr generally had a catridge-box (Patronentasche) with 36 cartridges, bayonet, and hats (every land Battalions could have personal hats). Every Battalion had also to form a special section of snipers (Scharfschützen) generally armed with the best rifles.

In each province the Landwehr was split in two parts (Abtheilungen), the first formed by the best fit men, the second by the less fit to combat. In this second Corps were also the men aged from 45 till 50 years, the family fathers (hausväter) and all who owned a firearm (till the age of 50 years); provided, all the above mentioned, they were not completely fit for the Landwehr duty. This early prototype of Landsturm had the task to provide to the order and discipline of the inner land, to defend the inner ways of communications and villages, to garrison the fortresses and towns, to escort prisoners and other military services. The 2nd Class Landwehr had less difficult duties, often ordered directly by provinces. These civil governments provided also to the soldiers uniforms and equipments. During war-time these forces were led by former Officers in retirement, recalled on duty.

The Supreme Patent Act (Allerhöchstes Patent) of June 9, 1808, stated also that the towns, villages, in which was no military unit (regular or Landwehr) had to form (with armed citizens), during wartimes, Security patrols (Sichereitswachen) and had to give men for transports duties to the army.

UNIFORMS[10] LANDWEHR GEMEINE

The Hats. Landwehr hats must be common round black hats high 6 Zoll (15,80 cm) with a brim wide 3 ½ Zoll (around 9 cm). They had on both sides one black wool lace (loop with buttons) and on the left side of the hat they had a cockade large 3 Zoll (8 cm) bearing the national colours of the region.

The "Rock" or waistcoat: the act of June 1808 specified the uniform for Upper, Lower and Inner Austrian Landwehr districts being distinguished by their facing colours:

Styria (Steiermark), white and white-green cockade; Carinthia (Kärnten) red and yellow-red-white cockade; Trieste and Istria, red and yellow-red-blue cockade; Carniola (Krain), light blue and white-blue-red cockade; Salzburg, yellow facing and white-red cockade;

Upper Austria, red with white-red cockade; Lower Austria, red and blue-yellow cockade.

Uniform comprised a grey-green or dark green (Stahlgrün) [11] short coat with facing-coloured collar, cuffs and shoulder strap piping, and white buttons; white or pike grey breeches, black gaiters, and a 'round hat' six inches high, with a 3 inches brim usually turned up on one or both sides, bearing, as said, a cockade in provincial colours. White leather belts were worn, black for NCOs (but actually more widespread). The waistcoat was surmounted, on the breast, for 6 Zoll (16 cm) and was tied up by a double line of white buttons. The lenght of the waistcoat (also called Loden) reached the belly and after. The Collars had to be high 2/3 of the neck-band (which had to be generally black). Cuffs had to be wide 3 ½ Zoll (around 9 cm) and set on the forearm. Piping and turnbacks were of green tissue. On shoulders they had green shoulder straps, with regional colour piping, to guide the leather belts which sustained the bayonet and the cartridge bag.

The Gilet: was green with a single file of smaller white buttons. The Breeches: they were long, grey and had a german type bib and small belt. The Gaiters: were black with a lateral line of small leather buttons and long till the knee. Shoes: they were the classical Bundschuhe or short shoes. With bad time were allowed also boots or leather cover for gaiters. Belts: Landwehr men carried the bayonet with a 5 cm wide leather belt.

Corporals

They had the same uniform but had a cane and a sabre, which was carried near the bayonet in a black leather sheath. The laces of the sabre were of green wool with the regional colours (Egalisierungs farbe).

NCOs

NCOs also had sabres with regional colour knots, and the usual canes.

Officers

Hat: Officers wore bicorns high 11 Zoll (28,9 cm) in the back and 10 ½ Zoll frontally (27,6 cm), wide 5 Zoll (13 cm) and with a band wide 2 Zoll (5,26 cm). On the left side of the hat there was a silver loop - long 7 Zoll (18,4 cm) – wide 1/3 Zoll (0,87 cm) – with a small white button and the regional cockade. They had also silver silk tassels with the regional colours. Waistcoat: it was similar to that of the soldiers, but log up to the knees. Breeches: grey, long and with germans belt and bib with silk camel hair braid on the outer seams and as thigh knots (Stabs-officers had silver camel hair braid).

Boots: long up to the knees. They also carried a sabre with a silver and white knot on a black glazed shoulder belt with a Port d'Epée with silver silk laces and regional colours.

Rank markings were one, two or three silver loops (1cm wide) on the collar for Unterleutnant, Oberleutnant and Hauptmann respectively; field officers had silver-edged collar and shoulder straps, and silver braid on the breeches.

The Schützen (of Landwehr) who some author called also Jäger had the same uniform of the Landwehr. However they did not carry bayonet or cartridge-bag, they wore a waist belt (large 2 Zoll) with a cartridge box at the front instead of shoulder belts, and carried a powder horn on a green cord over the left shoulder; NCOs also carried a sabre.

Why oaks leaves on hats?

Austrian soldiers used to carry three oak-leaves on their helmets-shakos; but why?

In Germany oak were the Trees of the Homeland, the powerful war trees of the Teutons, whose leaves also served in war as a field mark. The oak was consecrated to the thundering god Donnar (Thor). Ancient Celts observed the oak's massive growth and impressive expanse. They took this as a clear sign that the oak was to be honored for its endurance, and noble presence. Further merit to its regal presence is its tendency to attract lightning. This was considered hugely powerful among the ancients and is associated with one of their foremost gods, Dagda. More, in the old German language of flowers they told: "Who carries oak leaves, indicates his own determination and that thereby nobody will can stop him. So it was recommended, therefore, to be careful with those carrying oak leaves, and, above all, to avoid jokes with these fellows, who didn't allow jokes." The weapons put "at rest" during wars and campaigns were often hung up on oaks. It was easy to understand why German (and Austrian) warriors went in the battle with oak leaves.

LOWER AUSTRIA (NIEDER-ÖSTERREICH) LANDWEHR ORGANIZATION:

1. Viertel Ober dem Manhartsberg (OMB)
2. Viertel Unter dem Manhartsberg (UMB)
3. Viertel Ober dem Wiener Wald (OWW)
4. Viertel Unter dem Wiener Wald (UWW)

Commanders: Archduke Maximilian and Earl von Bissingen

Viertel Ober dem Mannhartsberg
5 Battalions in the Brigade Ulbrecht in Krems, Division Anton Mittrowsky under O'Reilly

1st Battalion Krems
- Chevalier Ludwig Estevet de la Bussière
Before Aspern: with Brigade Rüffer at Linz then in the Brigade Nordmann, autonomous, VI Corps.
Before Wagram: assigned to Brigade Hammer, Division D'Aspre, Reserve Corps
after Wagram : merged in 2nd combined Battalion OMB and UMB (Commander: Lichtenberg)

2nd Battalion Waidhofen an der Thaya
- Major Anton Eisenkolb then Baron Major Clemens Beissel finally Major Count Franz Schönborn.
Between Aspern and Wagram: in the Brigade Sinzendorf, detached in Pressburg then autonomous, Army of Inner Austria.
Before Wagram: in Brigade Weiss, Division Radetzky, IV Corps later was with the Avant-garde Provenchères, Division Radetzky, IV Corps
After Wagram: attached to Brigade Murray, Division Prohaszka, Reserve Corps with the remnants of the 1st Battalion and 3rd OMB, 1-2-3-4 of the Mühlviertel, 1st Traunviertel it became the 1st combined Battalion OMB and UMB.

3rd Battalion Zwettl
- Major Cölestin Gasser then Prince Ferdinand Colloredo
Before Aspern: was in the Brigade Ulbrecht, or Garrison Enns and Mauthausen then to the Army of Inner Austria.
After Wagram: with the remnants of the 2nd and 4th OMB, 2nd and 4th UMB and one more Upper Austrian Battalion it became the 2nd Combined Battalion OMB and UMB (Battalion Lichtenberg).

4th Battalion Horn
- Major Friedrich von Stark then Major Count Joseph Gilleis
Between Aspern and Wagram: detached to the Brigade Sinzendorf at Pressburg then detached to the Brigade Weiss Division Radetzky, IV Corps.
After Wagram: to the Division Hohenlohe, IV Corps then with the remnants of the 2nd and 4th OMB, 2nd and 4th UMB and one more Upper Austrian Battalion it became the 1st Combined Battalion OMB and UMB (see also above).

5th Battalion Krems and Zwettl
- Major Landgraf Friedrich Egon Fürstenberg
Before Aspern: in the Brigade Ritter or Garrison Linz, then in the Army of Inner Austria Between Aspern and Wagram: Army of Inner Austria
After Wagram: with the remnants of the 2nd Landwehr Battalion OMB, 1st Battalion Landwehr UMB, 1st and 4th Battalion Landwehr Hausrückviertel, 1st and 2nd Salzburg Landwehr Battalion it became the: 3rd Combined Battalion OMB and UMB **Viertel Unter dem Mannhartsberg (UMB)**
4 Battalions of the Brigade Paar at Vienna, Division Anton Mittrowsky under O'Reilly

1st Battalion Weikersdorf
- Major Count Joseph Brenner then Major August Wolf von Eggenburg Before Aspern: deployed on the line of river Enns, then withdrawn till Styria Between Aspern and Wagram: its soldiers deserted "en Masse"

2nd Battalion Ernstbrunn
- Major Count Joseph Heinrich Obergfell then Major Count Franz Schönborn, also interim Major Count Hardegg Before Aspern: deployed on the line of river Enns, then withdrawn till Styria

Between Aspern and Wagram: detached in Pressburg. Later in the detached Brigade Sinzendorf in Pressburg, then in the detached Brigade Bianchi and in the detached Brigade Weiss. At Raab in the Brigade GM Legisfeld, Division FML Franz Jellačić.

▲ Austrian Infantry Landwehr uniforms regiments: Austria and Moravian volunteers

3rd Battalion Wolkersdorf
- Major Lerch von Mühlheim; then, At Aspern: Major Count Joseph Heinrich Obergfell Before Aspern: line of river Enns, then in the VI Corps.

Between Aspern and Wagram: detached in Pressburg.

Before Wagram: in the Brigade Peter Vécsey, Avant-garde with Colloredo as commander, in the Brigade Máriássy, Division Vincent, VI Corps

After Wagram: remnants in the 1st combined Landwehr Battalion OMB and UMB.

4th Battalion Poysdorf
Major Prince Ferdinand Colloredo Before Aspern: line of river Enns

Before Wagram: to Brigade Máriássy, Division Vincent, VI Corps

After Wagram: remnants in the 1st combined Landwehr Battalion OMB and UMB.

Viertel Ober dem Wiener Wald (OWW)
2 Battalions in the Brigade Paar in Vienna, Division Mittrowsky under O' Reilly

1st Battalion Herzogenburg, St Pölten
- Major Philipp Praschmar

Before Aspern: with Brigade Albrecht, in the detached from IV Corps, Division Dedovich Between Aspern and Wagram: Brigade Sinzendorf, Army of Inner Austria

Before Wagram: Brigade Adler, Division Hohenfeld, VI Corps

After Wagram: with the Army of Inner Austria. Then it was split, part to the 1st Battalion Landwehr UMB, part to the 2nd combined Landwehr Battalion OMB and UMB (Lichtenberg).

2nd Battalion Lilienfeld
- Major Sebastian von Steinsberg; Between Aspern and Wagram: Major count Albert Clary and After Wagram: Major Franz Rieben von Riebenfeld

Before Aspern: part of the river Enns line

Between Aspern and Wagram: in Styria Army of Inner Austria. At Raab in the Brigade GM Legisfeld, Division FML Franz Jellačić.

3rd Battalion Scheibbs
- Major Andreas von Rein

Before Aspern: with Brigade Rüffer, Garrison Linz Between Aspern and Wagram: in Styria

then the remnants merged in the 2nd combined Landwehr Battalion OMB and UMB (Lichtenberg)

4th Battalion Weikersdorf
- Oberstleutnant Count Thomas Plunquet

Before Aspern: with the Brigade Ulbrecht, Garrison Enns, Mauthausen Between Aspern and Wagram: 3 companies attached to the Corps Kerpen Before Wagram: with Brigade Weiss, Division Radetzky, IV Corps

After Wagram: At Raab in the Brigade GM Legisfeld, Division FML Franz Jellačić. The remnants in the 1st Battalion Landwehr OWW

Viertel Unter dem Wiener Wald (UWW)
6 Battalion of the Brigade Paar in Vienna, Division Anton Mittrowsky under O'Reilly

1st Battalion Fischamend
- Baron Major Leopold Büchler and after Wagram Hauptmann Richter Before Aspern: stood in Vienna

Before Wagram: with the Brigade Riese, Division Nordmann (Avant-garde 2nd Wing)

After Wagram: with the 5th Battalion Landwehr UWW into the new 1st combined Landwehr UWW

2nd Vienna Battalion - Wien (Neu-Lerchenfeld)
- Major Count Emanuel Quentin and from April Major Sebastian Steinsberg von Leidenthal Before Wagram: in the Brigade Riese, Division Nordmann (Avant-garde 2nd Wing)

3rd Battalion Traiskirchen
- Major Count Franz Xaver Fuchs

Between Aspern and Wagram: was in the detached Brigade Bianchi then in the detached Brigade Bach, finally in the Brigade Weiss, Army of Inner Austria and then also detached alone.

Before Wagram: Brigade Riese, Division Nordmann (Avantgarde 2nd Wing)

4th Battalion Wiener Neustadt
- Baron Major von Buol then Major Clemens Beissel

Between Aspern and Wagram: with Brigade Weiss, Army of Inner Austria Before Wagram: still with Brig Weiss, Division Radetzky, IV Corps

after Wagram idem but later merged in the 2nd combined Landwehr BattalionUWW

▲ Austrian Landwehr Infantry 1809 From Ottenfeld artwork

5th Vienna Battalion - City of Vienna
- Major Count Maximilian Cavriani and after Wagram Major Johann Weissenwolf Before Aspern: stood in Vienna
Before Wagram: in the Brig.Mayer, Div. Nordmann (Avant-garde 2nd Wing) After Wagram: with Brigade Weissenwolf

6th Battalion or 2nd Wiener Neustadt
- Major Count Ernst Hoyos
Before Wagram: with Brigade Mayer, Division Nordmann (Avantgarde 2nd Wing)
After Wagram: with the 4th BattalionUWW in the 2nd combined Landwehr BattalionUWW

Battalions raised in August 1809
1st Combined Battalion OMB and UMB
from the remnants of the 2nd, 3rd and 4th Landwehr Battalions OMB, 2nd and 4th Landwehr Battalion UMB
2nd Combined Battalion OMB and UMB
– Major Lichtenberg
from the 1st OMB and the 1st and 3rd Landwehr Battalions OWW
1st Combined Battalion UWW
also called 1st Combined Niederösterreich – Major Büchler from the 1st and 5th Landwehr Battalions.
2nd Combined Battalion UWW
also called 2nd Combined Niederösterreich – Major Hoyos from the 4th and 6th Landwehr BattalionUWW

3rd Combined Battalion OMB and UMB
– Major Fürstenberg

from the 1st and 4th Battalion Hausrückviertel, the 1st and 2nd Battalion Salzburger Landwehr the 2nd and 5th Landwehr Battalion OMB and from the 1st Landwehr Battalion UMB

Other than the OMB, UMB, OWW, UWW denominations, these Battalions were known by their commander name: Battalion Beissel alias 2nd Landwehr Battalion OMB and 4th Landwehr Battalion UMB: Battalion Colloredo alias 2nd Landwehr Battalion OMB and 4th BattalionLandw, UWW; Battalion Fuchs alias 2nd Landwehr Battalion UWW; Battalion Fürstenberg alias 5th Landwehr Battalion OMB and 2nd combined Landwehr Battalion OMB and UMB; Battalion Gilleis alias 4th Landwehr Battalion OMB; Battalion Haugwitz alias 1st Battalion-Landwehr Znaym; Battalion Obergfell alias 2nd Landwehr BattalionUMB; Battalion Plunquet alias 4th Landwehr Battalion OWW; Battalion Praschma alias 1st Battalion Landwehr OWW; Battalion Richter alias 1st Landwehr Landwehr UWW; Battalion Schönborn alias 2nd Battalion Landwehr UMB; Battalion Straka alias 1st Battalion Landwehr Innvierter and 1st Combined Oberösterreich (Innvierter); this unit was also listed as a niederösterreich Landwehr Battalion before Wagram, in the ranks of the Brigade Adler, Division Hohenfeldt, VI Corps.

UPPER AUSTRIA LANDWEHR (OBERÖSTERREICH) OBERÖSTERREICHISCHE LANDWEHR
Commander. Archduke Maximilian, Earl Bissingen Organization:
1. Hausrückviertel (4 Battalions)
2. Innviertel (3 Battalions)
3. Mühlviertel (Battalions)
4. Traunviertel (4 Battalions)

"Die Montur der Landwehr besteht bei uns in einem sich schliessenden Rocke von grauen Tuche mit rothen Aufschlägen. Dieser Rock muß weit und bequem genug seyn, um in Winter über die eigenen Kleider getragen werden zu können. Der gemeine Mann erhält einr Patron=tasche auf 36 Patronen an einen Gurte, dann eine Baionnet=Überschwung=Gurte, und am hute ein messingenes Schildchen, worauf der Kreis, zu welchem das Bataillon gehöret, so wie auch die Zahl des Bataillons zu ersehen ist. Dieses Schildchen wird an den gewöhnlichen runden Hut mit einem schwarzen Bande befestiget." [12]

Hausrückviertel
3 Battalions in the Brigade Nesslinger at Ried, 1 Battalion in the Brigade Sinzendorf at Linz, Division Anton Mittrowsky under O'Reilly.

1st Battalion St Georgen
- Major Heinrich Kampfmüller then Major Count Anton Engel

Before Aspern: at Salzburg (then lots of deserters and prisoners made by the Bavarians hardly reduced it), disbanded before Aspern, its remnants in the III combined Niederösterreich Landwehr Battalion Fürstenberg.

2nd Battalion Lambach
- Major Hamsa then Baron Major Moltke

As above disbanded after Aspern, the remnants formed the 1st combined Oberösterreich (Innviertler) Landwehr Battalion.

3rd Battalion Waizenkirchen
- Baron Major Johann Schottendorf

Before Aspern: with the Brigade Sinzendorf of the detached Division Dedovich, then 2 companies with Army of Inner Austria in the Division Jellachich. It was disbanded immediately after Aspern (end of May), the remnants formed the 1st combined Oberösterreich (Innviertler) Landwehr Battalion.

4th Battalion Linz
- Major Count Johann Künigl

Before Aspern: part in the Brigade Sinzendorf, detached Division Dedovich – then part in the Brigade Mc Dermott, autonomous brigade.

Between Aspern and Wagram: 2 companies concurred to the raising of the 2nd combined Oberösterreich (Mühlviertler) Landwehr Battalion. The remnants formed autonomous units and partially were in the new 3rd combined Niederösterreich Battalion Fürstenfeld. At Raab battle with Division FML Colloredo-Mannsfeld, Brigade GM Marziani.

Innviertel
3 Battalions in the Brigade Nesslinger at Ried, Division Mittrowsky under O'Reilly.

1st Battalion Raab
- Major Franz Straka von Kriegsfeld; later Major Count Johann Weissenwolf and finally again Straka.

Before Aspern: in the Brigade Nesslinger, detached Division Dedovich

before Wagram and After Wagram: in the Brigade Adler, Division Hohenfeld, VI. Corps

At the May end formed the 1st Combined Oberösterreich (Innviertler) Landwehr Battalion with remnants of the 2nd and 3rd Hausrücker, the 1st, 3rd and 4th Mühlviertler and the 2nd, 3rd and 4th Traunviertler Landwehr Battalions.

2nd Battalion Ried
- Major Andreas Hoffer.

Before Aspern: with the Brigade McDermott, autonomous brigade, Army of Inner Austria. At the April's end gave its men to the new 2nd Combined Oberösterreich (Mühlviertler) Battalion.

3rd Battalion Mattighofen
- Oberstleutnant Count Carl Sinzendorf.

Before Aspern: it was in the Brigade Sinzendorf, detached Division Dedovich. On May its remnants went into the 2nd Combined oberösterreich (Mühlviertler) Battalion.

Mühlviertel
4   Battalions in the Brigade Sinzendorf at Linz, Division Anton Mittrowsky under O'Reilly.

1st Battalion Markt Urfahr
- Major Count Ferdinand Weissenwolf

Before Aspern: it was with the Brigade Sinzendorf, autonomous, Army of Inner Austria. Still in May merged with the 3rd Battalionin the 1st combined Oberösterreich (Innviertler) Landwehr Battalion.

2nd Battalion Neufelden
- Baron Major Christian Lahrbusch; then Major Maximilian Ungerhofer and finally Baron Major Münchhausen.

Before Aspern: with the Brigade Mc Dermott, detached Division Dedovich and then committed to watch duties along the bavarian borders outposts.

Between Aspern and Wagram: it was with the Brigade Erhardt, Division Jellachich, Army of Inner Austria After Wagram: detached to the Brigade Bianchi

At the May's end, with 2 companies of the 1st Hausrücker Battalion, with the remnants of the 2nd Battalion Innviertel and those of the 1st, 2nd and 3rd Battalion Traunviertler Circle formed the new 2nd Combined Oberösterreich (Mühlviertler) Landwehr Battalion (Münchhausen).

3rd Battalion Leonfelden
- Major Count Franz Lichtenberg

Before Aspern: it was with the Brigade Sinzendorf, detached Division Dedovich and still before Aspern gave its remnants to (with the 1st Battalion) 2nd combined (Münchhausen) Landwehr Battalion.

4th Battalion Bergen
- Major Count Maximilian Althann

Before Aspern: with the Brigade Sinzendorf, detached Division Dedovich.

Between Aspern and Wagram: ½ Battalion in the der Army of Inner Austria. At Raab battle with Division FML Colloredo- Mannsfeld, Brigade GM Marziani.

After Wagram: its remnants were merged in the 1st combined Oberösterreich (Innviertler) Landwehr Battalion

Traunviertel

1st Battalion Gmunden
- Major August Kobelt

Before Aspern: in the Brigade Mc Dermott, detached Division Dedovich, autonomous,

Between Aspern and Wagram: its remnants to the 2nd Combined Oberösterreich (Mühlviertler) Landwehr Battalion At Raab battle with Division FML Colloredo-Mannsfeld, Brigade GM Marziani.

2nd Battalion Kremsmünster, Kirchdorf
- Major Baron Gfeller then Major Count Carl Clary.

Before Aspern: in the Brigade Mc Dermott, autonomous, Army of Inner Austria. At Raab battle with Division FML Colloredo- Mannsfeld, Brigade GM Marziani. Later the remnants to the 2nd combined (Mühlviertler) Landwehr Battalion.

3rd Battalion Steyr
- Major Prince Carl Lamberg then Baron Major Münchhausen,

Before Aspern: in the Brigade Mc Dermott, autonomous, Army of Inner Austria. At Raab battle with Division FML Colloredo- Mannsfeld, Brigade GM Marziani. Its remnants to the 2nd Combined Oberösterreich (Mühlviertler) Landwehr Battalion.

4th Battalion Neuhofen
- Baron Major Anton Eiselsberg

Before Aspern: Brigade Nesslinger, detached Division Dedovich.

Between Aspern and Wagram: remnants to the 1st combined Oberösterreich (Innviertler) Landwehr Battalion.

BATTALIONS FORMED DURING THE CAMPAIGN

1st combined Oberösterreich (Innviertler) Landwehr Battalion – Major Straka
remnants of the 2nd and 3rd Hausrücker Landwehr Battalion, the 1st Innviertler, the 1st, 2nd and 4th Mühlviertler, the 4th Traunviertler Landwehr Battalion.

2nd combined Oberösterreich (Mühlviertler) Landwehr Battalion – Major Münchhausen
remnants of the 4th Hausrücker, the 2nd Innviertler, the 3rd Mühlviertler and the 1st -2nd Traunviertler Landwehr Battalion.

Group of Upper Austria Landwehr
Before Aspern: they went with Jellachich, brig. Provenchères Between Aspern and Wagram: in the Division Colloredo Before Wagram: concurred at the formation of the Brig Adler. Remained 1 Battalion which, in August, merged into the new :

2nd Combined Ober- and Niederösterreich Landwehr Battalion (Lichtenberg)
(with the 1st and 3rd Landwehr Battalion OWW, the 1st till 4th Mühlviertler and the 1st Traunviertler Landwehr Batt.

THE LANDWEHR FROM SALZBURG
Commander: Count Saurau - 4 Battalion of the Brigade Legisfeld in Salzburg, DivisionAnton Mittrowsky under O'Reilly.
Salzburg had uniforms with green "Röcken" and yellow facing, white pants, black gaiters (or boots). In effects only Officers had this uniforms with the three City Companies. The other companies had grey Lodens. The 4th Battalion, Pinzgauer, Zillertaler, Brixentaler had brown waistcoats with yellow facings. They were committed by the Army Order of February 16, 1809. [13]
The organization was the following:
a) the Battalions got one number (1, 2, 3, etc.). Each had 800-1200 men and a Staff Officer as Commander.
b) each Battalion was divided into 4, 6 and even 8 companies if numbers allowed it.
c) each company was divided into 4 – 6 platoons (Züge) and each platoon in many Corporalschäften (squads) raised in the land's parishes.

1st Battalion City of Salzburg
- Major Johann Georg von Wilmanns

Before Aspern: Brigade Legisfeld, Div. Jellachich Between Aspern and Wagram: Brigade Legisfeld, Div. Jellachich .

2nd Battalion Laufen - Oberstleutnant Count Ernst Herberstein
Before Aspern: in the Brigade Legisfeld, Division Jellachich. At Raab in the Brigade GM Sebottendorf, Division FML Franz Jellačić. later disbanded, remnants given to 1st Battalion

3rd Battalion Radstadt - Major earl Thun
Before Aspern: in the Brigade Legisfeld, Division Jellachich Between Aspern and Wagram: in Styria

4th Battalion Mittersill - Major Sigmund Brank
Before Aspern: in the Brigade Legisfeld, Division Jellachich
disbanded remnants to the 1st Battalion . It was also called Gebirgsbataillon.

COMMANDERS OF THE LANDWEHR BATTALIONS 1808-1810
Lower UpperAustria and Salzburg, by Karel Sáček et al.

Commander of the Battalion	Nation.	Name of the Battalion	seq. of comm.
Althann Maximilian Count Major	Upper Austria	4th Battalion Bergen	1
Beissel, Clemens Baron von, Major	Lower Austria	4th Battalion Wiener Neustadt	I 2/2
	Lower Austria	2nd Battalion Waidhofen an der Thaya	II 2/2
Brank Sigmund Major	Salzburg	4th Battalion Mittersill	I
Breuner, Joseph Count Oberstl.	Lower Austria	1st Battalion Herzogenburg, St Pölten	½
Buol, Baron von, Major	Lower Austria	4th Battalion Wiener Neustadt	½
Cavriani, Maxmilian Count Major	Lower Austria	5th Vienna Battalion - City of Vienna	½
Clary, Albert Count Major	Lower Austria	2nd Battalion Lilienfeld	2/3
Clary Carl Count Major	Upper Austria	2nd Battalion Kremsmünster, Kirchdorf	1/1
Colloredo, Ferdinand Prince, Major	Lower Austria	4th Battalion Poysdorf	I 1/1
Colloredo, Ferdinand Prince, Oberstlieutenant	Lower Austria	3rd Battalion Zwettl	II 2/2
Colloredo, Ferdinand Prince, Oberstlieutenant	Lower Austria	1st combined Battalion Ober and Unter dem Manhartsberge (= 1st Comb. Niederösterreichische Batt.)	III
Eiselsberg Anton Baron Major	Upper Austria	4th Battalion Neuhofen	1
Eisenkolb, Anton, Major	Lower Austria	2nd Battalion Waidhofen an der Thaya	½

New Uniform

CARNEVILLE HUSSARS

▲ Austrian Infantry Landwehr uniforms regiments

Name	Region	Battalion	
Engel Anton Count Major	Upper Austria	1st Battalion St Georgen	I
Fuchs, Franz Xaver Count Major	Lower Austria	3rd Battalion Traiskirchen	1/1
Fürstenberg, Friedrich Egon Landgraf, Major	Lower Austria	5th Battalion Krems and Zwettl	I 1/1
Gasser, Cölestin, Major	Lower Austria	3rd comb. Batt. Ober a Unter dem Manhartsberg	II
Gfeller Baron Major	Lower Austria	3rd Battalion Zwettl	½
Gilleis, Joseph Count Major	Upper Austria	2nd Battalion Kremsmünster, Kirchdorf	1
Kampfmüller Heinrich Major	Lower Austria	4th Battalion Horn	2/2
Kobelt August Major	Upper Austria	1st Battalion St Georgen	I
Künigl Johann Count Major	Upper Austria	1st Battalion Gmunden	I
Hamsa Major	Upper Austria	4th Battalion Linz	1
Hardegg, Count Major	Upper Austria	2nd Battalion Lambach	I
Herberstein Ernst count, Oberstl.	Lower Austria	2nd Battalion Ernstbrunn	3/3
Hoffer Andreas Major	Salzburg	2nd Battalion Laufen	I
Hoyos, Ernst Count Major -Oberstl.	Upper Austria	2nd Battalion Ried	I
Hoyos, Ernst Count Major -Oberstl.	Lower Austria	6th Battalion or 2nd Wiener Neustadt	I 1/1
La Bussière, Ludwig Chevalier Estevenet de, Oberstlieutenant	Lower Austria	2nd combined Battalion Unter dem Wiener Wald	II
	Lower Austria	1st Battalion Krems	1/1
Lahrbusch Christian Baron Major	Upper Austria	2nd Battalion Neufelden	1
Lamberg Carl Prince Major	Upper Austria	3rd Battalion Steyr	1
Lerch von Mühlheim, Major	Lower Austria	3rd Battalion Wolkersdorf	½
Lichtenberg Franz Count Major	Upper Austria	3rd Battalion Leonfelden	1/3
Lichtenberg, Franz Count Major	Lower Austria	1st combined Ober- und Niederösterreichische Battalion	2/3
Lichtenberg Franz Count Major	Upper and Lower Austria	2nd combined Ober- and Niederösterreich Landwehr Battalion	3/3
Moltke Baron Major	Upper Austria	2nd Battalion Lambach	1
Münchhausen Baron Major	Upper Austria	2nd Battalion Neufelden	1/3
Münchhausen Baron Major	Upper Austria	3rd Battalion Steyr	2/3
Münchhausen Baron Major	Upper Austria	2nd comb. Oberösterreich (Mühlviertler) Land.Batt.	3/3
Obergfell, Joseph Heinrich Baron	Lower Austria	2nd Battalion Ernstbrunn	I 1/3
Obergfell, Joseph Heinrich Baron von, Major -Oberstlieutenant	Lower Austria	3rd Battalion Wolkersdorf	II 2/2
Plunquet, Thomas Count Oberstlieutenant	Lower Austria	4th Battalion Weikersdorf	1/1
Praschmar, Philipp, Count von	Lower Austria	1st Battalion Herzogenburg, St Pölten	1/1
Rein, Andreas von, Major	Lower Austria	3rd Battalion Scheibbs	1/1
Rieben von Riebenfeld, Franz, Major	Lower Austria	2nd Battalion Lilienfeld	3/3
Rüchler, Leopold Baron von, Major	Lower Austria	1st Battalion Fischamend	I 1/1
Schönborn, Franz Count Major	Lower Austria	1st combined Battalion Unter dem Wiener Wald	II
Schottendorf Johann Baron Major	Lower Austria	2nd Battalion Ernstbrunn	2/3
Sinzendorf Carl Count Oberstleutnant	Upper Austria	3rd Battalion Waizenkirchen	1
	Upper Austria	3rd Battalion Mattighofen	1
St. Quentin, Emanuel Count Major	Lower Austria	2nd Vienna Battalion - Wien (Neu-Lerchenfeld)	½
Stark, Friedrich von, Major	Lower Austria	4th Battalion Horn	½
Steinsberg, Edler von Leidenthal, Sebastian, Hptm.	Lower Austria	2nd Battalion Lilienfeld	I 1/3
Steinsberg, Edler von Leidenthal, Sebastian, Major	Lower Austria	2nd Vienna Battalion - Wien (Neu-Lerchenfeld)	II 2/2
Straka von Kriegsfeld Franz Major	Upper Austria	1st Battalion Raab	1/2
Straka von Kriegsfeld Franz Major	Upper Austria	1st comb. Oberösterreich (Innviertler) Landwehr Batt.	2/2
Thun earl, Major	Salzburg	3rd Battalion Radstadt	I
Ungerhofer Maximilian Major	Upper Austria	2nd Battalion Neufelden	2/3
Weissenwolf Ferdinand Count Major	Upper Austria	1st Battalion Markt Urfahr	1
Weissenwolf Johann Count Major	Upper Austria	1st Battalion Raab	I/2
Weissenwolf, Johann Count Major	Lower Austria	5th Vienna Battalion - City of Vienna	2/2
Wilmanns Johann Georg von Major	Salzburg	1st Battalion City of Salzburg	I
Wolff von Eggenburg, August, Major	Lower Austria	1st Battalion Weikersdorf	2/2

THE VIENNA MILITIA (WIENER BÜRGER-CORPS)

The citizens of Vienna or simply those who had no more military duties and were free from 1805-06 enlisted in the special Militia Corps of the city. This was a traditional very ancient corps (since the 1529 turkish siege) which originally had 4 companies, each with the name of a Vienna district (canton) Stuben, Schotten, Widmer and Kärnthen. The enlistment was only for volunteers, who swore to defend the city in case of hostile attack or danger. The Militia had also its own cavalry, which was abandoned in 1740 but again raised in 1805.
The City Council (the Mayor was also the Oberst of the Militia) armed its soldiers, but they had to provide to the uniforms by themselves.
The Staff of the WBK (Wiener Bürger Korps) was the following: Oberst, Oberstlieutenant, 2 Majore, Caplan, Stabs-Adjutant with Captain rank, Regiments-Adjutant with 1st Lieutenant rank, Regimentsarzt, Capellmeister, Stabs-Fourier, Regiments-Tambour. They had blue waistcoats with red facings.

1st City Regiment
In it were allowed only true citizens of Vienna and nobles. The uniform had blue waistcoats, red facings, white breeches in summer, grey "russian" pants with red lining in winter. Its 8 companies (2 Battalions) had to defend the inner city of Vienna (not the imperial court which had its own Guards).

2nd City Regiment
The Second could enlist also house proprietors from suburbs, manufacturers, artisans, employees etc. It had also 8 companies (2 Battalions). The uniform was dark green with blue facings.

City Cavalry
It had around 260 horses, so a Division. It recruited also in the suburbs and in the closest towns. Their uniform was blue with red facings and gold buttons (in Parade they wore epaulettes, white breeches and high boots, in campaign they had no epaulettes or garments, riding pants and common boots). The Division was made of two squadrons each with 4 Züge.

The City Grenadier Battalion
It was a Battalion of around 650 grenadiers (Staff apart) made by three Divisions. The 1st Division came from the 1st City regiment: dark blue waistcoat, scarlet red facings, golden epaulettes, golden buttons and white breeches. The 2nd Division was attached to the Sharpshooters (Scharfschützen Corps) and came from the same social environment of the 2nd regiment. It had dark green coats, scarket red facings, epaulettes, golden buttons and white breeches. The 3rd Division came from the 2nd regiment and was composed only by authorized personnel. It had dark grey coats, sky blue facings, white buttons and white breeches with gaiters.

The Sharpshooters
The correct title was K.K. priv. ritterlich-bürgerliches Scharfschützen-Corps and was composed by all social classes and authorized citizens who had honorary mentions. Gala uniform: dark green waistcoat, scarlet red facings, golden buttons and epaulettes, white breeches, military boots, bicorn reversed hats with green and gold rosettes, one golden band with, at its end, a hunting horn, which had in the middle a golden button with the letters F.I. surrounder by laurel symbol. The hats had a classic black-yellow plume.
Campaign uniform: coat and breeches dark grey, dark green facings and piping (shoulder straps). They were armed with the 63 cm Stutzen, steel sabre with golden-black porte d'epée, the powder-horn and cartridge bag.

The Bombers (Bürgen artillerie ombardiers Corps)
Wore bicorns, blue uniforms with red facings and white breeches. They managed the gun of the fortress and on the city walls.

The Academy of Arts Battalion (Corps der bildenden Künstler)
It had four companies of students who wore green coats and cherry red facings, golden buttons and white breeches.

1809 – Volunteers Units of Austria and German Lands
Free Corps Brunswick (Braunschweiger Freikorps or the "Schwarze Schar", the Black Bunch) formed by Jäger, Infantry and Hussars, Uhlans ?). Uniforms well known with its "Totenkopf". At side the image of Uhlans.
Commander: the Duke of Brunswick Friedrich Wilhelm zu Braunschweig-Oels. Before Aspern: autonomous unit. Between Aspern and Wagram: attached to the XI Corps Kienmayr then also in the Brigade Am Ende (autonomous) After Wagram: autonomous.

Free Corps Carneville
Inhaber (Owner) Commander: Oberst Count Franz Simon de Carneville. Jäger Battalion – commander Major August Docteur

Before Aspern: some attched them to the Brigade Gratze, Division Rohan, IV Corps while others put it in the Brigade Grill, Division Dedovich, IV Corps or maybe as autonomous Brigade Carneville, Division Rohan, IV Corps. Sometimes called as IX Feldjäger Battalion.
At Wagram: fought with Brigade Provenchères, Division Radetzky, IV Corps
Carneville Hussars – led by Count Franz Simon de Carneville Before Aspern: in the Brigade Gratze, Division Rohan, IV Corps
At Aspern: Brigade Carneville, Division Rohan, IV Corps then Brigade Stutterheim, Division Rohan, IV Corps
At Wagram: Brigade Provenchères, Division Radetzky, IV Corps.
Free Corps Dörnberg or (Westphälisches Scharfschützen bataillon) Commander: Oberst Baron Wilhelm Dörnberg.
Archduke Johann Jäger see under Salzburger Jäger
Fränkische Legion or Bayreuthische Legion Recruitment: Franconia and Brunswick.
Infantry Commander: Oberstleutnant Count Emmanuel Mensdorff
Cavalry Commander (Hussars and Uhlans) – (interim commander) Major Count Hermann Nostitz
Katt Freikorps
Before Aspern: insurgents volunteers in Prussia
Kurhessen Freikorps
Before Aspern: a very small unit engaged with brig. Am Ende
Salzburger Jäger or 2nd Innerösterreichisches Freibataillon (Archduke Johann Jäger) Owner (Inhaber): the Archduke Johann of Austria
Commander: Major-Oberstlieutenant Baron Paul Thurn-und-Taxis
Before Aspern: 2 companies with the Brigade Buol, Chasteler then other 2 companies in the Brigade Fenner, Chasteler – last 2 companies in the detached Division Jellachich. Later 3 companies with Taxis, Bartholdy amd 4 company with Martin Teimer. At Aspern: 4 company with Chasteler
Between Aspern and Wagram: with the detached brig. Buol then, at Reissenfels, with Hauptmann Taxis - 1 company with Oberstleutnant Taxis - 1 company with Teimer. They fought at Volders, in Vorarlberg and in the May Bergisel battle in Vorarlberg.
At Wagram: 2 companies attache to the Brigade Eckhart, Division Frimont. After Wagram: they remained with the Brigade Buol, Chasteler, corps.
Free Corps Schlegenberg (Schlägenberg, Schlagenberg) Freikorps
so Schlegenbergische freiwillige Jäger or Wiener freiwilligr Jägerkorps / Wiener freiwillige Jägerkompanie. Commander: Count Anton Schlegenberg
At Aspern: attached to the IR 39 Duka, Brigade Bianchi, VI Corps

VOLUNTEERS OF VIENNA - WIENER FREIWILLIGE
1st Battalion – Major Count Emmanuel Bigot de St Quentin
Before Aspern: in Brigade Rothhacker, Division Reuss Plauen, V Corps then Brigade Albrecht, Division Dedovich, VI Corps. Later in the Brigade Nordmann, autonomous, VI Corps. All volunteers Battalions of Vienna took part at the defence of Ebelsberg.
At Aspern: Brigade Nordmann, Avant-garde VI Corps
At Wagram: with the Brigade Mariassy, Division Vincent, Avant-garde I Wing VI Corps After Wagram: with the Brigade Wallmoden, Division Vincent, VI Corps.
2nd Battalion – Oberst Baron August Steigentesch
also commander of the Volunteers group.
Before Aspern: in Brigade Rothhacker, Division Reuss Plauen, V Corps then Brigade Albrecht, Division Dedovich, VI Corps. Later Brigade Nordmann ,autonomous, VI. Corps.
At Aspern: Brigade Nordmann, Avantgarde, VI Corps
At Wagram: Brigade Máriassy, Division Vincent, Avant-garde Reserve Wing VI Corps After Wagram: with the Brigade Wallmoden, Division Vincent, VI Corp
3rd Battalion – Major Count Franz Waldstein
Before Aspern: in the Brigade Rothhacker, Division Reuss Plauen, V Corps then Brigade Albrecht, Division Dedovich, VI Corps. Later with the Brigade Bianchi, Division Kottulinsky, VI Corps.

At Aspern: Brigade Hoffmeister, Division Kottulinsky, VI Corps then Brigade Bianchi, Division Vincent, VI Corps At Wagram: attached to Brigade Splényi, Division Kottulinsky, VI Corps

4th Battalion - Oberstlieutenant Johann Küffel von Küffelstein

Before Aspern: part of the Brigade Provenchères, Division Vincent, VI Corps then Brigade Albrecht, Division Dedovich, VI Corps. Later with the Brigade Hohenfeldt, Division Kottulinsky, VI Corps.

At Aspern: in the Brigade Hohenfeldt, Division Kottulinsky, VI Corps At Wagram: with the Brigade Splényi, Division Kottulinsky, VI Corps. **5th Battalion Major Count Rudolf Salis-Gigers (Zizers)**

Before Aspern: with the Brigade Provenchères, Division Vincent, VI Corps then Brigade Albrecht, Division Dedovich, VI Corps. Later part of an autonomous brigade of VI Corps.

At Aspern: in an autonomous brigade of VI Corps.

At Wagram: in the Brigade Pfluger, autonomous, V Corps then in the same Brigade Pfluger, Division Weissenwolff, V Corps After Wagram: always with Brigade Pfluger, autonomous, V Corps.

6th Battalion – Major Chevalier Anton Managetta und Lerchenau

Before Aspern: with the Brigade Provenchères, Division Vincent, VI Korps then in the Brigade Albrecht, Division Dedovich, VI Korps . This Battalion was sent to Vienna as prisoner on "Parole".

Notes

1   De Serres Marcel M., Voyage en Autriche, essai statistique et géographique sur cette Empire, vol. 1- 4 Bertrand, Paris 1814.
2   Stanka, Julius: Geschichte des k. u. k. Infanterie-Regimentes Erzherzog Carl Nr. 3. Wien: 1894.
3   In effects the Depot Division of the regiment (someone told around 1000 men ?) had reached Vienna with the Division Dedovich and then the opposite Danube bank merging with the regiment and replacing the losses (the whole 2nd Battalion lost at Ratisbon). So it is possible the numbers of IR 3 at Aspern had been different than those referred. The regiment's history gives a number of losses (from April 1 to the end of May of 23 officers and 963 men). Stanka, Julius ibidem pag. 432.
4   Amon von Treuenfest, Gustav Ritter von: Geschichte des k. k. Infanterie-Regimentes Hoch- und Deutschmeister Nr. 4. Wien: 1879.
5   Dragoni Edler von Rabenhorst, Alfons: Geschichte des K. u. K. Infanterie-Regimentes Prinz Friedrich August, Herzog von Sachsen, Nr. 45. Von der Errichtung bis zur Gegenwart. Brünn: 1897.
6   The regimental history tells that the Help Circle for the De Vaux recruitment was Rzeszòw in Galicia and so justifies its disbanding after the lost of the outer recruitment district. Otherwise Wrede et al. do not refer of galician Circles for IR 45 (nor any depot company 45 appears in any army list for Galicia). Probably the outer "helping" Circle of the De Vaux was Judenburg in Styria and the reason of the disbanding was the loss of large parts of the Salzburg territory.
7   Auspitz, Leopold: Das Infanterie-Regiment Freiherr von Hess Nr. 49. Eine Chronik nach den Weisungen des Regiments- Commandanten Obersten Anton Juriskovic von Hagendorf.Teschen: 1889.
8   Leiler, Anton: Geschichte des k. k. Infanterieregimentes No. 59 seit seiner Errichtung 1682 bis zum Schlusse des Jahres 1855. Salzburg: 1864.
9   Capitulanten: former soldiers who did voluntarily extend their duty period (weiterdienen).
10   "Belehrungen zur Circular-Verordnung vom 23sten Juny 1808, die Landwehre betreffend." in Schallhammer, Anton von, Kriegerische Ereignisse im Herzogthume Salzburg in den Jahren 1800, 1805 und 1809, Verlag Mayr, 1853.
11   Upper and Lower Austria had mainly grey waistcoats and round shields with the number of Battalion on the hat. See the following note.
12   Upper and Lower Austria had so grey uniforms and hat badges. Kurz Franz, Geschichte der Landwehr in Oesterreich ob der Enns, Cajetan Hasslinger, Linz 1811. TR. "The uniform of our Landwehr consisten in a waist coat of grey tissue with red turnbacks. This waist coat had to be large and enough comfortable to allow, in winter, dressing it over the own common clothes. The common soldier got a cartridge bag sustained by a belt, with 36 cartridge and one belt to carry the bayonet, and also, on the hat, a small brass badge, which indicated the Circle from which came the Battalion together with the number of the same Battalion. This badge was fixed to the round hat by a black band".
13   Schallhammer, Anton von, Kriegerische Ereignisse im Herzogthume Salzburg in den Jahren 1800, 1805 und 1809, Verlag Mayr, 1853.

THE INNER-AUSTRIAN LANDWEHR INFANTRY
Innerösterreichische Landwehr

Landwehr 1809 Order of Battle
Commander: FML von Lippa.
1st Brigade GM Count Gavassini
Trieste - 2 battalions Adelsberg - 4 battalions Görz – 2 battalions
2nd Brigade GM von Munkácsy
Laibach - 3 battalions Neustädtl - 1 battalion
3rd Brigade GM Ritter von Fenner
Villach - 2 battalions Klagenfurt - 3 battalions
4th Brigade Oberst von Auracher
Judenburg - 2 battalions, Bruck an der Mur – 2 battalions
5th Brigade GM von Lutz Cilli - 2 battalions
Marburg - 2 battalions
6th Brigade GM Baron von Sebottendorf
Graz - 5 battalions
Reserve Troops
Commander: FML von Lippa Strassoldo-Infantry - 2 depot companies de Vaux- Infantry - 2 depot companies Lusignan- Infantry - 2 depot companies Frimont-Husaren - 1 depot squadron Grazer Landwehr - 2 depot companies Brucker Landwehr - 2 depot companies Judenburger Landwehr - 2 depot companies Marburger Landwehr - 2 depot companies Cillier Landwehr - 2 depot companies Grenzkordon - 3 companies
GM Graf Khevenhüller in Laibach Reisky-Infantry - 2 depot companies Simbschen-Infantry - 2 depot companies Laibacher Landwehr - 2 depot companies Neustädtler Landwehr - 2 depot companies Adelsberger Landwehr - 2 depot companies Görzer Landwehr - 2 depot companies Triester Landwehr - 2 depot companies Grenzkordon - 6 companies
GM Vogl in Klagenfurt
Hohenlohe . Bartenstein-Infantry- 2 depot companies Klagenfurter Landwehr - 2 depot companies Villacher Landwehr - 2 depot companies Grenzkordon - 3 companies Many of its units will be part of the later Division FML Jellačić de Buzim

CARINTHIAN LANDWEHR – KÄRNTNERISCHE LANDWEHR
Organisation:
1.   Circle of Klagenfurt (Klagenfurter Kreis - 3 battalions)
2.   Circle of Villach (Villacher Kreis - 2 battalions)
-   Before Aspern: the 7 Battalions of the carinthian and styrian Landwehr were with the Corps Chasteler (4 in the Brigade von Buol). At Raab in the Brigade GM Legisfeld, Division FML Franz Jellačić.

Circle of Klagenfurt
3 battalions in the Brigade Fenner in Klagenfurt, 2 depot companies in the Brigade Vogl in Klagenfurt, Division Lippa under Kerpen.
1st Battalion Klagenfurt - Major Count Franz Ursenbeck Before Aspern in the Brigade Buol, Corps Chasteler
2nd Battalion Althofen - Major Anton von Leiss
Before Aspern in the Corps Chasteler then in the Brigade Fenner.
3rd Battalion Lavamünd - Major Count Douglas Dietrichstein
Before Aspern and from Aspern till Wagram: in the Brigade Buol, Corps Chasteler or in the Brigade Fenner.
Circle of Villach
2 battalions in the Brigade Fenner In Klagenfurt, 2 depot companies in the Brigade Vogl in Klagenfurt, Division Lippa under Kerpen.
1st Battalion Villach - Major Count Johann Sardagna
Before Aspern: Brigade Fenner, Corps Chasteler later in the group Lodron then in the corps Reissenfels and finally in the Brigade Marchal.
2nd Battalion Sachsenburg - Major Count Hieronymus Maria Lodron
later under Major Count Anton La Motte
Before Aspern: in the Corps Chasteler, it was disbanded. Reorganized in June-July under the Army of Inner Austria.

Organization:

Landwehr of Styria - Steiermärkische Landwehr
1. Circle of Bruck (Brucker Kreis - 2 battalions)
2. Circle of Cillj (Cillier Kreis - 2 battalions)
3. Circle of Graz (Grazer Kreis - 5 Battalions)
4. Circle of Judenburg (Judenburger Kreis - 2 battalions)
5. Circle of Marburg (Marburger Kreis - 2 battalions)

Circle of Bruck (Brucker)
1st Battalion Mürzzuschlag - Major Franz von Stransky
- Before Aspern: with the Brigade Auracher, Corps Chasteler later with the autonomous Division Jellačić.
- till Wagram: with the Division Jellačić, Army of Inner Austria.

2nd Battalion Leoben – Major Ignaz von Gollnhofer
- Before Aspern: in the Brigade Auracher, Corps Chasteler then with the Brigade Fenner.
- till Wagram: with the Division Jellačić, Army of Inner Austria.
- After Wagram: was raised the 1st combined Steiermärkisches Landwehr Battalion from the 1st Battalion Mürzzuschlag and the remnants [7] of the 2nd Bn. Leoben.

The "Brucker" as a group:
- Initially 2 battalions with the Brigade Auracher in Leoben, 2 depot companies with the Brigade Lippa in Graz, Division Lippa under Kerpen then:
- Before Aspern: with the Corps Chasteler - 1 battalion with the Brigade Auracher, Corps Chasteler and also 3 more companies with the Brigade Auracher, Corps Lippa –2 more companies in the Reserve Truppen Lippa , then 1 battalion with the Brigade Fenner, Corps Chasteler. Finally 1 battalion with the Brigade Marchal, Corps Chasteler.
- till Wagram: 1 battalion with the Army of Inner Austria - 1/3 battalion with the Division Jellačić, Army of Inner Austria. At Raab in the Brigade GM Legisfeld, Division FML Franz Jellačić.

Circle of Cillj (today Celje – Slovenia) Cillier
1st Battalion Cilli - Major Johann Nepomuk Schmelzern
- from Aspern till Wagram: At the time of St.Michael battle (May 15) with Brigade GM Lutz, Division FML. Albert Gyulai. Then with the Division Jellačić, Army of Inner Austria. At Raab in the Brigade GM Gajoli, Division FML Franz Jellačić.

2nd Battalion Peilenstein - Major Baron Franz Leuzendorf
- Before Aspern: At the time of St.Michael battle (May 15) with Brigade GM Lutz, Division FML. Albert Gyulai. Then with Jellačić (autonomous)

The Cillier as a group:
2 battalions with the Brigade Lutz in Marburg, 2 depot companies with the Brigade Lippa in Graz, Division Lippa under Kerpen.
- Before Aspern: with Kerpen (Reserve of Inner Austria) with the Brigade Lutz, Corps Lippa 2 battalions with the Reserve "Truppen" Lippa 2 companies
- Before Wagram: 2/3 battalion with the der Army of Inner Austria - 1 battalion with the Division Colloredo, Army of Inner Austria.

Circle of Graz (Grazer)
1st Battalion Graz, Stadt Major Count Hrzan
then Major Sigmund Mahlern von Mahlenstein
- Before Aspern: with the IX Corps, Army of Inner Austria. depot companies in Graz.
- Before Wagram: in Graz later with the Division Colloredo, Army of Inner Austria
- After Wagram: in Graz

2nd Battalion Eggenburg - Oberstlieutenant Johann Ludwig Hummel
- Before Wagram: with the Division Colloredo, Army of Inner Austria. At Raab with Brigade GM Lutz, Division FML Colloredo- Mannsfeld. Later, during the battle, it was detached with one battalion Strassoldo infantry in order to defend the Szabadhégy bridge (detachment Oberst Count von Salins).

3rd Battalion Wilden - Major Cäsar von Viola
then Major Ignaz Lescynsky
- Before Wagram: in Graz then with the Army of Inner Austria. depot companies in Graz.
- After Wagram: disbanded, its remnants to the 2nd Marburger battalion.

4th Battalions Fürstenfeld - Major Conte Joseph Zenone
- Before Aspern: with the Army of Inner Austria
- Before Wagram: Brigade Best, Division Colloredo, Army of Inner Austria. At Raab in the Brigade GM Gajoli, Division FML Franz Jellačić.

▲ Austrian Infantry Landwehr uniforms regiments

th Battalions Hartberg - Major Baron Joseph Kottulinsky
- Before Aspern Brigade Best, Division Colloredo, Army of Inner Austria
- Before Wagram: At Raab in the Brigade GM Gajoli, Division FML Franz Jellačić.

The Grazer as a group: 5 Battalions with the Brigade Sebottendorf, 2 depot companies with the Brigade Lippa in Graz, Division Lippa under Kerpen
- Before Aspern: with the Brigade Sebottendorf, Corps Lippa 5 Battalions and with the Reserve Truppen Lippa 2 companies. At the time of St.Michael battle (May 15) all five battalionswere with the Brigade GM Sebottendorf by Mobiles Korps bei Villach: Division FML Frimont.

Circle of Judenburg (Judenburger)
1st Battalion Judenburg - Major Baron Tartler
then Major Baron Franz Werner
- Before Aspern: Brigade Auracher, Corps Chasteler then with the Division Jellačić (autonomous)
- Before Wagram: with the Division Jellačić. At Raab in the Brigade GM Sebottendorf, Division FML Franz Jellačić.

2nd Battalion Rottenmann - Major Johann Nepomuk Schiffer
- Before Aspern: with the VIII Corps, disbanded at the May end, remnants merged with the 1st battalion
- Before Wagram: 1st and 2nd battalionswere merged (1/2 battalions) and remained with the Division Jellačić, Army of Inner Austria.

Judenburger as a group: 2 battalions with the Brigade Auracher in Leoben, 2 depot companies with Lippa in Graz, Division Lippa under Kerpen
- Before Aspern: with the Brigade Auracher, Corps Lippa 2 battalions and later with the Reserve "Truppen" Lippa, 2 companies.
- Before Wagram: with the Division Colloredo or Frimont, Army of Inner Austria

Circle of Marburg (today Maribor Slovenia) Marburger
1st Battalion Marburg - Major Count Alois Khuenburg
- Before Aspern: with the main Reserve for the borders defence. At the time of St.Michael battle (May 15) with Brigade GM Lutz, Division FML. Albert Gyulai.

2nd Battalion Pettau - Major Heinrich Spormacher
then Major Ignaz Leszinsky (After Wagram: Battalions Schenkel)
- Before Aspern: with the main Reserve at Klagenfurt later with the Brigade GM Lutz,Division Albert Gyulai, VIII Corps . The two Battalions were merged Before the battle of Aspern.
- Before Wagram: again raised in Pettau and with Raab.

As a group: 2 battalions with the Brigade Lutz in Marburg, 2 depot companies with the Brigade Lippa in Graz, Division Lippa under Kerpen and then with the Brigade Lutz, Corps Lippa, 2 battalions finally with the Res. Truppen Lippa 2 companies.

Landwehr of Carniola – Istria – Gorizia and Coastlands (Krain-Küstenländische - Istrische) Landwehr Org.:
Circle of Adelsberg (Postojna) (Adelsberger Kreis - 4 battalions)
5. Circle of Görz (Görzer Kreis - 2 battalions)
6. Circle of Ljubljana (Laibacher Kreis - 3 battalions)
7. Circle of Neustädtl (Neustädtler Kreis - 4 battalions)
8. Circle of Trieste – Free Port of Trieste (Triester Kreis - 2 battalions)

Circle of Adelsberg (Postojna) Adelsberger
4 battalions with the Brigade Gavassini in Trieste, 2 depot companies with the Brigade Khevenhüller in Laibach (Ljubljana), Division Lippa under Kerpen.

1st Battalion Mitterburg (Pisino) - Major Emerich Pisino de Villa de Castella
then Hauptmann Carl von Schiwitzhoffen
- Before Aspern: with the Army of Inner Austria. At the time of St.Michael battle (May 15) with Brigade GM Lutz, Division FML. Albert Gyulai, then in Croatia.

2nd Battalion Lippa - Major de Pretier
then Major Baron Joseph Lazarini
It was with the der Army of Inner Austria then at Fiume **3rd Battalion Adelsberg - Major Baron Joseph Lazarini** disbanded before Aspern.

4th battalion Loitsch - Major Luxetich von Lichtenfeld
- Before Aspern: practically destroyed on the battlefields.

No other available data upon the single Battalions The whole group:
- Before Aspern: with the Brigade Kálnássy, IX. Corps with the Brigade Gavassini, 2nd Hauptkolonne Knesevich (4 battalions)

with the Brigade Gavassini, Corps Lippa, Army of Inner Austria (4 battalions) with the Brigade Khevenhüller, Reserve troops in the South 2 companies. then with the detached brig.Tommasich, Army of Inner Austria.
- Between Aspern and Wagram: 4 battalions with the IX Corps. At Raab in the Brigade GM Sebottendorf, Division FML Franz Jellačić.

Circle of Görz or Gorizia (Görzer)
2 battalions with the Brigade Gavassini in Trieste, Division Lippa under Kerpen.

1st Battalion Görz – Major Count Peter Coronini-Cronberg
- Before Aspern: with the Brigade Kálnássy, IX Corps then with the Brigade Gavassini, IX Corps.

2nd Battalion Tolmein - Major Elias von Bubanovich
- Before Aspern: at Prewald and Obtschina, then with the Brigade Gavassini, IX Corps. In June was in Croatia. As a group: before Aspern 4 companies with the Brigade Dumontet, IX Corps. After were with the Brigade Gyurkovich, 2nd Hauptkolonne Knesevich and also in the Brigade Gavassini, Corps Lippa, Army of Inner Austria (2 battalions). Later they were with the Brigade Khevenhüller, Reserve troops in South with 2 companies Finally the 2 battalions were deployed along the Isonzo river. Before Wagram 2 battalions with the IX Corps.

Circle of Laibach (Laibacher)
1st battalion Laibach – Major Count Joseph Thurn von Bleyburg
- Before Aspern: At the time of St.Michael battle (May 15) with Brigade GM Lutz, Division FML. Albert Gyulai. Then was with the Brigade Kálnássy, IX Corps . Before Wagram in Croatia.

2nd Battalion Radmannsdorf - Major Vitalis von Pasquali
- Before Aspern: It was surprised at Ljubljana and made prisoner on „parole".

3rd Battalion practically not raised (disbanded Before the war) – under Millautz ??

Laibacher as a group:
2 battalions with the Brigade Munkácsy in Laibach, 2 Depotkomp. with the Brigade Khevenhüller in Laibach, Division Lippa under Kerpen.
- Before Aspern: 2 battalions with the Brigade Munkácsy, 2nd Hauptkolonne Knesevich, Army of Inner Austria. One battalion was on watch along the Isonzo river but was also part of the Brigade Munkácsy, Corps Lippa, (2 battalions) Then 2 companies were with the Brigade Khevenhüller, Reserve troops in South.
- Before Wagram: the 2 battalions with the IX Corps.

Circle of Neustädtl (Neustädtler)
1st Unterkrainer battalion Neustädtl - Oberstleutnant Friedrich von Reuttenberg
then Hauptmann Franz Xaver von Langer
- Before Aspern: at Sachsenburg as garrison (till the end of May). Then returned to Neustädtl. In June, when Du Montet occupied Laibach, it reached the Du Montet Streifskorps. After the armistice marched till Szamobor (Croatia) . There the main part of the battalion deserted.

2nd Battalion Gottschee - Major Franz von Borwitz
then Major Joseph Albrecht
- Before Aspern: at Prewald - After Wagram: disbanded

3rd Battalion Tschernembl - Major Dabrovich
then Major Franz Scherer
- Before Aspern: with the VIII Corps with garrison tasks.

4th battalion not completely raised - Hauptmann Millautz ?? or Major Baron Carl von Obermayer ?
- other possible commanders Baron Obernberg ? or Major Vitali. ??

Neustädtler as a group:
- Before Aspern: 4 battalions at Prewald then to the build up of the fortress of Laibach also with the Brigade Kálnássy, IX Corps . As for other sources: with the Brigade Munkácsy, 2nd Hauptkolonne Knesevich, Army of Inner Austria and also with the Brigade Munkácsy, Corps Lippa (all 4 battalions). Later committed with the Brigade Khevenhüller, Reserve troops in the South, 2 companies. After Aspern 3 battalions with the IX Corps - After Wagram: in Krain (Krajna).

Note: Rudolfswerther Kreis = Neustädtler Kreis

Free City of Trieste
Trieste City Volunteers or Thurnsche (Thurn's) Jäger see also Triester Freikorps [8]
Trieste Free-Corps or Triester Freikorps = Triester freiwillige Jägerkorps
Recruitment: practically it was the Landwehr of Trieste, but recruited by volunteering. The depot companies were 2 with the Brigade Khevenhüller in Laibach, Division Lippa under Kerpen.
On June 28, 1808 the archduke Johann and the Inner Austria commissioner Count Franz Saurau came in Trieste

in order to organize the defense on the new borders After the Pressburg treaty. The citizens were liberated from military duties providing they raise some Landwehr units, which had the task to protect the traffic from sea to the territory (supplies, ammunitions etc.).

The basic uniform of this new Cordon soldiers was:

light grey trousers (in summer also like current "bermuda" pants), green coat with red facings, golden buttons and round hats with red-white-red cockade (similar to that of Krain). The men were recruited in the Trieste's territory and the officers were assigned by the Governor. The Cordon battalion was ready in March 1809. The pay was 10 Kreuzer per day.

Citizen Paul Hammer launched a private subscription which granted to soldiers an utter 5 Gulden (Fl.) fee per month. Major Count Paul Brigido, son of the former Trieste's Governor, was the first commander; then followed Major Count Raimund Thurn, as commander of the territorialmilz.

1st Battalion Triester Stadtmiliz or battalion Triester Freikorps – Major Count Paul Brigido also called City Jäger. The 1st Battalion under Brigido gathered itself in the Lazareth barracks by March 26.

Before Aspern: battalion Brigido reached the army in Friuli (a fusilier battalion with 2 Jäger companies); they went with Brigade Gavassini, IX Corps Gyulai. The Triester Corps (3 Battalions under Brigido) were, on May 16, at Prewald. The following day the were attacked by the French of Broussier. The Triester lost 182 men and lots of wounded. The fact alarmed the city while the French approched from Opicina. With the French occupation the Trieste garrison (2000 men) was made prisoner and sent to France. On June 3 the French general Schilt ordered to give all weapons, austrian badges to the Police. On June 25 at Neustadtl and Rann the three Trieste Battalions were disbanded but Thurn decided to continue the fight. See After.

2nd Battalion Triester Territorialmiliz or 2nd Bn. Triester Freikorps – Major Count Raimund Thurn also called Thurn's (Thurnsche) Jäger. In March the 2nd Battalion under Thurn gathered near Prosecco.

Before Aspern: part of the battalion was committed, under the military governor Major Baron von Cazzan, for the seizing of Capodistria (together with the 3rd hungarian battalion of the town and some cavalry). The operation was concluded in April with thesupport of a British frigate from the sea. Later a second Miliz battalion was raised, always under Thurn, and followed Brigido in Friuli with Brigade Gavassini, IX Corps Gyulai. The Triester task force (3 battalions) had task to defend Palmanova and Medea. The Thurn's Battalions then reached the lower Krain till June 25, when the 3 battalions were disbanded. Otherwise it was allowed to Count Thurn to raise a volunteer Jäger battalion and to march with them towards Styria. Under FML Gyulai at Graz (June 25) 2 companies fought in the Avant-Garde GM Splényi.

3rd Battalion Triester Territorialmiliz raised in March 1809 under Count Thurn. Disbanded June 25. Triester Jäger-Freikorps (2 compagnies)

Volunteer Battalion of Merchants and Noblemen.

Lands Circles – regional Districts	Number of Battalions	Summary of the Landwehr units on 1809 year (by Lubomír Uhlíř)
	Styria	
Graz	5	
Judenburg	2	
Marburg	2	
Bruck	2	
Cilli	2	
Total	13	
	Carinthia	
Klagenfurt	3	
Villach	2	
Total	5	
	Carniola	
Laibach	3	Oberkrain had the whole Bezirk Kranj (Krainburg), and part of the Bezirk Ljubljana (Laibach). Unterkrain was the southern part of the Bezirk Ljubljana (Laibach), cities of:Novo mesto (Rudolfswert), Kočevje (Gottschee), Krško (Gurkfeld), Postojna (Adelsberg).
Görz	2[9]	
Adelsberg	4	
Neustädtl	4	
Trieste	2[10]	
Total	15	

1809 – VOLUNTEERS UNITS OF INNER AUSTRIA

Free Corps of Dalmatia (Dalmatiner Freikorps) – Major Michael Ugarovich
Never in battles. Group of dalmatian volunteers did fight at Gospic.

Volunteers of Inner Austria (Innerösterreichische Freibataillone)
Volunteers from Kärnten, Steiermark, Krain-Küstenland

1st Battalion Graz und Bruck – Major Chevalier Nikolaus Fitzgerald
- Before Aspern: split with Chasteler
- Before Wagram: part with Kerpen part with Plunquet At Raab battle with Division FML Colloredo-Mannsfeld, Brigade GM Marziani.

2nd Battalion Salzburger Jäger (see After)

3rd Battalion Klagenfurt – Major Count Anton Triangi
- Before Wagram: with the Brigade Schmidt
- After Wagram: idem and then with von Buol

4th battalion Laibach – Major Baron Joseph Dumontet
- Before Aspern: with IX Corps . Major Dumontet (Du Montet) organized a special Streifscorps with which he captured the capital town Laibach in June. Then it was assigned to him the title of Commander of the Observation Corps in Krain.

Free Corps of Istria (Istrier Freikorps)
- ??? no mention.

Free Corps Luxheim (Freikorps Erzherzog Johann Freiwilige) commander Baron Ferdinand Luxheim.
- After Wagram: in Pustertal (East Tyrol)

Salzburger Jäger or 2nd Innerösterreichisches Freibataillon
- Owner: Archduke Johann of Austria (see also Salzburg)
- Commander: Major Baron Paul Thurn-und-Taxis
- Before Aspern:
2   companies in the Brigade Buol, Chasteler then 2 companies in the Brigade Fenner, Chasteler 2 companies in the detached Division Jellačić
3   companies with Taxis, Bartholdy
4   companies with Martin Teimer insurgents.
- at Aspern: 4 companies with Chasteler
- Between Aspern and Wagram: with the detached Brigade Buol then in the Group Reissenfels – with Hauptmann Taxis - 1 companies with Oberstleutnant Taxis - 1 companies with Teimer and also in Vorarlberg with Camichel . At Raab in the Brigade GM Sebottendorf, Division FML Franz Jellačić.
- at Wagram: 2 companies in the Brigade Eckhart, Division Frimont, Army of Inner Austria.
- After Wagram: Brigade Buol, Chasteler.

Trieste's Volunteer Battalion of Merchants and Noblemen.
(Kaufleute und Patrizier Corps) Had mainly port control duties. During the first days of the new French (Italian Kingdom) occupation the most important traders and merchants of Trieste, around 30 citizens, were sent (arrested) at Palmanova fortress in Friuli. The Landwehr was then disbanded.

Notes
1   As a possible Austrian sea-victory Robert Goetz told this:
"There is also the little action of Porto Quieto, but there the Austrians had a little help from their friends.
23 March 1797: The French army marches into Trieste and the Austrian Trieste flotilla (the 14-gun shebeks/xebecs Coloredo and Henrici plus 12 x 3-gun gunboats) under the command of Captain Simpson put to sea, escorting approx. 40 merchantmen that were evacuating artillery and stores from Trieste. 20 miles south of Trieste they encountered a French squadron - Brune (22), Bonaparte (8), Liberateur d'Italie (8), Corse (10) and two storeships under the command of Captain Sibille. Simpson put into the Venetian harbor of Porto Quieto, forming his flotilla in line across the harbor mouth. The French closed for the attack and the opposing forces exchanged "hot fire", but the Venetian SoL Eolo (70) which just happened to be in the harbor brought her broadside to bear and drove off the French. The convoy was then able to proceed unmolested. Without the Eolo it's hard to say what may have happened. Simpson had more guns, but Sibille had the bigger vessels.
That's about the closest to Austrian naval victory I can come up, and it hardly matches the glory of the Delphino! "
2   Other source put the regiment with the Oguliner still with GM Gavassini but the official history tells the Reinskt was with GM Kálnássy. Mandel Fryderyk, Geschichte des k. u. k. Infanterie-Regiments Guidobald Graf von Starhemberg Nr. 13. Krakau: 1893.
3   There the Generalmajor Franz Marziani got, as award, the surname "von Sacile".
4   Letter from FZM Kerpen to Archduke John: " …. Major Hacker is no more in Graz. The command of the

Schlossberg garrison is now assigned to Hauptmann Mayer von Rystel which has 800 men from the Lusignan and Strassoldo Depots and from Landwehr depot units."
Hans von Zwiedineck-Südenhorst, Die Geschichte des Krieges von 1809 in Steiermark: Regesten und Actenstücke aus dem Nachlasse das Herzogs Johann im Gräflichen Meran'schen Archive zu Graz, Leylam, Graz 1892.

5   The return of Marquis Chasteler from Tyrol was very difficult. On June 9 he wrote to the Archduke John from Weitenstein: "Today I am at Weitenstein with 3 Bns. Johann Jellacic infantry, 2 Bns. Hohenlohe Bartenstein, 1 weak battalion Archduke Franz Karl, 3 Comp. of Banat, 5 sqns. Hohenzollern Chevaulégers, 1 Bn. Carinthian Landwehr, 1 Bn. Stirian Landwehr, the 9th Jäger, 2 pieces of 6 pdrs., 5 guns of 3 pdrs. and 1 howitzer." Zwiedineck-Südenhorst op.cit. pag. 21.

6   In Lower Carniola (Unterkrain) was raised a special Group (Streifcorps) led by Baron Du Montet (Dumontet), commander of the 4th battalion of Inner Austria Volunteers. It was left behind when Gyulai retreated inside Croatia. The Group was formed by 2 Comp. of Simbschen regiment, six companies of Croatian Landwehr, the 4th Inner Austria Volunteers (people from Gorizia, Trieste and Carniola) and 1 squadron of Frimont hussars. At the time Ljubljana had a French seizing garrison of 1200 men and 200 cavalrymen in the castle. On June 27 Du Montet attacked. The town was assaulted by four columns: the main of Du Montet and another, from an opposite direction, by Hauptmann Ballerini at the city gates. A third column (Hauptmann Colson) was launched against the Carlstädt bridge and finally a 4th column (Hauptmann Francolini) entered the walls along the river Laibach by boats.
August Dimitz, Geschichte Krains: Vom regierungsantritte Leopold I. (1657) bis auf das ende der französischen herrschaft in Illyrien (1813) Band 4 Von der ältesten Zeit bis auf das Jahr 1813. Mit besonderer Rücksicht auf Culturentwicklung, Verlag I. v. Kleinmayr & F. Bamberg, 1876.

7   The term "remnants" here relates above all upon losses by desertion, instead of men lost on battlefields.
8   Löwenthal, I., Geschichte der Stadt Triest, Band 2, Verlag Lloyd, 1859.
9   Residents never organized a third battalion
10   The battalions were known as Triester Volunteers Jäger or (Triestes Freijäger-Corps). The 1st battalion originated from the Trieste town milice (Stadt-Miliz). The 2nd battalion from the territorial milice (Territorial-Miliz) and were also called as Thurn Jäger.

THE MORAVIAN-SILESIAN LANDWEHR INFANTRY
ordered by recruitment district

Mährische Landwehr- Moravia
Commander Archduke Ferdinand and Burggraf Wallis Organization:
1.   Brünner Kreis (4 Battalions)
2.   Hradischer Kreis (3 Battalions)
3.   Iglauer Kreis (3 Battalions)
4.   Olmützer Kreis (5 Battalions)
5.   Prerauer Kreis (3 Battalions),
6.   Teschener Kreis (2 Battalions)
7.   Troppauer Kreis (3 Battalions)
8.   Znaymer Kreis (2 Battalions)
-     before Wagram: 9 Battalions

The Czechs and the Slavic People
Moravians (Moravané or colloquially Moraváci in Czech) were (and are) the West Slavic inhabitants of Moravia, the easternmost part of Bohemia, also in Moravian Slovakia. They speak Moravian dialect of the Czech language and standard Czech. The state has been a state of present-day Moravians and Slovaks. The western part of Great Moravia's core (=present-day Moravia) was finally conquered by Bohemia in early 11th century and its population was "czechicized" in the 19th century. The eastern part of the core (=present-day Slovakia) was finally conquered by the Magyars (Hungarians) in the 11th-14th century and its population developed into present-day Slovaks in the 10th century. The inhabitants of the core of the state were designed as "Slovieni" (which is an old Slavic word basically meaning "Slavs" and was also used by (future) Slovenians and Slavonians at that time) or "Moravian peoples" by Slavic texts, and as "Sclavi" (i.e. Slavs), "Winidi" (i.e. Slavs), "Moravian Slavs" or "Moravians" by Latin texts. The present-day terms "Slovaks" / "Slovakia" (in Slovak: Sloveci / Slovensko) and "Slovenes" / "Slovenia" (in Slovene: Slovenci / Slovenija) arose later from the above "Slovieni".
As for Slovaks they can be divided into:
1)   Hungarian Slovaks dwelling the northern hungarian counties of Nyitra, Trentschin, Türok, Arva, Lip-

tau, Söhl, Bars, Hont, Gömör, Neograd etc.

2) Moravian Slovaks also called Charvatians dwelling the Moravian lowlands and hills. They were mostly in the areas of Hradisch (were they were called Ungarische – Hungarians) and partially around Brünn, Gaya, Ostrau, Lundenburg and on both banks of the river Morava (March in German – Marchland = Morava land). Mountain people who inhabited the highlands of the Prerau and Hradisch districts were also called Walachians (like the rumenians) but they were people similar to Hungarians in dress, language and costumes. [20]

3) Silesian Slovaks dwelling the northern part of Moravia being the lesser part of the Slovak gender.

The Olmütz District was also inhabited by Hannaques, a people of farmers with dress, customs different from Slovaks. Their principal wealth consisted in their cattle and flocks. They probably were the most ancient slavic Moravian tribe. They lived, at the time, in an area between Olmütz, Wischau, Kremsier and Prossenitz, around 20000 square meter wide. Three small rivers (Hannah, Trzebowka and Blata) granted and extreme fecundity to the ground.

The Poles

Frederick II the Great of Prussia seized Silesia from the Habsburg heiress Maria Teresa in the War of the Austrian Succession (1740– 48). After Prussia's victory, Austria retained only the Silesian districts of Krnov (Jägerndorf), Opava (Troppau), and Cieszyn (Teschen), which constituted extreme south-southeastern Silesia. Austria's Silesians (Silesian: in Polish Ślązacy; in German Schläsinger) were considered as being Poles. While the Lower Silesian language was considered a German dialect, spoken in Lower Silesia (Prussia), mainly in southwestern Poland, but as well as in northeastern Bohemia they spoke a slavic (rather polish) Silesian idiom.[21]

In every case they were considered to be part of Moravia. These districts were united to Moravia until 1849. Silesians apart, the Poles were of other two types:

1) the true Poles, of Galician origins, with the two people of Gorales (from Hora or Gora = mountain; a mountain people of ancient Sarmatian origin) and Masuraques (dwellers of the lowlands near Lublin, Oswiecim till Tarnow, heirs of the ancient Polish noblemen);

2) the Rusnjaks (Rusyn) (who were called also Ruthenians and came from Bielorussia) dwellers of the southern mountains (Carpathian) till the northern Hungary counties. A group among them were the Pokutiens, confined in the Carpathian mountains.

All these people dwelled mainly in the Galician lands.

Brünner Kreis (Brno)

1 Battalion of the BrigadeWodniansky in Olmütz, 3 Battalions of the BrigadeChorinsky under Argenteau

1st Battalion Brünn - Oberstleutnant Count Franz Chorinsky then major Count Johann Taafe.
- before Wagram: BrigadeBuresch, Division Brady, II Corps
- after Wagram: with remnants of III Battalion became the I Comb. Brünner Landwehr Battalion.

2nd Battalion Cernahora - major Count Leopold Bukowsky
- after Wagram: for the main part was merged in the III combined Moravian volunteers Battalion (Boxberg)

3rd Battalion Austerlitz - major Count Richard Longueval, then major Count de Ségur
- before Wagram: BrigadeBuresch, Division Brady, II Corps
- after Wagram: with remnants of the I Battalion became the I Comb. Brünner Landwehr Battalion.

4th Battalion Seelowitz major Friedrich Hoffmann von Mondsfeld
- before Wagram: in the BrigadeNeustädter, autonomous, V Corps while (for others) in BrigadeNeustädter, Division Weissenwolf, V Corps
- after Wagram: BrigadeNeustädter, autonomous, V Corps. In August with 2 comp. of I Battalion became the II Comb. Brünner Landwehr Battalion.

Hradischer Kreis

3 Battalions of the BrigadeDunoyer in Ung. Hradisch, Division St.Julien under Argenteau

1st Battalion Strassnitz Oberstleutnant Count Franz Anton Magnis (Magny) then Hauptmann Johann Schindler
- before Aspern: in Olmütz
- before Wagram: BrigadeClary, Division Fresnel, I Corps,
- after Wagram: in Olmütz (merged with the III Battalion)

2nd Battalion Holleschau major Johann Wurmb
- before Aspern till after Wagram: in Cracow

3rd Battalion Buschlowitz - major Count Leopold Berchtold then major Joseph Höger (after Wagram)
- before Wagram: BrigadePaar, Division Brady, II Corps then in the IV Corps
- after Wagram: BrigadeQuallenberg, Division Buresch, II Corps

later merged in the I Battalion Combined Hradischer Landwehr Battalions

Iglauer Kreis

1st Battalion Iglau - major Joseph Crehan
- before Wagram: BrigadeNeustädter, autonomous, V Corps then of the VI Corps
- after Wagram: BrigadeNeustädter, autonomous, V Corps

2nd Battalion Iglau - major Baron Ernst von Boxberg
- no available data

Olmützer Kreis

2 Battalions (IV and V) of the brig. Pietsch in Troppau, Division St.Julien under Argenteau. 3 battalions in Olmütz (brig. Wodniansky)

1st Battalion Olmütz district Hauptmann Fichtl (ad interim) later **major Franz Count Silva-Taroucca**
- Olmütz town, Brigadebaron Wodniansky

2nd Battalion Olmütz district major Sylverius von Spannwald
- Mährische Schönberg, Brigadebaron Wodniansky

3rd Battalion Olmütz district major Franz Count Longueval
- Hohenstadt, Brigadebaron Wodniansky

4th Battalion Olmütz district - major Johann Bayer then **major Count Ségur**
- with Oberst von Romberg at Troppau then with V battalion

5th Battalion Olmütz district major Franz Schmidt then **major Count Khuenburg**
- before Wagram: with Oberst von Romberg at Troppau later BrigadeNeustädter, autonomous, V Corps then with the VI Corps
- after Wagram: BrigadeNeustädter, autonomous, V Corps

Prerauer Kreis

2 Battalions of the brig. Pietsch in Troppau, Division St.Julien under Argenteau

1st Battalion Prerau district major baron von Bereczko
- Teschen

2nd Battalion Prerau district major baron Ferdinand von Stücker
- Friedek

3rd Battalion Prerau district major Joseph von Khann then **Major Count Leopold Bukowsky (Bukuwky)**
- Olmütz with GM baron Bojakowsky

Teschener Kreis

2 Battalions of the brig. Pietsch in Troppau, Division St.Julien under Argenteau

1st Battalion Teschen - major Förster von Felsenburg then **major Nepomuk Hallász von Fischenbach**
- in Cracow

2nd Battalion Friedeck - major Willibald Henzler von Lehnaburg
- Division Egermann, VII Corps, commanded to watch the Jablunkapaß

Troppauer Kreis

3 Battalions of the BrigadePietsch in Troppau, Division St.Julien under Argenteau

1st Battalion Troppau - baron major Ignaz Wrbna
- Division Egermann, VII Corps

2nd Battalion Jägerndorf - baron major Ignaz Jókay
- in Cracow

3rd Battalion Zuckmantl - major Count Conrad Plunquet
- in Cracow

Znaymer Kreis

2 Battalions of the BrigadeRamberg in Znaim, Division St.Julien

1st Battalion Namiest - major count Ernst Ludwig Haugwitz
- before Wagram: BrigadeSwinburne, Division Rohan, IV Corps
- after Wagram: Division Radetzky, IV Corps then in Olmütz later merged with the II Battalion in the Combined Znaymer Landwehr Battalion.

2nd Battalion Znaym - major Joseph Sterzl
- before Wagram: BrigadePaar, Division Brady, II Corps

- after Wagram: later merged with the I Battalion in the Combined Znaymer Landwehr Battalion

3rd Battalion not raised
- after Wagram: the Znaym Landwehr were all combined together.

Combined Znaymer Landwehr Battalion Major Count Ernst Ludwig Haugwitz The Combined Mährisches Landwehr Battalion (Major Boxberg)
- before Aspern: BrigadeAdler, Division Hohenfeld, VI Corps
- before Wagram: BrigadeSplényi, Division Kottulinsky, VI Corps

then called the 3rd Mährisches Landwehr Battalion (Major Praschma)
- after Wagram: Brig Adler, Division Hohenfeld, VI Corps

Commanders of the Landwehr Battalions - years 1808-1810; Moravia and Silesia [22]

Commander of the Battalion	Nation	Name of the Battalion	Seq of Com
Bayer, Johann, Major	Silesian-Moravian	4th Battalion Olmutz	2/2
Bereczko, Freiherr von, Major	Silesian-Moravian	1st Battalion Prerau	1/1
Berchtold, Leopold Graf, Major	Silesian-Moravian	3rd Battalion Hradisch	1/2
Boxberg, Ernst Freiherr von, Major	Silesian-Moravian	2nd Battalion Iglau	1/2
Bukowsky (Bukuwky), Leopold Graf, Major	Silesian-Moravian	2nd Battalion Brünn	I 1/1
	Silesian Moravian	3rd Battalion Prerau	II 2/2
Crehan, Joseph, Major	Silesian-Moravian	1st Battalion Iglau	1/3
Fichtl, Hptm. (ad interim)	Silesian-Moravian	1st Battalion Olmutz	2/2
Förster von Felsenburg, Major	Silesian-Moravian	1st Battalion Teschen	1/2
Hallász von Fischenbach, Nepomuk, Major	Silesian-Moravian	1st Battalion Teschen	2/2
Haugwitz, Ernst Ludwig Graf, Major	Silesian-Moravian	1st Battalion Znaim	I 1/1
	Silesian-Moravian	Combined Znaym Battalion (1st Battalion and part of 2nd Battalion)	II
Henzler von Lehnaburg, Wunibald, Major	Silesian-Moravian	2nd Battalion Teschen	1/1
Hoffmann von Mondsfeld, Friedrich, Major	Silesian-Moravian	4th Battalion Brünn	I 1/1
	Silesian-Moravian	2nd Combined Brünner Battalion (4th Bn and part of 1st Battalion)	II
Höger, Joseph, Major	Silesian-Moravian	3rd Battalion Ungarisch Hradisch	2/2
	Silesian-Moravian	Combined Hradisch Battalion (3rd Battalion and 1st Battalion)	II
Chorinsky, Franz Graf, Obtl.	Silesian-Moravian	1st Battalion Brünn	1/2
Jókay, Ignaz Freiherr von, Major	Silesian-Moravian	2nd Battalion Troppau	1/1
Khann, Joseph von, Major	Silesian-Moravian	3rd Battalion Prerau	1/2
Khuenburg, Graf, Major	Silesian-Moravian	5th Battalion Olmutz	1/2
Longueval, Franz Graf, Major	Silesian-Moravian	3rd Battalion Olmutz	1/1
Longueval, Richard Graf, Major	Silesian-Moravian	3rd Battalion Brünn	1/2
Magny, Franz Anton Graf, Obtl.	Silesian-Moravian	1st Battalion Ungarisch Hradisch	1/2
Nesselrode, Max Graf, Major	Silesian-Moravian	1st Battalion Iglau	2/3
Plunquet (Plonguier), Conrad Graf, Major	Silesian-Moravian	3rd Battalion Troppau	1/1
	Silesian-Moravian	4th Battalion Olmutz	I(?) 1/2
Ségur, Graf, Major	Silesian-Moravian	3rd Battalion Brünn	II(?) 2/2
	Silesian-Moravian	1st Combined Brünner Battalion (3rd Bn and part of 1st Battalion)	III
Schindler, Johann, Hptm.	Silesian-Moravian	1st Battalion Ungarisch Hradisch	2/2
Schmidt, Franz, Major	Silesian-Moravian	5th Battalion Olmutz	2/2
Silva-Taroucca, Franz Graf, Major	Silesian-Moravian	1st Battalion Olmutz	1/2
Spannwald, Sylverius von, Major	Silesian-Moravian	2nd Battalion Olmutz	1/1
Sterzl, Joseph, Major	Silesian-Moravian	2nd Battalion Znaim	I 1/1
	Silesian-Moravian	1st Battalion Iglau	II 3/3
Stücker, Ferdinand Freiherr von, Major	Silesian-Moravian	2nd Battalion Prerau	1/1
Taaffe, Johann Graf, Major	Silesian-Moravian	1st Battalion Brünn	2/2
Wrbna, Eugen Graf, Major	Silesian-Moravian	1st Battalion Troppau	1/1
Wurmb, Johann, Major	Silesian-Moravian	2nd Battalion Ungarisch Hradisch	1/1
Würth, Carl, Hptm.-Major	Silesian-Moravian	2nd Battalion Iglau	2/2

Lands	Source: Lubomír Uhlíř	Summary of the Landwehr units on 1809 Moravia and Silesia	
District – region	Number of Battalions	District –Region	Number of Battalions
Brünner Kreis	4	Prerauer Kreis	3
Iglauer Kreis	2 [23]	Olmützer Kreis	5
Hradischer Kreis	3	Troppauer Kreis	3
Znaymer Kreis	2	Teschner Kreis	2
Total	24		

Notes:

1 Maybe it was only in Reserve during the action at Teugen, in which the III Corps attacked.
2 Pizzighelli, Cajetan: Geschichte des k. k. Infanterie-Regimentes Kaiser Franz Joseph Nr. 1. 1716 - 1881. Troppau: 1881.
3 Amon von Treuenfest, Gustav Ritter von: Geschichte des kaiserl. u. königl. kärnthnerisches Infanterie-Regimentes Feldmarschall Graf von Khevenhüller Nr. 7. Wien: 1891.
4 Gartner Edler von Romansbrück, Anton: Geschichte des k. u. k. Infanterie-Regimentes Erzherzog Carl Stephan No. 8 von der Errichtung des Regimentes bis auf die Gegenwart. Brünn: 1892.
5 Geschichte des k. u. k. Infanterie-Regimentes Oskar II. Friedrich, König von Schweden und Norwegen, Nr. 10. Wien: 1888.
6 It seems extremely contradictory what affirms the history of the regiment at page 255: "the colonel and regiment commander Weigl, to whom, few time before, the wounded general major Henneberg the brigade command had assigned". Was the regiment under Clary or Henneberg?
7 Johann, Erzherzog: Geschichte des k. k. Linien-Infanterie-Regiments Erzherzog Wilhelm Nr. 12. Wien: 1877-80.
8 Latterer von Lintenburg, Adolf Ritter: Geschichte des k. k. 15. Infanterie-Regiments Adolf Herzog zu Nassau. Prag: 1874.
9 Many sources say the regiment recruitment was in Bohemia, depot Chrudim. This was the previous Kreis (1781-1800) but Wrede referred its levy was then transferred to the Moravian Silesian area with Kader at Mährische Schönberg and Myslenice. However there are some references of personal soldiers military Papers which still listed Chrudim as recruitment center for Zach's troopers.
10 When colonel Murray was wounded (in the Hausen woods) Bresslern had to take the command. However he was also wounded in the same battle and did not take the command of the regiment. On May 26 oberst Murray became major general and the command was given to Bresslern, who resigned on June 25 for the severe wounds.
11 Amon von Treuenfest, Gustav Ritter von: Geschichte des k. k. Infanterie-Regimentes Nr. 20 Friedrich Wilhelm. Kronprinz des Deutschen Reiches und Kronprinz von Preussen. Wien: 1878.
12 In the Orders of battle it can be found that the regiment had 2 battalions and 4 companies. This is correct . In effect companies n. 17 and n. 18 had been formed later and had not yet reached the regiment.
13 Hubka von Czerncžitz, Gustav Ritter: Geschichte des k. u. k. Infanterie-Regiments Graf Lacy Nr. 22 von seiner Errichtung bis zur Gegenwart. Zaza: 1902.
14 Hödl, Rudolf Edler von: Geschichte des k. u. k. Infanterieregiments Nr. 29 Gideon Ernst Freiherr von Laudon. Temesvár: 1906.
15 Zwiedineck-Südenhorst Hans von, "Die Brigade Thierry im Gefechte von Abensberg am 19. und 20. April 1809".
16 Relation Pflüger, KA., FA. 1809 Deutscliland Hauptarmee VI1/200.
17 Joseph Mittrowsky had died on March 2, 1808 at Paskau (Moravia).
18 Janota, Robert: Geschichte des K. und K. Infanterie-Regimentes Graf Daun Nr. 56. Teschen: 1889.
19 Pillersdorff, A.: Das 57. Infanterie-Regiment Fürst Jablonowski und die Kriege seiner Zeit. Wien: 1857.
20 I effect there were a bit of confusion upon the mountain people of Moravia (and Silesia). Walachians wee different from Slovaks but had a similar dialect and were also different from the Hannaques, which were rather confused with Slovaks. Walachians had other denominations, one different for each village (they were mostly shepherds): Kopaniczares, Chorobates, Passekarsches or Sallaschener. In Rohrer, Versuch über die slawischen Bewohner der österreichischen Monarchie. 1804, VolunteerI, p. 29.
21 There is some contention over whether Silesian is a dialect or a language in its own right. Some Polish linguists consider Silesian to be merely a prominent regional dialect of Polish. However, many Silesians regard it as a separate language belonging to the West Slavic branch of Slavic languages, together with Polish and other Lechitic languages, as well as Upper and Lower Sorbian, Czech and Slovak. In July 2007 the Silesian language was recognized by the Library of Congress in USA.
22 Courtesy of Karel Sáček
23 The 3rd Battalion was not completed, the men were attached to the 3rd Moravian volunteers Battalion.

Unterofficier und Mann der Salzburger Landwehr 1809.

▲ Austrian Infantry Landwehr uniforms of Salzburg regiments. Ottenfeld's artwork

1809 – VOLUNTEERS UNITS OF MORAVIA - SILESIA

On 1 March 1809, it was allowed the creation of volunteer battalions. The 1808 Landwehr Patent contained many exemptions, especially for students, skilled workers and townspeople, but they could volunteer for "Freiwillige" units, augmented by Landwehr prepared to serve outside their district. Volunteers signed up for the duration of the war. All officers and NCOs had to have military experience and so were retired or drafted regulars. The distinguishing uniform feature of all western volunteer battalions was the cuffs red.

Mährische Freiwillige – Moravian Volunteers
= Mähr. Freikorps = Mähr.-Schles. Freiwillige = Mähr. Legion, (part of the Legion Archduke Carl ??)

1st Moravian volunteers Battalion or Mährische Jäger – major Johann Seyffert
- Recruitment: in the Landwehr district Brünn
- before Aspern: BrigadeReinhardt, Div. Schustekh, V Corps then to the BrigadeD'Aspre, II Res. Corps
- at Aspern: BrigadeReinhardt, Division Schustekh, V Corps (never engaged).

2nd Moravian volunteers Battalion or Mährische Jäger – major Count Felix Vetter von der Lilie
after: major baron Joseph Le Breux
- Recruitment: in the Landwehr districts Olmütz - Prerau
- before Aspern: BrigadeGratze, Division Rohan, IV Corps
- at Aspern: BrigadeGratze, Division Dedovich, IV Corps
- between Aspern and Wagram: IV Corps
- at Wagram: BrigadeProvenchères, Division Radetzky, IV Corps then autonomous in the Division Radetzky, IV Corps

3rd Moravian volunteers Battalion – major baron Ernst Boxberg
later: major Bernhard Dobler von Friedberg.
- Recruitment: in the Landwehr districts II Olmütz and II Iglau.
- before Aspern: BrigadeMesko, Division Vincent, VI Corps
- at Aspern: BrigadeAdler, Division Kottulinsky, VI Corp then BrigadeSplényi, Division Vincent, VI Corps. Later BrigadeHofmeister, Division Vincent, VI Corps
- at Wagram: BrigadeSplényi, Division Kottulinsky, VI Corp Generic addenda for all units:
in April: 1 Battalion BrigadeBojakowsky in Olmütz, 1 BrigadePöck, Division St.Julien under Argenteau.
- before Aspern: Battalions Moravian VolunteerJäger in the BrigadeNostitz, Division Fresnel, I Corps -- 1 Battalion Moravian VolunteerJäger BrigadeWinzingerode, Division Fresnel, I Corps
- after Wagram: 1 company Moravian VolunteerJäger BrigadeAdler, Division Hohenfeldt, VI Corps

THE GALICIAN LANDWEHR INFANTRY

Territorial commander Bellegarde and Wurmser. This Corps practically were never raised. Only some unit of volunteers were organized entering the campaign against the Poles and the Saxons.

The 1809 Volunteers Units of Galicia The Galician Volunteers battalions (Galizische Freiwillige) [17]

I   Battalion Ostgalizien – major count Hussey
Raised with 4 companies, it was always in Upper Hungary without getting any contact with enemies.
- after Wagram: it was reinforced by 4 companies of fusiliers and 1 company of Jäger (Freikorps Schill).

II   Battalion Westgalizien „Erzherzog Ferdinand"– major Adam Rétsey de Retse
Raised with 4 companies it was always in Galicia with garrison duties. It fought however aginst the Poles at Gorżice and other clashes.

III   battalion "Kaiserin Lodovica" – Hauptmann-major count Franz Neuhaus von St.Mauro
As above. Never in battle, it was always in Bohemia.

Arnauten Corps Bukowina [18] **and Bukowinaer Freiwillige battalion Major Chevalier Friedrich Forget de Barst**
It was raised too late to fight (October) from the previous Arnauten of Bukowina and volunteers of East Galicia.

Galician Cossacks or Kosackenkorps (Österreichisches Kosakenpulk -Galizische Freikosaken
- Commander: major Baron Franz Fichtl.

In Galicia, the only volunteer cavalry unit formed was a corps of dismounted cossacks (Freikosaken-Abtheilungen zu Fuss) who wore native dress, fur or felt busby, bluejackets faced red, baggy red or blue trousers, with knife and pistols in the belt or red girdle; as there was a shortage of muskets, many carried only lances or pikes.
- Recruitment: Galicia reinforced by 3 Sqns. of the Schlesischen Freikorps Schill.
- they always acted in the VII Corps.

Schill Freikorps – major Ferdinand von Schill [19]
- Recruitment: from 2nd prussian Hussars Rgt Brandenburg, 1 prussian light infantry battalion of Mecklenburg-Strelitz later (between Aspern and Wagram) attached to the Hussar-Uhlans cavalry (Husaren Ulanen Reitende Jäger), Infantry = some swedish-pomeranian Landwehr units, with some austrian elements.
- before Aspern: they acted in Mecklenburg – Pommern.

Schlesisches Freikorps Schill – Oberstleutnant Johann Georg Schill (unit different from the above) [20]
- Recruitment: Silesia and Poland

THE BOHEMIAN LANDWEHR INFANTRY
Ordered by Recruitment District
Bohemia commanders Archduke Ferdinand and BurgCount FZM Wallis

1	Berauner Kreis	(2 Bn.)	10	Königgrätzer Kreis	(5 Bn.)
2	Bidzower Kreis	(4 Bn.)	11	Leitmeritzer Kreis	(5 Bn.)
3	Budweiser Kreis	(3 Bn.)	12	Pilsener Kreis	(3 Bn.)
4	Bunzlauer Kreis	(6 Bn.)	13	Prachiner Kreis	(4 Bn.)
5	Caslauer Kreis	(3 Bn.)	14	City of Prague	(2 Bn.)
6	Chrudimer Kreis	(4 Bn.)	15	Rakonitzer Kreis	(2 Bn.)
7	Elbogener Kreis	(3 Bn.)	16	Saazer Kreis	(2 Bn.)
8	Kaurimer Kreis	(2 Bn.)	17	Taborer Kreis	(2 Bn.)
9	Klattauer Kreis	(3 Bn.)			

BERAUNER Kreis – Beraun
The 2 Bns. were in the Brig and Div. Franz Kinsky in Prague under Riesch and Loudon
- I Bn. Seltschau – Major Count Wrtby
- - at Wagram: brig. Wratislaw, Div Vukassovich, III Corps
- - after Wagram : brig. Schneller, Div. Vukassovich, III Corps
- II Bn. Hostomer - Major Count Wilhelm Klebelsberg
- - at Wagram: brig. Schneller, Div. Vukassovich, III Corps
- - after Wagram.: brig. Wratislaw, Div. Vukassovich, III Corps

BIDZOWER (Bydzower) Kreis - Bydzow
The 4 Bns. were in the Brig Szénassy (fortress Jaromir-Josefsstadt) under Riesch and Loudon.
- I Bn. Hohenelbe – Major Krisar later Major Count Carl Khevenhüller.
- - Facts: reserve in Josefstadt.
- II Bn. Jićin – Oberstleutnant Heinrich von Hoffmeister later Major Joseph von Borwitz
- - Facts: reserve in Josefstadt.
- III Bn. Miletin – Major Joseph Fils.
- - Facts: reserve in Josefstadt.
- IV Bn. Bidzow – Major Count Leopold Kinsky later Major Baron Joseph Ottlilienfeld.
- - Facts: reserve in Josefstadt.

BUDWEISER Kreis – Budweis (České Budějovice)
The 3 Bns. in the Brig and Div. GM Richter at Pisek under Riesch and Loudon
- I Bn. Budweis - Major Count Carl Wratislaw
- - Recruitment: in Böhmerwald (Bohemian Forest) region.
- - Facts: along the border of the Böhmer Wald.
- II Bn. Wittingau - Major Leonhard Halpert.
- - Facts: not known.
- III Bn. Krumau - Major Anton von Künstlern after Major Alois von Reisinger
- - Facts: not known.

BUNZLAUER Kreis (Jung-Bunzlau)
1 Bns. was in the brig. and Div. Schönthal at Leitmeritz, 5 Bns. were in the Brig Novak, Div. Schönthal under Riesch and Loudon.
- I Bn. Niemes-Gabel - Major Friedrich Clam-Gallas
- - Facts: in Reserve along the Iser.
- II Bn. Reichenberg (Liberec) - Major Christian Clam-Gallas
- - Facts: in Reserve along the Iser, then at Prague.
- III Bn. Turnau - Major Carl von Pflüger
- - Facts: Theresienstadt (Terezín) garrison
- IV Bns. Münchengrätz - Major Count Ernst Waldstein
- - Facts: Reserve at Prague.
- V Bns. Nimburg - Major Franz Prizichowsky
- - Facts: along the Iser, in the Bayreuth campaign at Gefrees.
- VI Bn. Melnitz - Major-Oberstleutnant Prince Anton Isidor Lobkowitz.
- - Facts: at Theresienstadt, then with Am Ende, at Dresden.

ČASLAUER Kreis – Časlau
The 3 Bns. in the brig. Oberdorf at Časlau, Div. Franz Kinsky under Riesch and Loudon.
I   Bn. Deutsch Brod (Havlíčkův Brod) - Oberstleutnant Wenzel Sporck then Major Plauser
-    Facts: in the Bayreuth campaign
II   Bn. Časlau - Major Plauser , later from Aspern to Wagram: Major Prince Wilhelm Auersperg
Facts: in Oberösterreich, it fought at the battle of Urfahr-Linz.
III   Bn. Kuttenberg (Kutná Hora) - Major Count Sebastian Trautmannsdorf.
-    Facts: in the Bayreuth campaign

CHRUDIMER Kreis – Chrudim
The 4 Bns. in the Brigade Bautin at Chrudim-fortress and Königgrätz under Riesch and Loudon.
I   Bn. Leitomischl (Litomyšl) - Oberst Count Georg Waldstein later Major Count Anton Borosini von Hohenstern
-    Facts: before Aspern did a Mutiny, then in the III Corps (Kolowrat)
II   Bn. Landscron (Lanškroun) - Major Carl Strauss
-    Facts: in Königgrätz.
III   Bn. Pardubitz (Pardubice) - Major Count Johann Breda
-    Facts: in Königgrätz .
IV. Bns. Hermann-Mestetz (Hermanuv Mestec) - Major Christian von Geisztler
-    Facts: at Eger, then in the III Corps (Kolowrath)

ELBOGENER Kreis – Elbogen (Loket)
The 3 Bns. in the Brig Ullrich, Div. K. Kinsky under Riesch and Loudo
I   Bn. Eger (Cheb) - Major Carl Frasmüller Edler von Weidenburg later Hauptmann Johann Werbeck, finally Major Sérenyi
-    Facts: in the Bayreuth campaign
II   Bn. Schlackenwerth - Major Peter von Pfisterer
-    Facts: in the Bayreuth campaign
III   Bn. Buchau - Major Fortunatus Erdelly
-    Facts: in the Bayreuth campaign

KAURZIMER Kreis - Kaurzim (Kouřim)
The 2 Bns. in the brig. Oberdorf in Caslau, Div. Franz Kinsky under Riesch and Loudon I Bn. Brandeis - Hauptmann Fischer
-    Facts: in Prague, then in the III Corps (Kolowrath)
II Bn. Schwarz-Kosteletz - Major Count Prokop Wratislaw
-    Facts: along the Iser, then in the III Corps (Kolowrath)

KLATTAUER Kreis – Klattau (Klatovy)
The 3 Bns. in the brig. Rosenhayn at Horazdiowic, Div. Richter under Riesch and Loudon I Bn. Bischofsteinitz - Major Baron Wenzel Kotz von Dobrz
-    Facts: along the Bohemian border.
II   Bn. Klattau - Major Count Anton Thun
-    Facts: in the Böhmerwald
III   Bn. Nepomuk - Major Count Friedrich Schönborn
-    Facts: in the Böhmerwald

KÖNIGGRÄTZER Kreis – Königgrätz (Hradec Králové)
First 5 Bns. in the brig. Szénassy in Jaromirz-fortress Josefsstadt under Riesch and Loudon
I   Bn. Trautenau - Major Count Franz Deym
-    Facts: in Josefstadt
II   Bn. Nachod - Major Michael Mayer
-    Facts: in Josefstadt
II Bn. Opocus - Major Johann von Bohunek
-    Facts: in Josefstadt
V   Bns. Geyersberg - Major Joseph von Nostitz
-    Facts: at Prague, then in the Bayreuth campaign
VI   Bn. Königgrätz - Major Joseph von Borwitz, later Hauptmann Carl Würth (Wörth)
-    Facts: at Dresden, then at Theresienstadt

LEITMERITZER Kreis – Leitmeritz (Litoměřice)
First 3 Bns. in the brig. Waldstein at Pilsen, other 2 Bns. in the Brig Schönthal, Div. Schönthal under Riesch and Loudon
1. Bns. Leitmeritz and Theresienstadt - Major chevalier von Chlumecsansky
-    Facts: in Saxony with the corps Am Ende, then at Paschkopole, corps Am Ende, then at Theresienstadt.

Böhmische und mährische Landwehr 1809.

▲ Bohemian and Moravian landwehr uniforms regiments. ottenfeld's artwork

II   Bn. Bilin - Obst Count Joseph Waldstein then Major Canal von Ehrenberg
- Facts: in Saxony with the corps Am Ende, then at Paschkopole, corps Am Ende, then at Theresienstadt.
III   Bn. Tetschen - Major Count Carl Clary
- Facts: in Saxony with the corps Am Ende, then at Paschkopole, corps Am Ende, then at Theresienstadt. After Wagram was with the brig. Bianchi
IV.   Bns. Auscha - Major Georg von Dangl, then Obstltn. Nowak
- Facts: in Saxony with the corps Am Ende, then at Paschkopole, corps Am Ende, then at Theresienstadt.
V.   Bns. Rumburg – Major Count Johann Salm
- Facts: in Saxony with the corps Am Ende, then at Paschkopole, corps Am Ende, then at Theresienstadt.

PILSENER Kreis - Pilsen
3 Bns. in the brig. and Div. K. Kinsky in Pilsen under Riesch and Loudon
I   Bn. Groß Marep (Haide) - Oberstleutnant Joseph Obermeyer von Ebernberg
- Facts: at Wagram in the III Corps
II   Bn. Plan - Major Mathias chevalier von Godart
- Facts: in the III Corps (Kolowrath), then in Moravia.
III   Bn. Pilsen - Major Baron Johann Hildebrand
- Facts: was in Upper Austria

PRACHINER Kreis
2 Bns. in the Brig Rosenhayn in Horazdiowic, Div. Richter, 1 Bns. in the brig. and Div. Richter in Pisek under Riesch and Loudon
I   Bn. Pisek - Major Count Carl Berchtold
- Facts: in the Böhmerwald, then in the III Corps (Kolowrath).
II   Bn. Brzeznitz - Oberst Hartmann von Hartenthal later Major Count Prokop Hartmann von Klarstein
- Facts: before Aspern was part of the brig. Richter, IV Corps. At Wagram was sent in the Böhmerwald
III   Bn. Schüttenhofen - Major Count Leonhard Rumerskirch
- Facts: before Aspern was part of the brig. Richter, IV Corps.
IV. Bns. Welschbirken - Oberst Wenzel chevalier von Puteani, then Major Prokop Neukirchen
- Facts: before Aspern was part of the brig. Richter, IV Corps. At Wagram was in the outposts of the Böhmerwald

PRAGUE city District
1st Bn.in the brig. and Div. Franz Kinsky in Prag under Riesch and Loudon.
I   Bn. - Oberst Count Johann Wratislaw
- Facts: was at Prague and in Bohemia till Wagram, then was split in parts.
II   Bn. – Major Count Johann Pachta
- Facts: was at Prague and in Bohemia till Wagram, combined with the 1st battalion before Aspern and then was split in parts taking the name :
Combined Landwehr battalion of Prague- Oberst Count Johann Wratislaw
- Facts: brig. Wratislaw, Div. Vukassovich, III Corps . After Wagram brig. Wratislaw, Div. Schneller, III Corps -

RAKONITZER Kreis
1   Bns. in the brig. and Div. Schönthal in Leitmeritz, 1 Bat in the brig. and Div. Franz Kinsky under Riesch and Loudon
I   Bn. Welwarn - Major Prince Ferdinand Kinsky, then, interim, Hauptmann A.. Hubel, later Major J. Kurz
- Facts: in Theresienstadt.
II   Bn. Rakonitz - Major Joseph Hofmann later Major Baron Bohusz.
- Facts: in Theresienstadt.

SAAZER Kreis
- 2 Bns. in the brig. and Div. Karl Kinsky in Pilsen under Riesch and Loudon **I Bn. Komotau** - Oberstleutnant Prince Joseph Lobkowitz
- Facts: first was at the Paschkopole, then in Theresienstadt .
II Bn. Saaz - Major Baron Anton Wodniansky
- Facts: not known.

TABORER Kreis
2   Bns. brig. Richter under Riesch and Loudon
I   Bn. Pilgram - Major Joseph Kriegern von Maisdorf
- Facts: in the Bayreuth campaign.
II   Bn. Tabor - Major Count Joachim Woracsiesky later Major-Oberstleutnant Baron Vinzenz Zesner
- Facts: was a previous battalion of the Legion Archduke Charles. Not known others.

Alphabetic Index of the Landwehr Battalions Commanders - 1808-1810 - Bohemia) Karel Sáček

Commander of the Battalion	Nation	Name of the Battalion	seq. of com
Auersperg, Wilhelm Fürst, Major	Bohemian	2nd battalion Časlau district	1/2
Berchtold, Carl Graf, Major	Bohemian	1st battalion Prachin district	1/1
Bohunek (Nohynek), Johann von, Major	Bohemian	3rd battalion Königgrätz district	1/1
Bohusz, Freiherr von, Major	Bohemian	2nd battalion Rakonitz district	2/2
Borosini von Hohenstern, Anton, Major	Bohemian	1st battalion Chrudim district	2/2
Borwitz, Joseph, Major	Bohemian	2nd battalion Bydzow district	I 2/2
	Bohemian	5th battalion Königgrätz district	II 1/3
			III 3/3
Breda, Johann Graf, Major	Bohemian	3rd battalion Chrudim district	1/1
Call, Freiherr von, Major	Bohemian	2nd battalion Saaz district	1/2
Clam-Gallas, Christian Graf, Major	Bohemian	1st battalion Jungbunzlau district	1/1
	Bohemian	2nd battalion Jungbunzlau district	1/2
Clary, Carl Graf, Major	Bohemian	3rd battalion Leitmeritz district	1/1
Dangl, Georg von, Major	Bohemian	4th battalion Leitmeritz district	1/2
Deym, Franz Graf, Major	Bohemian	1st battalion Königgrätz district	1/1
Erdelly, Fortunatus, Major	Bohemian	3rd battalion Elbogen district	1/1
Fils, Joseph, Major	Bohemian	3rd battalion Bydzow district	1/1
Fischer, Hauptmann	Bohemian	1st battalion Kaurzim district	1/2
Fronmüller Edler von Weidenburg, Carl, Major	Bohemian	1st battalion Elbogen district	1/3
Geisztler, Christian von, Major	Bohemian	4th battalion Chrudim district	1/1
Godart, Matthias Ritter von, Major	Bohemian	2nd battalion Pilsen district	2/2
Halpert, Leonhard, Major	Bohemian	2nd battalion Budweis district	1/1
Hartmann von Hartenthal, Oberst	Bohemian	2nd battalion Prachin district	1/2
Hartmann-Klarstein, Prokop Graf, Major	Bohemian	2nd battalion Prachin district	2/2
Hildebrand, Johann Freiherr von, Major	Bohemian	3rd battalion Pilsen district	1/1
Hoffmeister, Heinrich von, Oberstleutnant	Bohemian	2nd battalion Bydzow district	1/2
Hoffmeister, Oberstleutnant	Bohemian	2nd battalion Klattau district	1/2
Hofmann, Joseph, Major	Bohemian	2nd battalion Rakonitz district	1/2
Hubel, Ambros, Hauptmann (ad interim)	Bohemian	1st battalion Rakonitz district	2/3
Chlumeczansky, Adalbert Ritter von, Major	Bohemian	1st battalion Leitmeritz district	1/1
Khevenhüller, Carl Graf, Major	Bohemian	1st battalion Bydzow district	2/2
Kinsky, Ferdinand Fürst, Major	Bohemian	1st battalion Rakonitz district	1/3
Kinsky, Leopold Graf, Major	Bohemian	4th battalion Bydzow district	1/2
Klebelsberg, Wilhelm Graf, Major	Bohemian	2nd battalion Beraun district	1/1
Kotz von Dobrz, Wenzel Freiherr von, Major	Bohemian	1st battalion Klattau district	1/1
Kriegenr von Maisdorf, Joseph, Major	Bohemian	1st battalion Tabor district	1/1
Krisar, Major	Bohemian	1st battalion Bydzow district	1/2
Künstlern, Anton von, Major	Bohemian	3rd battalion Budweis district	1/2
Kurz, Joseph von, Major	Bohemian	1st battalion Rakonitz district	3/3
Lažansky, Graf, Oberstleutnant	Bohemian	2nd battalion Pilsen district	1/2
Lobkowitz, Anton Isidor Fürst, Maj.-Obtl.	Bohemian	6th battalion Jungbunzlau district	1/1
Lobkowitz, Joseph Fürst, Maj.-Obtl.	Bohemian	1st battalion Saaz district	1/1
Malowetz, Ernst Freiherr von, Hauptmann	Bohemian	1st battalion Kaurzim district	2/2
Mayer, Michael, Major	Bohemian	2nd battalion Königgrätz district	1/1
Neukirchen, Prokop, Major	Bohemian	4th battalion Prachin district	2/2
Nostitz, Joseph Graf, Major	Bohemian	4th battalion Königgrätz district	1/1
Novak, Oberstleutnant	Bohemian	4th battalion Leitmeritz district	2/2
Obermayer von Ebernberg, Joseph, Oberstleutnant	Bohemian	1st battalion Pilsen district	1/1
Ottlilienfeld, Joseph Freiherr von, Major	Bohemian	4th battalion Bydzow district	2/2
Pachta, Johann Graf, Major	Bohemian	2nd battalion města Prahy	1/1
Pfisterer, Peter von, Major	Bohemian	2nd battalion Elbogen district	1/1
Pfluger, Carl von, Major	Bohemian	3rd battalion Jungbunzlau district	1/1
Plauser, Major	Bohemian	2nd battalion Caslau district	I 2/2
Przichofsky, Franz Graf, Maj.-Obtl.	Bohemian	1st battalion Caslau district	II 2/2
Puteany, Wenzel Ritter von, Oberst	Bohemian	5th battalion Jungbunzlau district	1/1
Reisinger, Alois von, Major	Bohemian	4th battalion Prachin district	1/2
	Bohemian	3rd battalion Budweis district	2/2
Rumerskirch, Leonhard Graf, Major	Bohemian	3rd battalion Prachin district	1/1
Salm, Johann Graf, Major	Bohemian	5th battalion Leitmeritz district	1/1
Serényi (Serinni), Major	Bohemian	1st battalion Elbogen district	3/3
Schönborn, Friedrich Graf, Major	Bohemian	3rd battalion Klattau district	1/1
Sporck, Wenzel Graf, Oberstleutnant	Bohemian	1st battalion Caslau district	1/2
Storr, Ferdinand, Major	Bohemian	2nd battalion Jungbunzlau district	2/2

Strauss, Carl, Major	Bohemian	2nd battalion Chrudim district	1/1
Thun, Anton Graf, Major	Bohemian	2nd battalion Klattau district	2/2
Trauttmansdorff, Sebastian Graf, Major	Bohemian	3rd battalion Caslau district	1/1
Waldstein, Ernst Graf, Major	Bohemian	4th battalion Jungbunzlau district	1/1
Waldstein, Georg Graf, Oberst	Bohemian	1st battalion Chrudim district	1/2
Waldstein, Joseph Graf, Oberst	Bohemian	2nd battalion Leitmeritz district	1/2
Werbeck, Johann, Hauptmann	Bohemian	1st battalion Elbogen district	2/3
Wodniansky, Anton Freiherr von, Maj.	Bohemian	2nd battalion Saaz district	2/2
Woracziczky, Graf, Major	Bohemian	2nd battalion Tabor district	1/2
Wratislav, Carl Graf, Major	Bohemian	1st battalion Budweis district	1/1
Wratislav, Johann Graf, Oberst	Bohemian	1st battalion města Prahy	1/1
Wratislav, Prokop Graf, Major	Bohemian	2nd battalion Kaurzim district	1/1
Wrtby, Graf, Major	Bohemian	1st battalion Beraun district	I 1/1
Wrtby, Graf, Major	Bohemian	Combined Berounský battalion	II
Würth (Werth ?), Major	Bohemian	5th battalion Königgrätz district	2/3
Zesner, Vincenz Freiherr von, Maj.-Obstl.	Bohemian	2nd battalion Tabor district	2/2

Maj.-Obstl. = Major-Oberstleutnant --- města Prahy = City of Prague Notes:

1 Capitulanten: former soldiers who did voluntarily extend their duty period (weiterdienen).
2 Franz Kurz, Geschichte der Landwehre in Oesterreich ob der Enns, Band I – II, Verlag Haslinger, 1811.
3 Haythornthwaite Philip, Fosten Bryan, Austrian Army of the Napoleonic Wars (I): Infantry, Osprey Publishing Men at Arms Series # 176.
[iv] Allmayer-Beck Johann Christoph - Lessing, Erich. "Das Heer unter dem Doppeladler. Habsburgs Armeen 1718-1848", Wien, 1981. p. 215
4 From Zehetbauer, Ernst, „Landwehr gegen Napoleon. Österreichs erste Miliz und der Nationalkrieg von 1809", Vienna 1999 and from „History ck zeměbraneckého Kromeriz Infantry Regiment No. 25" (edited by Karel Langer), Kroměříž, 1909.
6 Frankenberger, Otakar, „Landwehr of Czech lands in 1809". In: Historie a vojenství, n. 2/1969, s. 227.
7 Radimský, Jiří, "Contributions to the history of military reform in the year 1808" In: Časopis Vlasteneckého spolku musejního v Olomouci, roč. (Journal of the Homeland Association of Olomouc Museum), Vol. 57, 1948, No. 209 and 210, p. 51.
8 Hollins Dave - Younghusband Bill. "Austrian Auxiliary Troops 1792-1816", Osprey Publishing, Men-at-Arms, 1996 (reprint 2002), s. 34. Although the central processing of English history should be approached very critically and with great caution, it was not the case of Hollins' "Ospreys". His knowledge, also under relative absence of appropriate references to sources, currently is
specialized in military uniforms and it is well known the author is a reference guide for several military historians about life and culture of the Austrian Empire. Only in the case of attribution of facings with the same color as their territorially competent ordinary infantry regiments, just the lacking of the source can raise doubts that Hollins made a mistake in the description of the state of 1813.
9 Zástěra Karel, "Acts and attractions, cultural and other images from the Bohemian East." Skutč, 1896, s. Works, 1896, p. 223.
223. Referring to the above provisions for the Austrian battalions is wrong to assume that Landwehr were not uniformed. They had only to issue uniform coats only during fire exercises.
10 Tanestry = tornistry, pagnety = bayonets. Řezníček, Vácslav. Naše zlatá matička, Díl II. "Our golden nut", Storm, Prague, 1923, p. 140.
11 Source: Austrian Landwehr in 1809: the Uniform Plates of Joseph Eder. Also in the Napoleon Series (Copyright by Markus Stein).
12 In Saxony came the X Corps of Am Ende (June 1809) which included six battalions of Bohemian Landwehr: 2, 3, 4, 5 Leitmeritz, the 6th of Hradec Kralove and the 6th of Boleslav. Coincidentally, in the city historical museum of Leipzig there is an Austrian
Landwehr hat of 1809 - the classic Corsican type.
Hollins – Younghusband, "Austrian Auxiliary Troops", p. 39. It is very interesting also the similar representation of the Czech Landwehr of 1813, which comes from the Lipperheide Berlin gallery. Soldier has his "blanket" on head, which Hollins describes as "Corsican hat".
13 Similar headgears between Bohemian Landwehr 1809 and Czech volunteers of 1800 became the cause of several mistakes. The first was committed by Gilbert Anger,"Illustrirte Geschichte der kk Armee", II. Band, Vienna, 1887, p. 1772 - 1178, whenunder the image of a 1800 volunteer he placed the label "Czech Landwehr", while the following text clearly shows that it was 1809 Landwehr. The same mistake repeated Haythornthwaite Philip - Fosten Bryan, "Austrian Army of the Napoleonic Wars (I): Infantry", Osprey
Publishing, Men-at-Arms, 1986, s. 31 which were apparently inspired by Anger.
14 Zehetbauer, „Landwehr gegen Napoleon", p. 269, 293 (see above).
15 Zehetbauer, „Landwehr gegen Napoleon", p. 238, 245.
16 Řezníček Vácslav, "Naše zlatá matička", Díl II. Bouřky, kapitola Stíny. Praha, 1923

▲ Austro-Hungarian Pontooner, sapper and miner 1809 about. From Ottenfeld artwork

THE HUNGARIAN INSURRECTIO AS IN 1809

(from: *Exercier Reglement für die Insurrection des Adels von Ungarn. Pesth 1809, Erstes Hauptstück*t. Erster Abschnitt. Stell und Abteilung.)

The Landwehr system was extended also to Hungary and to a part of the Croatia by the Pressburg (Pozsony-Bratislava) parliament (Landstag) (August 20 – November 5, 1808), which decided to raise a force of about 20.000 men for the national line regiments and by direct proposal of the Kaiser Franz, in the case of a direct threat against the hungarian Crown lands, decided to raise a Personal Insurrection Levy.

	Insurrectio Line or Light battalion		
1	Stabsoffizier und Kommandant	1	Bataillons Adjutant
1	Fourier	1	Bataillons Tambour
	Insurrection Line or Light Coy		
1	Hauptmann	1	Oberlieutenant
2	Unterlieutenant	2	Feldwebel
12	Corporale	2	Tambour
1	Zimmerman		

The Coy had two Feldwebeln like the regular units in war (because the Insurrectio was raised only as wartime units). Here the equivalent terms in Hungarian (the language of Insurrectio)

	Magyar Insurrectio gyalogos zászlóalj		
1	Zászlóaljparancsnok	1	zászlóalj segéd
1	zászlóalj raktáros őrmester	1	zászlóalj dobos
	Magyar Insurrectio gyalogos csapat		
1	Százados	1	Főhadnagy
2	Hadnagy	2	Őrmester
12	Káplár or Tizedes	2	Század-Dobos
1	Katonai ács		A variable number of
	Utász		honvédelem katonai (Privates)

A brief History of the Hungarian Insurrectio
by István Nagy (and Enrico Acerbi)

That's a great problem in the Hungarian history of the 18th and the 19th century. The insurrectio was generally "der adelige Aufstrand", the feudal militia of the noblemen. But in the truth, at the beginning of the 19th century, the Hungarians weren't able to determine, who must go to war when the insurrectio was called.
The Insurrectio had been called four times: in 1797, 1800, 1805 and 1809; but only in 1809 the insurgents did fight.
The Military Borderlands were part of the Hungarian Crown lands (as well as Croatia. The Croatian Kingdom was under the rule of the Hungarian Crown, but, in effects, it was governed by the Banus of Croatia).
However the Border was under the direct control of the Hofkriegsrat, not of the King of Hungary (the Kaiser himself). The serfs in the Border weren't paying any tax but directly served as soldiers when called. In the war against the Turks (1788-1791) more Grenzer troops were raised than before and this happened also later, in 1796, and until 1848-1849. It was not a special event because it was allowed by the law.
The "Magyar" or Hungarians was actually a dependant of the Hungarian Crown. So the born Croatian, Serbs, Romanians were called as being hungarians (this happened many years before the spreading of nationalism), provided they live in hungarian lands, Frontier apart. However the Croatian, Serbs, Romanians, who lived in the Borderlands, were only Grenzer, militarized citizens of that lands.
In order to push back enemies through the borders and in order to achieve the so called "Tregua Domini" (by the Lord a Truce), the higher Prelates, the royal barons and the hereditary lands barons (landowners) had to raise their own troops, under their own standards (Fähnlein) or **Banderia**. This was the:
- **Insurrectio Banderialis**: noblemen and the Holy-orders had to raise hussars regiments (banderia. Singular Banderium) according to their financial wealth. These men were organised into the "Banderia" (at least 50 men, namely 1/8 of the full 400 men banderium force) of the noblemen owner (or Holy-order). It fought under the colour (standard) of the "Owner". If the noble was not so wealthy to raise 50 hussars, the eventual enrolled men were sent under the colour of the County (Banderium of the county). The King, the Queen, the Lords, Higher Prelates and some Holy-order could retain their own Banderia.

Even the lesser nobility, but enough in wellfare to get money for raising troops, could have their small armies and join the Insurrectio (here called **Particularis**). These were an Insurrectio mode, which had some character of volunteers-call to arm (at least for the commanders).

In effects, there were two ways to call for Insurrectio:

1. **Insurrectio Partialis**: whenever only one or two (of the former three feudal Lords) components were called to arms nationwide or in some regions of the country.

2. **Insurrectio Generalis**: all components were called to arms, nationwide. In this case "all and each" Prelates, hereditary or acquisite barons with their subordinate vassals (for Croatia, the Summalisten), must raise troops paying directly them and for them. The poorer noblesmen had to enroll "personally under the King's Flags" for the so called:

3. **Insurrectio Personalis**: where all the hungarian nobles (personalis = persons, but even organizations Ie. the free cities) had to stand up (but this was restricted more times). So the insurrectio personalis was a personal insurrection of the nobles and of all their cities, towns and other corporations, which held the noble title. The nobles didn't pay taxes, but were compelled personally to defend the Country. They had the opportunity to send deputy soldiers instead of themselves; but this, actually, was not common;

In every case there were also standard rules to understand the richness degree of the nobles. They simply counted the number of rural farms (Porta) in order to have a measure of the landowner wellfare. So many paid and raised troops along with this rating value.

4. **Insurrectio Portalis**: the poorer Vassals (and sometimes with the higher nobles aid) raised hussars and footsoldiers according to what stated by law. The "porta" is a term which means house. The earlier origin is not known. It was, therefore, the taxation standard units, when taking off money from each farmhouse, owned by a landowner. In the Hungarian Kingdom (as above mentioned, they were not the same thing as the lands of the Hungarian Crown) there were 5405,5 Porta. The country-soldiers were formally volunteers, but the recruiting was not always free from violence.

The portalis and the banderialis Insurrections were often mixed and combined. The banderialis and portalis Insurrections had not different Statutes. The Statutes were so complicated that it was impossible to keep them as the original statement. Actually, except in the personalis component, nobles and aristocrats raised as many troops as they wanted; usually more than the number fixed by the Statutes. In reality the laws changed very fastly and the called insurrections were never the same in strenght or in organization.

Croatian Insurrectio

At Agram (Zagreb) the Insurrectio recruitment had specific legislative Council Committee. Their proposal in 1809 was to raise up to 10.000-12.000 insurgents. This was not a Landwehr statement but only a privilege of nobles and High Clergymen. The Insurrectio could have been general or a mass-recruitment (Generalis or Massalis) or partial (Insurrectio particularis or partialis). Also in Croatia it was splitten between personal, banderial or portal (Insurrectio personalis, banderialis, portalis). A personal Insurrectio came from nobles (Turopoljce, Kalničane, through the countryside of SV Ivan Zeline free towns and others), namey from people who, for personal ethical wish, did go into war with a "personal" Banal regiment. The Banderial occurred in the case when someone organized a Banderial regiment, in which men would have been recruited (lend) for a larger period. The Banderials were volunteer-soldiers under the flag (Banderium) of some border feudal Lord (or, in the 1809 event, under the Holy flags of the Church, the "Zagrebački" Bishop Maksimilijan Vrhovac). Also there the countryland nobility was burdened with the so called "portalis insurrectio" according to the number of their taxation fees (used to estimate the number of the bondmen to be enrolled).

Practically, the Agram's bishop, Maksimilijan Vrhovac, actually the Ban's Lieutenant, in 1809, raised 17.726 insurgent, whereof 15.742 were common infantrymen, and 1.984 horsemen. Among this fellows, therefore, he could count on 1.042 "personalis" staff insurgents (Officers), about 10.000 "portalis" insurgents through the counties, only 29 volunteers and 1.644 soldiers enrolled in his "banderial" Insurrectio. This was the utmost number of soldiers raised there as Insurgents. However they were rather undrilled, mostly rude peasants, many reaching their battalions as irregular crowds of youngmen and boys. The commander was there the Ban, Fieldmarshal Ignaz Gyulai helped by the vice- commander of the Croatian Kingdom, the "podmaršal" Vinko Knežević. The cavalry was led by the Colonel Joseph Drašković, while the infantry had, as commanders, the colonels Patačić, Amadeo, Peharnik and Berković.

This mass of soldiers did participate to the 1809 larger engagements (St. Michael, Graz, Raab and Wagram) only in a nominal part. Most of them were employed to defend the Bosnian borders against Turks and against Marmont and in repressive duties during the internal riots in their Homeland.

Insurrectio in napoleonic times
In 1715 the King gave to the Reichstag nobles a Proposition by which (ex art. 8) he explained what would have to be really the Personal Insurrectio of his Vassals and that of their "Banderias". "Quandoquidem Nobiles et omnes illi, quos sub nomenclationem hac, in Ungaria lex complectitur, pro Regni defensione militare, adeoque personaliter insurgere, suaque respectiva Banderia producere et praestare teneantur". They must raise troops and must act in the name of the Crown.
In 1796 the Insurrectio was called two times, in 1797, 1800 one time; all calls did not go till the first line in battles. The first call raised a contingent of 17969 Hussars (erste Aufgebot) and 3556 soldiers (in the same time around 50000 recruits reached the Depots of the regular hungarian infantry). The second call gave a contingent of 10778 cavalry, 26606 infantry and, for the first time, 6416 Croatians (a total of 47916 men).
From 1800 the Insurrectio had the character of expecial emergency. From 1805 till 1808 all was clearly stated in the Reichsprotokoll. Hungary (apart of Croatia and Slavonia) had to raise 17214 hussars and 21230 soldiers, the K.K. Frei Städten (Free Towns) and the special Districts had to raise 4000 more Bürger zu Pferd (mounted civilians). It was a grand total of 41000 men called to defend Homeland, which had to be counted with 1952 Scharfschützen (snipers in volunteers units) and around 20000 recruits for the regular army. Under the Rule Law of 1808 this service had to continue for at least three years (after the King's call), with the advantage they will remain (and eventually fight) in their Homeland territories.

The "Insurrectio" hungarian Cavalry (Hussars) in 1809
Besides the Insurrection units of the present list (under), many Counties and free City formed both divisions or single squadrons (also half-sqns) as volunteers cavalry units. These cavalry was ready to fight around August, but, having never met the enemies, yjey were mainly disbanded or used to replenish other units. Only the Hont's division was attached, as 5th division, to the 2nd hussars Archduke Joseph regiment.

▲ Hungarian Insurrectio military uniforms from an ancient print of J.Eder

District		District Commander	Name of		Counties and free Cities	Forces		Notes
			Regiment (division)	Commander	Recruiting the Rgt.	Sq.	Men	
On left Danube bank	The Danube	FMZ baron Paul Davidovich	Preßburg (Pozsony)	Oberst GNepomuk Esterházy	Preßburg (Pozsony), Trentschin (Trencsén)	6	1039	The Regiment was at the Waag and fought at Raab (battle) and Papa
			Neograd (Nógrád)	Oberst Garnika	Neograd (Nógrád), Bars, Jazygier and Kumanen district,	6	1074	
			Bars	Oberst Simonyi	Hont, Sohl (Zólyom), Liptau (Liptó), Turócz, Arva	6	858	Deployed at the Waag, fought at Raab (battle) and then was at Jablunka Pass
			Pest	Oberst Gosztóny	Pest	6	1056	Deployed at the Waag, independent unit of Arch. John Corps fought at Raab (battle) and Karakó
Trans: On right Danube bank		FML baron Mecséry	Sümegh	Oberst Pászthory	Sümeg (Somogyi), Baranya, Tolna and Komorn (Komárno)	6	1106	The regiment fought at Raab (battle)
			Veszprém	Oberst Zichy	Vészprem, Stuhlweißenburg (Székesfehérvár)	6	1007	independent unit of Arch. John Corps fought at Raab (battle) and Karakó
			Zala	Oberst Foky	Zala, Eisenburg (Vás county)	6	1071	Raab (battle) battle
			Eisenburg	Oberst Batthyányi	Eisenburg (Vás), Raab (Győr), Wieselburg (Moson)	6	1098	These two units fought at Raab (battle) and then were transferred to the 2nd Reserve Corps
			Ödenburg	Oberst Festetics	Ödenburg (Sopron)	2	374	
On left Tisza bank	The Theiss Tisza	GM Graf Hadik de Futak	Zemplén county	Oberst Kantó	Zemplén, Abaujvár, Sáros, Zips (Szepes), Ungvár	6	1234	Both regiments began the war with the Arch. John army, then were under division Egermann in Galicia
			Heves county	Oberst Almássy	Heves, Borsod, Gömör, Torna	6	1033	
Trans: On right Tisza bank		FML baron Duka	Szabolcs	Oberst Kallay	Szabolcs, Haiducken Städte (Hajdú), Debrecen	6	1135	The troops from these districts were concentrated at Pest, detached to the Bakonyer-Wald. They did not fight at Raain the Parte of them were at Wagram with the VI Corps Hiller (infantry) and the I and II Reserve Corps (cavalry)
			Bihar	Oberst Doboszy	Bihar, Békés, Csongrád	6	1055	
			Torontál	Oberst Lázár	Torontál, Temes, Arad, Krassó	6	1063	
			Szatmár	Oberst Vecsey	Szatmár, Ugocsa, Bereg, city of Szegedin (Szeged), Csánad, Mármaros	6	1019	
			Arad	Major Edelspacher	Torontál, Temes, Arad, Krassó	6	??	Had to be raised on October
Croatian and Slavonian			Banderial Insurrection	Oberst Petar Knezevich		8	??	Only four of these 12 Sqns. Reached the Ban Corps. They took partial part in the Graz battle. The others remained in Croatia as garrison
			Personal			4		
			Slavonian-Syrmian (serbs)	??		2	??	

Units not Insurrectional

Regular army regiments	Primartial	Oberst Luszeńsky	Gran (Esztergom) and Primartial region	6	1023	Both regiments were raised to be part of the main Army. They had all regular Army officers. These two regiments fought at Wagram and then marched to the Schütt
	Neutra (Nyitra)	Oberst Berényi (after Ürményi)	Neutra (Nyitra)	6	1011	The Neutra regiment had the name of Queen regiment (Kaiserin)

The "Insurrectio" hungarian Infantry in 1809

District		District Commander	Name of			Counties and free Cities	Forces	
			N°	Battalion	Commander	Recruiting the Rgt.	Co.	Men
On left Danube bank	The Danube	FMZ baron Paul Davidovich These four battalions were deployed on the Schütt and on the lower Waag, fought at Raab (battle) and then were detached to the Jablunka-pass	1	Preßburg (Pozsony)	Oberst Borbély	Preßburg (Pozsony), Trentschin (Trencsén)	6	1212
			2	Pest	Oberst Podhorszky	Pest, Bács, Hont	6	1224
			3	Neutra	Oberstltn. Ordödy	Neutra (Nyitra), Bars, Turócz	6	1186
			4	Nógrád	Major Szabo	Neogrard (Nógrád), Arva, Gran (Esztergom), Sohl (Zólyom), Liptau (Liptó)	6	1262
Trans: On right Danube bank		FML baron Mecséry These six battalions were concentrated near Raain the They fought all at Raab (battle) and then formed the garrison of the Komorn fortress	5	Eisenburg (Vás)	Oberstltn. Carl Erdödy	Eisenburg	6	1191
			6	Eisenburg (Vás)	Major Tersztyánsky	Eisenburg (Vás), Raab (Győr), Ödenburg (Sopron), Wieselburg (Moson)	6	1028
			7	Komorn (Komárno)	Major Kmosko	Komorn (Komárno), Raab (Győr)	6	1148
			8	Zala (Szala)	Oberst Ghilány	Zala, Sümegh (Somogyi)	6	1172
			9	Veszprém	Oberst Markus	Veszprém	6	1207
			10	Stuhlweißenburg (Székesfehérvár)	Hauptmann Pribek	Stuhlweißenburg (Székesfehérvár), Tolna, Baranya	4	490
On left Tisza bank	The Theiss (Tisza)	GM Graf Hadik de Futak The infantry of these districts had one battalion at Dukla, another on the upper Arva, the remaining deployed near Erlau. They did not take part at the Raab battle and after were part of the II Reserve Corps (then detached to the VII corps - Egermann division in Galicia)	15	Heves county	Major Tibad	Heves	-	1133
			16	Borsod county	Oberstltn. Szemere (after Bay)	Borsod	-	1191
			17	Gömör county	Oberstltn. Fáy	Borsod, Gömör	-	1541
			18	Zemplén county	Oberstltn. Széntessy	Zemplén, Ungvár	-	1137
			19	Abaujvár county	Oberst Keller (then Hándo)	Abaujvár, Torna, Sáros, Zips (Szepes)	-	1200
Trans: On right Tisza bank		FML baron Duka All the troops from these districts were concentrated around Pest. They did not fight at Raab, some detached to the Bakonyi-Wald. Part stood with Hiller at Wagram	11	Szatmár	??	Szatmár	6	1191
			12	Szatmár	??	Szatmár, Bereg, Ugocsa	3	760
			13	Mármaros	??	Mármaros	6	1071
			14	Bihar	Oberstltn. Poroszlay	Arad, Bihar	3	545

APPENDIX B

HUNGARIAN INSURRECTIO INFANTRY 1809

Commanders:
1 - left Danube bank or Cis-Donau: Davidovich
2 - right Danube bank or Trans-Donau: Mécsery
3 - left Tisza bank or Cis-Theiss: Hadik
4 - right Tisza bank or Trans-Theiss: Duka

Districts cis-Donau (Commander Davidovich), **battalions**:
Preßburg I, Pest II, Neutra III, Neograd IV

Districts trans-Donau (Commander Mécsery), **battalions**:
Eisenburger V, II Eisenburger VI, Komorn VII, Zala VIII, Stuhlweißenburg X,

Districts cis-Theiss (Commander Hadik), **battalions**:
Heves XV, Borsod XVI, Gömör XVII, Zemplin XVIII, Abaujvár XIX

Districts trans-Theiss (Commander Duka), **battalions**:
I Szatmárer IX, II Szatmárer XI, Máramaros XIII, Bihar XIV

HUNGARIAN INSURRECTIO

- Commander: archduke Joseph, but probably the first was archduke Rainer

ABAUJVÁR, Insurrectio batt. n° 19 - oberst Keller then oberst Hánlo
- Recruitment: from counties of Abaujvár-Torna, Sáros, Zips (Szepes).
- was at Dukla, Arva or Erlau, later with II Reserve Corps, finally attached to Div. Egermann, VII Corps

BIHAR, Insurrectio batt. n° 14 - Oberstleutnant Poroszlay
- Recruitment: from Bihar and Arad
- in Pest, then in the Bakonyer Wald, after Wagram part with VI part with I and II Reserve Corps

BORSOD, Insurrectio batt. n° 16 - Oberstleutnant Szemere then Oberstleutnant Bay
- Recruitment: from Borsod
- was at Dukla, Arva or Erlau, later with II Reserve Corps, finally attached to Div. Egermann, VII Corps

1st EISENBURGER Insurrectio batt. n° 5 - Oberstleutnant Karoly Erdödy
- Recruitment: from Eisenburg (Vasvár) – Vas County.
- before Aspern: on the Schütt
- before Wagram: battle of Raab (battle), then to the Jablunkapaß

2nd EISENBURGER Insurrectio batt. n° 6 - major Terczánsky
- Recruitment: from Eisenburg, Raab (Györ), Ödenburg (Sopron), Zwieselburg
- between Aspern and Wagram: at Raab (battle), then at Komarom fortress
one among I or II Batt. (not known):
- between Aspern and Wagram with div. Jellachich or Colloredo, Inner Austria army

GÖMÖR, Insurrectio batt. n° 17 - Oberstleutnant Fay
- Recruitment: from Gömör and Borsod.
- was at Dukla, Arva or Erlau, later with II Reserve Corps, finally attached to Div. Egermann, VII Corps.

HEVES, Insurrectio batt. n° 15 - major Tibad
- Recruitment: from Heves
- was at Dukla, Arva or Erlau, later with II Reserve Corps, finally attached to Div. Egermann, VII Corps

KOMORN Insurrectio batt. n° 7 - major Kmosko
- Recruitment: from Komorn (Komarno) and Raab (Györ)
- between Aspern and Wagram: with div. Colloredo, VIII Corps

MÁRAMAROS, Insurrectio batt. n° 13 – commander not known
- Recruitment: from Máramaros County
- Pest, Bakonyer Wald and, after Wagram, part with VI Corps, part with I and II Reserve

NEOGRAD, Insurrectio batt. n° 4 - major Szábo
- Recruitment: from Neograd (Nógrád), Árva, Gran (Esztergom), Liptau (Liptó), Sohl (Zólyom)
- Schütt, Waag, Raab (battle), Jablunkapaß

NEUTRA, Insurrectio batt. n° 3 - Oberstleutnant Ordody
- Recruitment: from Neutra (Nyitra), Bars, Turócz
- Schütt, Waag, Raab (battle), Jablunkapaß

PEST, Insurrectio batt. n° 2 - major Podhorsky
- Recruitment: from Pest, Bács, Hont.
- Schütt, Waag, Raab (battle), Jablunkapaß
sometimes (between Aspern and Wagram) also with the Inner Austria army

PRESSBURG, Insurrectio batt. n° 1 - oberst Borbély
- Recruitment: from Preßburg (Pozsony or Bratislava) and Trentschin (Trencsén)
- Schütt, Waag, Raab (battle), Jablunkapaß.

STUHLWEISSENBURG, Insurrectio batt. n° 10 - Hauptmann Pribek
- Recruitment: from Stuhlweißenburg (Székesfehévár), Tolna, Baranya
- Schütt, Waag, Raab (battle), Jablunkapaß

SZALA (Zala), Insurrectio batt. n° 8 - oberst Ghilány
- Recruitment: from Szala (Zala) and Szümegh (Somogy)
- Schütt, Waag, Raab (battle), Jablunkapaß.
sometimes (between Aspern and Wagram) 2 batt. with the Inner Austria army.

1st SZATMÁRER Insurrectio batt. n° 11 – comm. not known
- Recruitment: Szatmár
- Pest, Bakonyer Wald, after Wagram part with VI part with I and II Reserve Corps

2nd SZATMÁRER Insurrectio batt. n° 12 – comm. not known
- Inhaber: Kaiserin Maria Ludovica
- Recruitment: Szatmár, Bereg, Ugocsa
- Bakonyer Wald, after Wagram part with VI part with I and II Reserve Corps

VESZPRIM, Insurrectio batt. n° 9 - oberst Markus
- Recruitment: Veszprim (Veszprem)
- Schütt, Waag, Raab (battle), Jablunkapaß
between Aspern and Wagram with the Inner Austria army. (div. Colloredo or Jellachich) then with Div. Jellachich.

ZEMPLIN, Insurrectio batt. n° 18 - Oberstleutnant Szentessy
- Recruitment: Zemplin (Zemplen) and Ungvár
- was at Dukla, Arva or Erlau, later with II Reserve Corps, finally attached to Div. Egermann, VII Corps.

HUNGARIAN INSURRECTIO CAVALRY
- Organization:
districts cis-Donau (Davidovich): regiments Preßburg, Neograd, Bars, Pest.
districts trans-Donau (Mecséry): regiments Szümegh, Vészprim, Szala, Eisenburg, Ödenburg.
districts cis-Theiss (Hadik): regiments Zemplin, Heves.
districts trans-Theiss (Duka): regiments Szabocs, Bihar, Torontál, Szatmár, Arad

ARAD Hussars raised in October 1809
- between Aspern and Wagram: Rgt with brig. Mécsery, left Wing army of Inner Austria

BARS - oberst Knesevich Hussars
- Recruitment: from Hont, Sohl, Liptau, Turocz, Arva
- Raab (battle), then Jablunkapaß

BIHAR - oberst Doboszy Hussars
- Recruitment: from Bihar, Békés, Csongrád
- detached in Bakonyer Wald, then with II Reserve Corps

EISENBURG - oberst Batthyány Hussars
 Recruitment: from Raab (Györ) and Eisenburg
- between Aspern and Wagram: at Raab (battle), then II Reserve Corps

HAIDUCKEN
see Palatinal hussars Rgt n° 12 and Insurrectio cavalry of Rgt Szabolcz

HEVES - oberst Almássy Hussars
- Recruitment: from Heves, Borsod, Gömör, Torna
- between Aspern and Wagram: with Hadik, Inner Austria army with then Div. Egermann, VII Corps.

HONT see volunteers

JAZYGIER and KUMANIER
see Insurrectio cavalry of Rgt Neograd and with Palatinal hussars n° 12.

NEOGRAD - oberst Garnika Hussars
- Recruitment: from Bars, Neograd and the Jazygier and Kumanier districts
- between Aspern and Wagram: at Raab (battle) and Pápa

NEUTRA KOMITAT Husaren see Volunteers

ÖDENBURG - oberst Festeticz Hussars
- Recruitment: from Ödenburg
- between Aspern and Wagram: brig. Mécsery, left Wing of Inner Austria army then with II Reserve Corps

PEST - oberst Gosztóny Hussars
- Recruitment: from Pest, Bács
- between Aspern and Wagram: with brig. Andrassy, Inner Austria army then with brig. Mécsery, left Wing of Inner Austria army .

PRESSBURG - oberst Esterházy Hussars
- Recruitment: from Preßburg and Trentschin
- at Raab (battle) and Pápa with brig. Bianchi, Inner Austria army, Pressburg bridgehead
- after Wagram: idem

PRIMARTIAL Hussars see Volunteers

SZABOLCZ - oberst Kallay Hussars
- Recruitment: from Szabolsz and the Haiduk cities
- detached in the Bakonyer Wald, then II Reserve Corps

SZALA – ZALA oberst Foky Hussars
- Recruitment: from Szala, Eisenburg
- between Aspern and Wagram: with Div. Frimont, right Wing of Inner Austria army

SZATMÁR oberst Vécsey Hussars
- Recruitment: from Szatmár, Ugocsa, Bereg, Szeged and Csanád
- detached in the Bakonyer Wald, then II Reserve Corps

SZEKLER see the Hussar Regiment n° 11 in the regular cavalry section.

SZÜMEGH - oberst Pásztory Hussars
- Recruitment: from Szümegh, Baranya, Tolna, Komorn
- between Aspern and Wagram: with Div. Frimont, right Wing of Inner Austria army

TORONTÁL - oberst Lázár Hussars
- Recruitment: from Torontál, Temes, Krásso, Arad
- detached in the Bakonyer Wald, then with II Reserve Corps

VESZPRIM - Oberstleutnant Zichy Hussars
- Recruitment: from Veszprim and Stuhlweissenburg
- between Aspern and Wagram: with brig. Andrassy, Inner Austria army later with brig. Mécsery, left Wing of Inner Austria army

ZEMPLIN - oberst Kantó Hussars
- Recruitment: from Zemplin, Abaujvár, Sáros, Zips, Ungvár
- between Aspern and Wagram: with Hadik, Inner Austria army then Div. Egermann, VII Corps

INSURRECTIO CROATIAN-SLAVONIAN-SERBIAN
see also the table above.

BANDERIAL-PERSONAL-MASSAL INSURRECTIO INFANTRY
- Commander: Oberstleutnant Draskovich
- between Aspern and Wagram: 2 batt. with brig. Munkácsy, IX Corps then 2 batt. with brig. Kengyel, IX Corps

BANDERIAL, PERSONAL, SLAVONIAN-SERBIAN INSURRECTIO HUSSARS
- Commander: oberst Knesevich
- before Aspern: with IX Corps in Croatia, partially in formation.
- between Aspern and Wagram: with brig. Amade, IX Corps then 3 Sqns. with brig. Splényi, IX Corps. Later 2 Sqns. were with brig. Gavassini, IX Corps and finally 4 Sqns. with IX Corps, and 4 Sqns. in Croatia

PORTALIS. Note: Magnates of Hungary raised 5 cavalry Div. (2 Sqns. each) for the regular Hussars regiments.

SIEBENBÜRGISCHE INSURRECTIO, (Infantry and Hussars) never organized. was only a project.

1809 – VOLUNTEERS UNITS OF HUNGARY

FREIWILLIGE or the true free-corps of Volunteers (often also Jäger battalions or only Jäger named), set up in the empire by nobles (who called themselves also as proprietaires) or early nationalist (Schill) or a mixture of both (the Duke of Brunswick - Braunschweig, i.e.) and the Freiwilligenbataillone (Freibat. in the contemporary literature).
They follow here an alphabetic order in accordance with their denominations.

ARADER GEBIRGSJÄGERKORPS - Hauptmann Joseph Nagy
Units which made only service by chasing deserters in the inner country.

BUKOWINAER Freibataillon – major Chevalier Friedrich Forget de Borst
Was never in battles.

ERZHERZOG KARL Husaren see Siebenbürgische Hussars

HONT Hussars
- Recruitmen: in the Hont County
- Organization: 1 Div = 2 Sqns.
- army of Inner Austria but they were never in battle.

MARIA LUDOVICA Freikorps see Siebenbürgisches Freikorps

NEUTRAER Regiment freiwillige Husaren - Insurrectio
They were also considered a regular-like Hussars regiment, apart for the Insurrectio call-to-arms time:
- Owner "Kaiserin Maria Ludovica" – Commander: Oberst Bérenyi then oberst Ürményi.
- Recruitment: County of Neutra (Nyitra)
- before and at Aspern: in the Brig. Kerekes, Div. Kienmayer, II Reserve Corps (remained in Bohemia)
- at Wagram: Brig. Kerekes, Div. Schwarzenberg, Reserve Corps
- after Wagram: Brig. Kerekes, Div. Nostitz, Reserve Corps

PRIMATIAL (Primartial) Regiment freiwillige Husaren - Insurrectio
At the service and paid by the archduke Carl Ambrosius
Comm.: oberst Luszensky.

- Recruitment: Gran (Esztergom) County and Primartial
- before and at Aspern: in the Brig. Kerekes, Div. Kienmayer, II Reserve Corps (remained in Bohemia)
- at Wagram: Brig. Frehlich, Div. Nordmann, Avantgarde II Wing later in the Brig. Vécsey, Div.Nordmann, Avantgarde II Wing
- after Wagram: Brig. Kerekes, Div. Nostitz, Reserve Corps

SIEBENBÜRGISCHES Jägerkorps Maria Ludovica – Transylvanian Chasseurs
- Owner: Kaiserin Maria Ludovica

I Bat. (Saxon) - Oberstleutnant Kolb
In Hungary, never engaged.

II Bat. (Hungarian) - Hauptmann Simon Christof
In Hungary, never engaged.

SIEBENBÜRGISCHE HUSAREN Erzherzog Karl
Data not available

Notes

1 - rom: Exercier Reglement für die Insurrection des Adels von Ungarn. Pesth 1809, Erstes Hauptstückt. Erster Abschnitt. Stell und Abteilung.Courtesy of Jeff Lewis, NapSeries.

2 - These numbers was those of the Enrollment Lists but they were rather lower in the battlefields (unfit, ill and deserters).

3 - The **combat of Papa** (12 June 1809) was a rearguard action fought during Archduke John of Austria's retreat towards the Danube after the failure of his invasion of Italy. Prince Eugène himself reached Papa on the morning of 12 June, to find the Archduke's entire army camped before him, but the rest of the French troops were slow in arriving. By the time Grenier's division arrived, at about 2pm, most of the Austrian infantry were already on their way north. A rearguard, consisting of two battalions of regular hussars, one battalion of regular infantry, one of frontier infantry (Grenzer) and three of Insurrection Hussars (a militia raised in an emergency), was left around Papa under the command of FML Frimont. Frimont posted his cavalry to the south-west of Papa, facing the French, and his infantry to the north

The French were finally ready to attack at around 2pm. Eugène sent troops to outflank the Austrians on both sides, then ordered Montbrun, the Badeners and two chasseur regiments to charge the Austrian centre. The first attack failed, but the second succeeded, and the town fell to the French, while the Austrians fled north. The French made something of a mess of the pursuit, only using their light cavalry, while the 1st Dragoon Division wasn't used all day. Despite this failure they inflicted around 600 casualties on the Austrians, many of the prisoners, three times their own losses of around 200 men. On the following day the French continued the pursuit, and on 14 June they inflicted a major defeat on the Archduke at Raab.From http://www.histoire-empire.org.

4 - **Karakó combats**: June 8, 1809. Eugene arrived with 18,000 men at Steinamanager (Szombathely). Lauriston drove 4,000 men to Sárvár, who was caught by chasseurs and Baden cavalry of Colbert. On June 9, 1809, he formed a junction, east of Sárvár, with the main army. The cavalry hold the following positions:

division Sahuc at Gógáufa - General Colbert 9th Hussars at Karakó, the 20th chasseurs at Merse and the 7th chasseurs at Kenyeres; Montbrun occupied Pápócz (1st chasseurs), Asszonyfa (2nd chasseurs) et Marcaltö (7th hussars) .

The defenders, under command of colonel Gosztonyi (a division of Pest cavalry, 230 Gradiskaner under major Taza) withdrew by Jánosháza up Karakó. But the next day, they were attacked again, about two o'clock in the afternoon. This time, they managed to push back the 900 cavalry of general Marollet, despite three attacks.

The French so tried to pass the Raab river at Bodonhely rather than at Marcal. General Andrássy stopped them with his troops stationed on the Marcal: Pest Cavalry (628 men), Veszprém (1143 men), and the Archduke Joseph Hussars (739 men) at Gógánfa.

June 8 saw new troop movements. The Szala cavalry (1100 h.) and the Insurrectio battalion n. 2 (1094 men) were

▲ Hungarian Insurrectio military uniforms

ordered to go to Tét, the cavalry regiment Somogy (1272 riders) moved to Pápa. They should strengthen the Andrássy cavalry.

On 10 June, general Macdonald reached Körmend. The same day, at 13 pm, Karakó was again attacked. The French have gathered at Jánoshásza seven cavalry divisions and two infantry battalions. General Andrássy moved to Dobróka two cavalry divisions (Veszprém), a hussars archduke Joseph division, a division of Blankenstein hussars and a half battery of horse artillery.

At three o'clock in the afternoon, two infantry battalions and three cavalry divisions did attack again the hungarian Colonel János Gosztonyi at Karakó. Despite heavy losses, they pushed up them till Dobróka, followed by the 9th hussars (general Debroc), who drove against the infantry, bound to decline in mass.

Blocked by the muddy ground, Hungarian cavalry could not attack at that time. The French put in battery, at a distance of 2500 paces, four pieces of eight and two howitzers. The Archduke Joseph hussars and part of the Veszprém cavalry threw themselves on the French, which retreated immediately. However a counterattack with two cavalry divisions regained the lost ground. Gosztonyi lost 300 men.

Archduke John withdrew towards Pápa, which he reached during the night. Eugene now expected that archduke John was to take position at Papá to fight. From http://www.histoire-empire.org.

5 - Insurrectio banderialis: noblemen and the holy order had to raise hussars according to their wealth. These men were organised into "banderium" (at least 50 men, the 1/8 of the full 400 men banderium) of the noblemen (and holy order). It fought under the color (standard) of the "raiser". If the noble not so wealthy to raise 50 hussars theese men were sent under the color of the county (banderium of the county). The king, the queen, the lords and some holy orders had their own banderium. (note by István Nagy 2007)

6 - Insurrectio personalis: the mandatory stand-up of all the noble persons (and organisations f.e. the free cities) (it was restricted more times).

7 - Esztergom was the seat of the *primás* (Primate) of the Roman Catholic Church in Hungary.

8 - Bakony (German: Bakonyer Wald) is a mountainous region in Transdanubia, Hungary. It forms the largest part of the Transdanubian Medium Mountains. It is located north of Lake Balaton and lies almost entirely in Veszprém county. The Bakony is divided into the Northern and Southern Bakony through the Várpalota-Veszprém-Ajka-Devecser line.

9 - The Dukla Pass is a strategically significant mountain pass in the Carpathian mountains on the border between Poland and Slovakia, and close to the western border of Ukraine. It is the lowest mountain pass in the Carpathian mountains main range. Located south of Dukla in Poland and northeast of Prešov in Slovakia, the Dukla pass is acknowledged as an area where Eastern and Western Slavic cultures meet..

10 - Arva county in northern Hungary.

11 - Eger (German: Erlau) is a city in northern Hungary, the county seat of Heves, east of the Mátra Mountains. The defence of the northern Hungary was decided after the Russian threats and their intervention during the campaign in Poland.

12 - Two islands in the Danube, situated in the Hungarian plain between Pressburg and Komorn Great Schütt Island is bordered by the Danube proper on the south and west, and by the Little Danube and the Schwarzwasser (Oeregduna) It is 58 miles long, from 10 to 20 miles wide, and is subject to the floods of the rivers, being low and even. Owing to its rich soil, it is called the Golden Garden of Hungary. It has several towns, including Komorn, which is situated in the southeast corner of the island. Little Schütt Island, bordered by the Danube proper on the north and east, and by the Wieselburger Danube, and lying to the southwest of Great Schütt Island, is 28 miles long.

13 - The Váh (German: Waag; Hungarian: Vág) is the longest river entirely in Slovakia. A left tributary of the Danube river, the Váh is 406 km long, including its Čierny Váh branch. Its two sources, the Biely Váh (White Váh) and the Čierny Váh (Black Váh), are located in the High Tatras and Low Tatra mountains, respectively, and it flows over northern and western Slovakia and finally pours into the Danube near Komárno (Komarom).

14 - Jablunka Pass (Czech: Jablunkovský průsmyk) is a mountain pass in the Beskids, located in the elevation of 553 m above sea level, currently in the Czech Republic, near the border with Poland and Slovakia. It separates the Moravian-Silesian Beskids and the Silesian Beskids mountain ranges. It is one of the most important transport routes in the Western Carpathians. Road from Žilina to Těšín runs here. Košice-Bohumín railway line also runs here. It was an important route from the Middle Ages, connecting Upper Hungary with Silesia, more precisely Cieszyn Silesia.

THE LOST DISTRICTS

Austrian Recruitment System

When the foreign mercenaries were not enough to make war, in the 17th century, came into the scene the "standing armies", changing the recruitment systems. Instead of being hired for explicit military operations, mercenaries were now recruited as permanent elements of armies. So called "standing armies" often required replacements of troopers lost through deaths, illnesses, desertions and discharges in peacetime, and, of course, of those killed in battles. The peacetime attrition for desertion was relatively low, running at approximately from a 6 per cent of total strength each year in Prussia till about 10 per cent in other German armies and Austria. War more than doubled these rates, in particular for Austria during the operations in the Balkans against the Turks. Native fellow citizens, who were not volunteers, had an high rate of desertions in comparison to who chose to make war as a job or for necessity. So many armies continued to enroll foreigners (Ausländer).

Foreign recruitment was part of what was called the "company economy", a system largely devolved to officers who had to maintain their units in return for fixed costs. So many recruiting parties often clashed over the right to recruit in particular areas, causing friction with the local authorities. Adherence to constitutional propriety was vital for the Habsburgs, who had to preserve a certain German goodwill.

To minimize troubles, the monarchy began, in the early eighteenth century, to entrust its recruitment within the Reich (Reichswerbung) to a general, who coordinated the recruiting areas of different regiments and negotiated with the local princes for authorizations. This system, revised in 1765 and part of a wider reform of Habsburg recruitment, had this requisite:

- the possibility to enroll men from the Habsburg hereditary lands (called Erbländer) assigning each infantry regiment to one of the new created recruitment districts (Werberayons). These districts were almost determined by the administrative and geographical Kreis structure.

A central management was allowed by the organization of a permanent office of the "Reichswerbungs-Direktor" or Director of Recruitment within the Reich in Frankfurt. They also actually offered to the men standardized enlistment agreements (Capitulationen) for several year periods.

This Reichswerbung system was initially intended to provide one third of the German infantry, with the residue coming from the Habsburg inner lands. Surplus recruits were to be sent to other military branches or even to the cavalry, which were otherwise excluded from Reichswerbung, as the higher social prestige and better wages of the "riders" attracted always many native volunteers. The monarchy's Italian, Netherlandish and Hungarian infantry regiments drew on local fellows, though it was obvious that units stationed in Italy were actually permitted to recruit in the Reich territory.

Till 1806 Austrian recruited in the former Holy Roman Empire territories (das Reich) or their hereditary lands as the Emperor, Kaiser Franz II, was also the Holy Roman Emperor. The Empire was formally dissolved on August 6, 1806 when the last Holy Roman Emperor Francis II (from 1804, Emperor Francis I of Austria) abdicated, following a military defeat by the French under Napoleon (see Treaty of Pressburg). Napoleon reorganised much of the empire into the Confederation of the Rhine, a French satellite. Franz, now only I, was forced to abandon the Reichswerbung and to issue new recruitment provisions.

It was so stated to create a sort of National Borders Enlistment system in order to allow the "catching" either of foreigners, either of former Austrian "Roman Empire" citizens, who wanted to serve under the "doubleheaded eagle" banners. This was called the Konfinen Werbung and substituted the former enrollment organization.

Now the recruits came from the national inscriptions to the levy lists (Assentierung), from volunteering and from the foreigners (Ausländer).

The old external recruitments were a dangerous, but often lucrative activity for all military personnel. The officers and men sent out to recruit not only received special bonuses, but were outside the routine surveillance of their superiors. The success of their mission depended on finding sufficient men and bringing them safely back to their garrison, with or without the consent of the local authorities. The easiest way was to recruit by establishing a post in an inn and parading through the streets in dashing uniforms, accompanied by attractive women, while bandsmen played trumpets and drums and others swigged mugs of beer and sang army songs. Officers generally stayed well out of the way of such action which was left to trusted NCOs, often with local knowledge, who would bring their recruits across the frontier to where their superiors were waiting, frequently in a coach hired from a nearby imperial city. The system remained the same, otherwise acting immediately at the borders of the Empire, not abroad, and attracting recruits with higher fees than regular enlisted men.

The Austrian Netherlands
The Netherlands had 17 provinces, seven of whom "... renouncing the Spanish Crown, and abjuring the Religion, generated a republic named Heretical Netherlands or United Provinces of Holland; this last name taken from their main province. Other 10 territories formed the Catholic Netherlands, or Flanders, a territory which was mainly Austrian, partially French and partially Dutch." This told an ancient Encyclopaedia.
Austria ruled on these provinces:
Brabant: divided into Dutch and Austrian. The Dutch Brabant had four Cantons: Bergue-op-Zoom, Breda, Herzogenbusch (Bois-le Duc), Maastricht, on the Liegeois, which was an important place on which Austria claimed some rights. The Austrian Brabant also had 4 cantons: Brusselles, the capital of all Austrian territories, Antwerpen, Mechelen or Malines and Leuween (Lovanium).
Austrian Flanders: divided into 3 parts (Quartiers): Gantz or Ghent, Bruges and Ypres. This territor had two ports at sea: Ostende and Nieuport.
County of Hannonia (Hainaut): with the capital Mons. County of Namur
County of Artesia (Artois): capital Arras County of Cambresis: capital Cambrai
County of Liege: Duchy of Limburg Duchy of Luxemburg
Austrian Netherlands lasted from 1713 till 1794 when were seized by France (1794-1815). This region comprised most of modern Belgium (except the officially lower Rhinesh Prince-Bishopric of Liège) and Luxembourg (including the homonymous present Belgian province).
The term more used to indicate the troops coming from those regions was: Wallonien regimenter. To many modern Walloons, Wallonia means "land of the valleys". This could be the real etymology of the word, as the part of Wallonia where Walloon language is traditionally spoken (the provinces of Liege, Namur and Luxembourg) is one of the hilliest region of Europe, and contrasts sharply with the flatness of Flanders.
Till 1794 there were recruited the personnel for regiments n. 9, 30, 38, 55, 58.

The Austrian Northern Italy
In Italy, Austria had recruited, above all, in Lombardy and Milan (former spanish Milanesado) the two historical italian regiments n. 44 (once Belgiojoso) and n. 48 (once Caprara). After Campoformido (1797) and for a short time, Austria recruited in Venetia (reg. n. 63 and n. 46) and Friuli (reg. n. 13). Obviously in 1809 with Eugène de Beauharnais ruling the Italian Kingdom and Bavaria ruling Trento, Austria did not have any italian district for recruitment.

The „Further Austria" (Vorder-Österreich)
Further Austria or Anterior Austria (German: Vorderösterreich, die Vorlande) was the collective name for the old possessions of the Habsburgs in Baden and Swabia (south-western Germany), Alsace and in Vorarlberg after the focus of the Habsburgs had moved to Austria.
Further Austria comprised the Sundgau (southern Alsace) and the Breisgau east of the Rhine (including Freiburg im Breisgau after 1368) and included some scattered territories throughout Swabia, the largest being the margravate of Burgau in the area of Augsburg and Ulm. Some territories in Vorarlberg that belonged to the Habsburgs were also considered part of Further Austria. In the Peace of Pressburg of 1805, Further Austria was entirely dissolved and the formerly Habsburg territories were assigned to Bavaria, Baden and Württemberg.
The austro-german soldiers from Breisgau, Ortenau and Nellesburg were always recruited in the IR 41.

Tirol and the Vorarlberg
Following defeat by Napoleon in 1805, Austria was forced to cede Tirol to the new Kingdom of Bavaria after the Peace of Pressburg.
Tirol as a part of Bavaria became a member of the Confederation of the Rhine in 1806. The Tiroleans rose up against the Bavarian authority and succeeded twice in defeating Bavarian and French troops trying to retake the country. Austria lost the war of the Fifth Coalition against France, and got even harsher terms in the Treaty of Schönbrunn in 1809. Often glorified as Tirol's national hero, Andreas Hofer, the leader of the Insurgency, was executed in 1810 in Mantua, having lost the final battle against the French and Bavarian forces. Tirol remained divided under Bavarian and Italian authority for another four years before being reunified and returned to Austria following the decisions at the Congress of Vienna in 1814.
Vorarlberg was a part of Further Austria, and parts of the area were ruled by the Counts Montfort of Vorarlberg. However, its recruitment mainly followed the same ways of the Tirolean units. It recruited for the IR 41 of Further Austria and for the Tirolean IR 46, which was disbanded in 1807 in order to raise the Jäger regiment, from which came the idea to form the Feldjäger battalions of 1809.

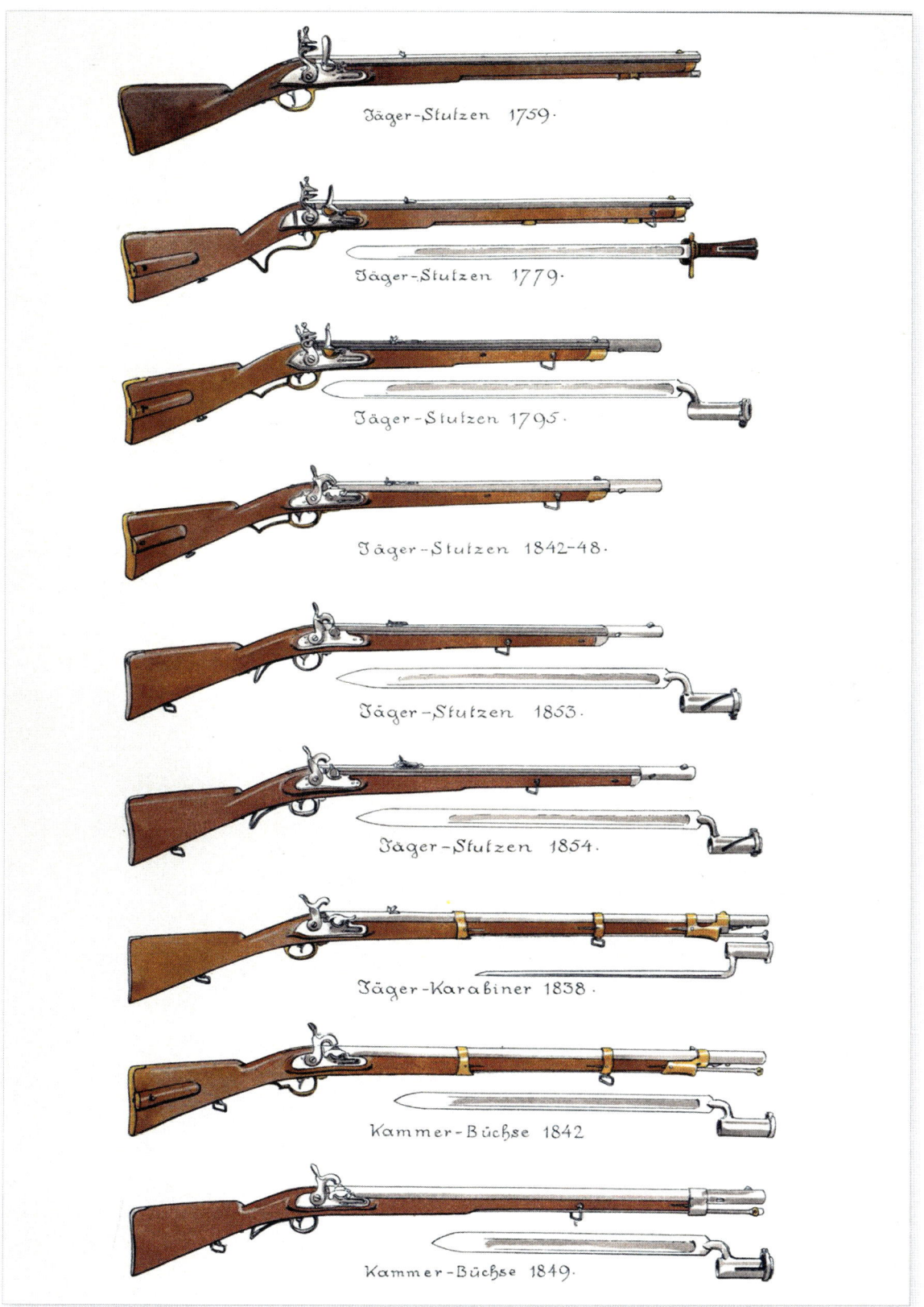

▲ Austrian rifle and weapons of jäger 1809. From Ottenfeld artwork

▲ Austrian cornet and drummer of jäger 1809. From Ottenfeld artwork

THE AUSTRIAN FELDJÄGER BATTALIONS

In 1792 four Freikorps units were on duty with the Austrian army, the Tyroler-Schärfschützen-Corps, D'Aspre-Feld-Jäger-Corps, Le Loup-Feld-Jäger-Corps and Wurmserische-Frei-Corps, each consisting of about 1,000 men organised into two battalions.
With the organisation of the Light Infantry battalions in 1798, the D'Aspre-Feld-Jäger was absorbed into this new system whilst the Le Loup and Wurmserische Corps continued to act independently. The Tyroler-Jäger, however, was reorganised into two battalions of six companies each and, although remaining a Freikorps unit, was brought into line with the organization of the line regiments. With the dissolution of the Light Infantry Battalions in 1801, a regular jäger regiment was formed from the cadre of troops existing and titled the "Tyroler-Jäger-Regiment", and established with three battalions each of six companies organised in the same manner as the line infantry fusiliers. The majority of the soldiers already had experience working as Jägers with the Tyroler- Schärfschützen- Korp and Le Loup-Feld-Jäger and the balance of recruits were taken from volunteers of regiment n. 46, whose recruitment area was in the Tyrol. From the beginning the Jägers operated as independent battalions, assigned to the various brigades, as required, and soon proved their worth in the field. [1] In 1805 the Regiment was officially taken into the line, given the number 64 and exclusive recruitment in Tirol and in 1808 seven new battalion were formed around experienced officers and N.C.O.s promoted from the existing battalions from recruits found in the Tirol, and skilled marksmen taken from other infantry regiments and the various estates throughout the Bohemian, Galician and Moravian regions, virtually denuding the country of skilled gamekeepers and hunters, as one prominent landowner of the day complained. An eleventh battalion was raised in 1809. However, in order to fill the companies to full strength, only nine battalions took the field that year and in 1810 the battalions were cut back to a single division each of two companies plus a depot company. In 1812 moves were again made to bring the Jäger battalions up to full strength and nine full battalions, each with six companies of full 120 jäger strength, were fielded for the 1813 campaign and by the end of 1814 three new battalions, bringing the Regiment up to twelve full battalions, had been raised.

The force in peacetime of one of the 9 Jäger-divisionen was ruled by the Hofkriegsrat Anordnung of August 15, 1808, with the Patrouilleführer introduction of November 16, 1808 and the Ärzte (Medical) organization of August 14, 1811.

Staff	Jäger division		
1	Stabsoffizier as Commander	1	Ober-Arzt
2	Unter-Arzt	2	Fourieren
1	Fourierschützen	6	total

	Jäger division (two companies)		
2	Hauptmann	or 2	Capitan-Lieutenant
2	Oberlieutenant	4	Unterlieutenant
4	Oberjäger	16	Unterjäger
20	Patrouilleführern	2	Fourierschützen
4	Trompetern	2	Zimmerleuten
6	Privatdiener	240	Gemeinen Jäger
6	Gemeinen Jäger zu Privatdiensten	282	Total
		260	of which, firearms

The Jäger divisions had to form a battalion in war-time. In the case of a war they prewieved these upgrades:

	Jäger division companies (each)		
4	Unterjäger	10	Patrouilleführer
1	Zimmermann	10	Jäger (ober and unter ?)

On November 16, 1808, the Hofkriegsrat disposed: [2]
"The current set up and dislocation of the Jäger divisions and the management of their Reserve, proves itself the need that, currently being these divisions already six and afoot, just more compagnien must divide themselves by serving detachments. So a fast recruitment of the original battalion will be possibly prepared and brilliantly facilitated, without causing an important expenditure...."

Therefore, we dispose that, each of the existing 6 Jäger divisions, from December 1st, must organize itself, under the command of their current field officers, into a battalion of 6 companies, and that they have to be considered and to be treated as Cadres for the raising of the whole battalion.

The complete peacetime strength of such battalion of 6 companies it will be of 860 men:

Staff	Jäger battalion		
1	Stabsoffizier as Commander	1	Ober-Arzt
1	Bataillons-Adjutanten	5	Unter-Ärzten
4	Fourieren	1	Fourierschützen
1	Privatdiener	14	total
	Jäger battalion's company		
1	Hauptmann or Capitan-Lieutenant		
1	Oberlieutenant	2	Unterlieutenant
2	Oberjäger	8	Unterjäger
10	Patrouilleführern	1	Fourierschützen
2	Trompetern	1	Zimmerleuten
3	Privatdiener	110	Gemeinen Jäger
		141	**Total in peacetime**
	Jäger battalion	6	companies
6	Hauptmann or Capitan-Lieutenant		
6	Oberlieutenant	12	Unterlieutenant
12	Oberjäger	48	Unterjäger
60	Patrouilleführern	6	Fourierschützen
12	Trompetern	6	Zimmerleuten
18	Privatdiener	660	Gemeinen Jäger
860	Total with Staff	846	lesser Total

The provisional strength of the companies and their organisation was calculated only according to the actual effectiveness of every division, after which would had lacked approximately 50-60 men for every company. A Jäger battalion had to be commanded by a Major Oberstlieutenant or a Colonel, the company by a captain or by a Capitänlieutenant. [3] Companies' platoons were led by an Oberleutnant (o an Unterleutnant and eventually by an Oberjäger).

Initially the six companies of the same battalion had different garrisons, [4] one for each company, but, early in 1809 also the Jäger battalions raised their Depots. Early in 1809 it had also the Stabstrompeter (Staff trumpet). In wartimes a subaltern officer was appointed as Proviantmeister of the battalion; he had the task to command the Train and the transports director (Wagenmeister), the servants, the Train watching etc. In wartimes came also one Unterjäger as transports director, one Profos and one ordered gunsmith (Büchsenmacher).

The recruitments of the officers took place between the pupils of the Neustadt Military Academy or good NCOs and Cadetten. The emperor appointed the Staff officers, the Hofkriegsrath appointed the High officers.

The complements came from the inscriptions to the levy lists (Assentierung) by the oldest pupils of the regiment's education houses (Regimentserziehungshäuser), by voluntary enrollment and by the way of the regular conscription positions.

Jäger battalions had to accept either lawful Austrian citizens (Inlander), either foreigners, with the residents having to be free from duty or coming from the regiment dismissed veterans, whilst it was necessary to have some trustworthiness about foreigners.

If the Jäger battalions could not fully cover the stated numbers for peacetime by own recruitment, they yearly became complete by conscription (Konskription) of appropriate people. First these "second hand" recruits were tested by the Jägers for four weeks; then the unsuitable ones, to Jäger duty, were checked by an official commission of the general command and without its authorization they were sent back to their pertaining regiments, by which they had been served.

Every Jäger division, which in wartimes had to form a whole battalion, had to have a Reserve division (two companies of Cadres). The Reserves (Cadres) could enroll even common citizens skilled in hunting, young hunters and those who were able to act as fine shooters, snipers, proven hunters serving local Lords, as also Schützen, who already exhibited their attachment to the Army. In the case those kind of fellows would have already enrolled for infantry Reserve, they had to be transferred directly into the Jäger Reserve.

Active military service lasted 10 years, after which began the Reserve duty (Reservedienstpflicht) till the age of 40.

▲ Jager 1798-1805. From Ottenfeld artwork

At the end of his military Duty time the soldiers could enter a futher enrollment or „Capitulation" for other 6-10 years and renew once again also this. The renewing enlistment men or Capitulanten enjoyed different promotions. In example retired soldiers had a farewell award, while badly dismissed men had a "Laufpass" (a jilting card).

The minimal height for a Jäger was 163 cm, but when the men lacked, they accepted also 160 cm men.

The common recruitment fee for the regular recruits amounted to 3 fl., [5] while the fee for the Konfinen recruits was 30-40 fl., for the Foreigners [6] it was 10 fl., for voluntary recruits, free from military Duty (Konskriptionsbefreite) was 15 fl.

Jäger gradually changed some items of the old uniforms, maintaining their original (Austrian) dark blue- grey (Hechtgrau) coats. The helmet was abandoned for the corsican hut, with a small green Plume and attached bands which closed, under the chin, with a small leather button; the hat plate, shaped as an hearth, had in the middle the battalion number. The prescribed gaiters, however still not available, had 18-14 buttons. Practically Jäger wore knee-long boots, as officers did, and obtained officially gaiters only in 1818. Also the little Plume was soon again abolished. The Capitulanten, also called Veterans, since July 11, 1807, at the moment of the new enlistment, received a small shield as award, with the word "Veteranis" overwritten, which was brought on the left chest side as a pin.

NCOs and the best Jäger (in the third rank) were armed with the short rifle (Jägerstutzen model 1795), for sniping fire, the first and second ranks had the Jägerkarabiner model 1807, which granted a less sharp fire volley. The short rifle had a barrel of 67 cm (same length of the bayonet) in malleable iron with a caliber of 13,7 mm. In campaign the NCOs had 30 ball-cartridges, Jäger with carbine 60 and Jäger with Stutzen 100;
each had 3-5 flintstones.

Jäger battalions moved in "Mass" formation. The Mass was useful to move a battalion so rapidly as possible from a place, to pivot it in new directions and to serve as a marching formation during the battles.

AUSTRIAN FELD-JÄGER BATTALIONS IN 1809

Feldjägerbataillon n. 1 – the "Lutz Jägers"

Commander: Major-Oberstleutnant Carl Lutz Recruitment: Bohemia

depot: Brüx (town Most, in northern Bohemia) then at Josefstadt (Bohemia)– 1 Reserve company (Kader) with Brig. Rosenhayn in Horaschdowitz (Horažďovice, Bohemia), Div. Richter under Riesch and Loudon in Bohemia.

- before Aspern: in January Brig. Count Carl Crenneville (Klattau) – Div. FML Carl von Hennequin (Prague) – deployed at Tauš (today Domažlice) at the bohemian border watching the road to Regensburg (Ratisbon in Bavaria). Later Brig. Winzingerode, light Div. [7] Fresnel, I Corps when it had a strength of 1010 men; April 8, Brig. Ignaz Hardegg, Div. Fresnel, I Corps while the 5th company remained in northern Bohemia under Am-Ende (Theresienstadt) to watch the Saxony border.[8]

It began the "Freedom for Europe" Archduke Charles' campaign. April 19 again with Brig. Winzingerode, light Div. Fresnel. During the retreat towards Bohemia was with rearguard brigade Nostitz; then the 3rd company covered the retreat fighting at Kehlheim (April 23). On April 28 the battalion was at Waldmünchen again under brigade Winzingerode. On May 12, it began the advance towards the Marchfeld (Aspern and Wagram) with the vanguard Div. of FML Klenau, reaching Lang-Enzersdorf.

- at Aspern: Brig. Ignaz Hardegg, Div. Klenau, avant-garde IV Corps: vanguard clash against the French bridgehead in front of Aderklaa. At Aspern was in the vanguard of the 4th and 5th columns,

led by Hardegg distinguishing in the Esslingen battle (lost 234 men).

- between Aspern and Wagram: with the avant-garde Nordmann (left Wing), then under Vécsey and after under Frelich. Von Lutz promoted to Colonel. On June 1st, the battalion had 5 companies with 457 men and 8 officers.
- at Wagram: Brig. Frelich, Div. Nordmann, I Corps attacked by the French brigade Conroux.
- after Wagram: during the retreat Nordmann chose castle Sachsengang as strongpoint. The 2nd, 3rd and 4th companies were taken prisoners, while the 1st and the 6th continued to fight (captain Count von Inzaghi). These two companies with the remnants of the 7th Jäger battalions were now under Radetzky rearguard of the IV Corps. From July 11 till 15 the "combined" battalion withdrew through Groß-Niemschitz, Austerlitz, Prossnitz till Nesamislitz where was reached by a division of the 8th Jäger, officially forming the "kombiniert Jäger" battalion under command of the Oberstleutnant Mumb (8th Jäger). On December 1809 under brigade Frelich, Div. Ulm.

Feldjägerbataillon n. 2 – "Arno" Jägers

Commander: Major-Oberstleutnant Baron Carl Schneider von Arno [9] Recruitment: Bohemia.

Depot: Freistadt in Muhlviertel (Upper Austria) near the Bavarian border - 1 Reserve company (Kader) with Brig. Rosenhayn in Horaschdowitz (Horažďovice, Bohemia), Div. Richter, (another) 1 Reserve company with Brig. Szénassy in Jaromirz under Riesch and Loudon.

- before Aspern: it was at Landskron (Lanškroun in the Pardubitz region, eastern Bohemia) under Brig. GM Wenzel Buresch von Greifenbach at Chrudim and under Prague Div. FML Thomas von Brady. Later brigade Hardegg, avant-garde Division Fresnel von Hennequin, I Corps Bellegarde, when fought at Ursensollen (April 14) and distinguished itself by seizing the citadel of Berching. Then was with Brig. Nostitz, Div. Fresnel, I Corps and later marched to Bohemia with avant-garde brigade baron Wintzingerode- Ohmfeld, 2nd Column FML Bellegarde.
- at Aspern: Brig. Winzingerode, Div. Fresnel, 2nd Column FML Bellegarde; involved in the frontal assault against the village of Aspern, when Wacquant brigade occupied the village, while Winzingerode seized the Auen houses, behind it. After the battle, Bellegarde did write an honorary mention for the commander Schneider, Hauptmann Brand and lieutenant Hartlieb. A golden medal for bravery was awarded by Oberjäger Finkenberger and Unterjäger Schasser, who drone themselves in middle of the French Guard units, attacking a captain of the enemy army. After then was with the Brig. Stutterheim, Div. Fresnel, I Corps and also avant-garde Hardegg.
- between Aspern and Wagram: service at the Higher Command (Hauptquartier).
- at Wagram: fought at Aderklaa under brigade Stutterheim, Division Fresnel, I Corps Bellegarde and was in the same unit till the battle of Znaim, where it was in the second line between Leschna and Kukrowitz.
- after Wagram: with Div. Frimont.

Feldjägerbataillon n. 3 – "Baroni" Jägers
Commander: Major-Oberstleutnant Daniele Baroni-Cavalcabò [10] Recruitment: Bohemia.
Depot: had to be at Eferding (Upper Austria), near the Bavarian border, but actually it was raised at Theresienstadt (today Terezin) under Oberleutnant Plisnier (coomander of the Depot company). The Kader company had 2 officers, 1 Oberjäger, 6 Unterjägern, 1 Unterarzt, 1 Fourierschütz, 1 Trompeter, 1 Zimmermann, 60 men, 1 Privatdiener (total of 74 men). The battalion's Train had 7 light wagons (Leiterwagen[11] with 7 drivers – Knechte – and 14 train horses) and 12 pack horse with related drivers. It had also a Marketender or supplies seller. [12] - 1 Reserve company (Kader) with Brig. Novak in Jungbunzlau (today Mladá Boleslav in central Bohemia), Div Schönthal under Riesch and Loudon.

- before Aspern: it was at Teschen (Bohemia) under Brig. GM baron Carl Am-Ende at Leitmeritz (Div. FML baron Josef von Ulm – Prague). Later Brig. Winzingerode, Div. Fresnel, I Corps – marched from Teschen on February 25 throug Aussig, Teplitz reaching the new quarters at Postelberg (current Postoloprty-Czech Rep.)on February 28. Later avant-garde Winzingerode, Div. Vogelsang, I Corps with which "invaded" Bavaria (April 10); April 14, five hours of fire combat at Ursensollen (Bavaria); lost 144 men. Then the Retreat to Bohemia, with the "now" Rearguard-division Fresnel (April 29 at Trasenau near Taus); actual strength 805 men (595 Jäger). On May 12 brigade Nostitz, Division Vogelsang of I Corps and then attached to brigade Weissenwolf (V Corps Reuss- Plauen) with the task to watch Danube banks at Stöckerau. Combats at Lang-Enzersdorf and Schwarzelaken-Au.
- at Aspern: was in the Brig. Weissenwolf, autonomous, V Corps. Fought at Aspern-Essling. On June 16 it had 796 men (672 Jäger).
- at Wagram: not fought the battle, was in the Brig. Klebelsberg, autonomous, V Corps then Rearguard Brig. Klebelsberg, Div. Weissenwolff, V Corps. July 10, combat at Schöngrabern then battle of Znaim where it was on the Pöltenberg under brigade Winzian, V Corps.
- after Wagram: Brig. Klebelsberg, autonomous, V Corps then in Hungary with Div. Schustekh. Later again with the brigade Bianchi and, at the year's end, under division Merville at the Bavarian border where it was reduced to two divisions.

Feldjägerbataillon n. 4 – "Piombazzi" Jägers
Commander: Major-Oberstleutnant Jakob Anton (Giacomo Antonio) Piombazzi [13]
Recruitment: Bohemia.
Depot: Gmunden in the Traunviertel, south of Linz.

- before Aspern: it was at Prachatitz (Brig. GM Johann von Schöntal at Budweis – Div. FML baron Josef von Ulm – Prague). Later Brig. Nostitz, Div. Fresnel, I Corps then brigade Hardegg, avant-garde Division Fresnel von Hennequin, I Corps Bellegarde, then Brig. Radetztky, Avantgarde, I Corps.

- between Aspern and Wagram: attached to Oberstleutnant Baron Scheibler (Streifkorps) [14]. During the battle of Aspern the Oberleutnant Rueber was assigned to the watch the entrenchments on Tabor island, at the confluence of river Enns into Danube, near Mauthausen. In the night of July 5 he made three assaults against the French-Bavarian detachments. For this assault Rueber was awarded with MTO Cross in 1810.
- at Wagram: Brig. Klebelsberg, autonomous, V Corps then brigade Count Klebelsberg, Division Weissenwolf, V Corps Reuss- Plauen. The battalion had rearguard tasks during the retreat and on July 9 fought at Schöngrabern were Piombazzi maintained the link with the IV Corps, with continuous and stressing struggles against the French patrols, being finally able to gather with the rest of the army.
- after Wagram: I Corps.

Feldjägerbataillon n. 5 – "Suden" Jägers
Commander: Major-Oberstleutnant Baron Georg Suden Recruitment: Moravia.
Depot: Tepl (current Teplá in western Bohemia, bavarian Border) - 1 Reserve company with Brig. Pietsch in Troppau, Div. St.Julien under Argenteau.
- before Aspern: was at Butschowitz (Brig. GM Timothäus von Kérékes at Brünn, Div. FML marquis Franz Lusignan, Brünn). Later Brig. Crenneville, Div. Klenau, II Corps then brigade Baron Peter Vécsey, 3rd column – I Reserve Corps prince Liechtenstein, detached from IV Corps, at Teugen-Hausen (Thann); at Abensberg was in the Right Wing brigade Vécsey, I Reserve Corps prince Liechtenstein. Fought at Eckmühl in the extreme right wing under Peter Vécsey autonomous brigade. Later Brig. Radivojevich, autonomous, III Corps.
Later it was assigned to the 1st Column (Marquis Sommariva) of the Corps Kolowrath and it was present at the Urfahr-Linz battle (May 17) occupying the Pöstlingberg hills near Linz. Partially the battalion was also with the detachment oberst Ignaz von Leuthner (Div. Sommariva). It was still employed in patrol and watch operations (Streif-commandos).
- at Wagram: fought at the clash of Altendorf (July 5) then followed the Sommariva's retreat in Bohemia.

Feldjägerbataillon n. 6 – "Zaborsky" Jägers
Major-Oberstleutnant Emerich Zaborsky de Zabora Recruitment: Moravia.
Depot: Mährisch-Neustadt (today Uničov in eastern Moravia at the Silesian border) - 1 Reserve company Brig. Pietsch in Troppau, Div. St Julien under Argenteau.
- before Aspern: was at Neustadt (Moravia) (Brig. GM Nikolaus von Kayser, Olmütz – Div. FML Count Franz St.Julien, Olmütz). Later Brig. Crenneville, Div. Klenau, II Corps. Brigade Baron Peter Vécsey, 3rd column – I Reserve Corps prince Liechtenstein, detached from IV Corps, at Teugen-Hausen (Thann); at Abensberg was in the Right Wing brigade Vécsey, I Reserve Corps prince Liechtenstein. Fought at Eckmühl in the extreme right wing under Peter Vécsey autonomous brigade. Then with Brig. Radetzky, detached, IV Corps then Brig. Crenneville, autonomous, III Corps and finally Brig. Radetzky, autonomous, V Corps.
- between Aspern and Wagram: assigned to the Kollowrath Corps in Bohemia on May 17 fought at Urfahr-Linz in the 2nd (main) Column of Vukassovich seizing the village of Katzbach and having comtas there, at Dornach and Gallneukirchen. Then he continued to perform its "small war" in the area between Neumarkt and Linz.
- at Wagram: part of the battalion reached the brigade Stutterheim, Division Fresnel, I Corps Bellegarde, during the battle, reinforcing the battered 2nd Jäger battalion.

Feldjägerbataillon n. 7 – "Steffanini" Jägers
Commander: Oberstleutnant Joseph (Giuseppe) Steffanini Count di Monte Airone then Oberst Baron Ludwig Steinmetz
Recruitment: Upper and Lower Austria – Salzburg - Vienna.
Depot: Mistelbach then Lietzen. It had 2 Reserve companies under Brig. Ulbrecht in Krems, Div. Anton Mittrowsky under O'Reilly's command.
- before Aspern: was at Herzogenburg (Brig. GM Josef von Mayer, St.Polten – Div. FML Fürst Franz Rosemberg-Orsini, Vienna). Later Brig. Peter Vécsey, Div. Klenau, II Corps then under Klenau direct command, avant-garde Div. Klenau, II Corps Carl Kolowrat-Krakowsky. In this period the battalion was the "link" between the I and II Corps and fought against a French detachment at Hirschau (April 11-12). With brigade Crenneville it was detached at Hemau near Ratisbon, avant-garde Div. Klenau, II Corps Carl Kolowrat-Krakowsky. Later was with Brig. P. Vécsey, autonomous, II Corps, and finally marched in Bohemia with 3rd Column - FML prince Hohenzollern, avant-garde brigade Vécsey.
- at Aspern: 3rd Column - FML prince Hohenzollern, avant-garde brigade Vécsey then Brig. Mayer, avant-garde II Corps. Later Brig. Peter Vécsey, autonomous, II Corps.
- between Aspern and Wagram: Brig. Vécsey, avant-garde Nordmann.
- at Wagram: Left Wing avant-garde brigade Frelich (Fröhlich), Division Nordmann.

Feldjägerbataillon n. 8 – the "Achter" or "Deutsche" Jägers
Commander: Oberstleutnant Hieronymus Mumb
Recruitment: provinces of the German Austria then Inner Austria.
Depot: Wels. 1 Reserve company (Kader) under Brig. Sinzendorf in Linz, Div. Anton Mittrowsky under O'Reilly.
- before Aspern: was at Wels (Brig. GM Carl Dollmayer von Provenchères, Wels – Div. FML baron Josef von Stipsicz, Linz). Later Brig. Peter Vécsey, Div. Klenau, II Corps then Brigade comte Carl Crenneville, avant-garde Div. Klenau, II Corps Carl Kolowrat-Krakowsky; detached at Hemau, had a small clash near Ratisbon (April 23) returning later to the Brig. Vécsey, again autonomous, II Corps. After the Archduke Charles retreat it destroyed the Nittenau bridge to cover the withdrawal and finally marched to Bohemia with 3rd Column - FML prince Hohenzollern, avant-garde brigade Vécsey.
- at Aspern: 3rd Column - FML prince Hohenzollern, avant-garde brigade Vécsey (right wing), lost 300 men in the battle. Then was with the Brig. Mayer, avant-garde, II Corps and also returned again to Brig. P. Vécsey, autonomous, II Corps.
- at Wagram: fought with Div. Siegenthal, brigade Hardegg, II Corps Hohenzollern.
- after Wagram: II Corps.

Feldjägerbataillon n. 9 – "Kärnten" or "Göldling" Jägers
Commander: Major-Oberstleutnant Baron Carl Göldlin von Tieffenau [15] Recruitment: (Carinthia, Styria) Inner Austria.
Depot: Villach (Upper Carinthia).
- before Aspern: was at St.Veit (in Krain) (Brig. GM Anton von Gajoli, Klagenfurt – Div. FML marquis Friedrich von Bellegarde, Graz. Later Brig. Wetzl, Div. Albert Gyulai, then Frimont, VIII Corps later Brig. Wetzl, Div. Frimont, VIII Corps. Attached to the Corps Chasteler in the Brig. Fenner and in detail:
- 3 comp. Brig. Buol - Chasteler comp. Brig. Fenner - Chasteler
- 3 comp. Brig. Marschal - Chasteler later 1 comp. with Taxis

Its Depot company was with the Brig. Hardegg (detached). On April 23 the commander, Oberstlieutnant Baron Göldin, marched towards Zambano and attacked general Fontanelli at Bosco di Velo, together with the Tiroler Landsturm. The day after two companies fought near Murazzo. On April 28 the battalion was split, 3 companies were on the Austrian left wing in South Tirol, the other on the right wing near Innsbruck; the remaining two companies were in Reserve. Half company was also involved in the heroic defense of pass Strub, with its commander Göldlin against the Bavarians of Division Wrede.
- between Aspern and Wagram: 2nd, 3rd, 5th and part of the 6th comp. with the Brig. Buol in Tirol. Some detachments were also involved in the May battle of Bergisel (Innsbruck), and then in the clashes at Trient, Kufstein, Andorf and Küffersfeld. Later in May

(29) they covered, under general Buol, the Chasteler retreat in the Upper Inn valley. The company of Trient also retreated up to Carinthia and joined the Archduke John Army. On June 17, near Papa, it gathered itself with the Inner Austria army. That company had also been attacked at Klagenfurt (June 6) and went, with its army, to Pressburg, and then to the Marchfeld. 1 Detachment was with Brig. Lutz, Div. Jellachich, Armée of Innerösterreich (army of Inner Austria) then to the Staff of the Armée of Innerösterreich. The Depot-company fought at Graz and Fürstenfeld and in the battle of Raab. At Raab the company was in the brigade Legisfeld, division Jellacich while one detachment was the Reserve brigade Ettingshausen, div. Davidovich.
- at Wagram: 2nd column brigade Eckhardt, Div. Frimont, army of Inner Austria – Archduke John.
- after Wagram: Brig. Buol (autonomous).

Notes:
Some Jäger companies, listed in the 1809 situations and army lists, were not part of the Feldjäger corps. Their real identity or origin is not known:
- between Aspern and Wagram: 2 Jäger companies with Div. Sommariva.
- at Aspern: the Jäger company of the 2nd column.
- after Wagram: 2 comp. from Linz.

Some quoted Jägers were companies of volunteers as the Salzburger Jäger (see also Volunteers):
- before Aspern: Corps Chasteler - with brigades Buol – Fenner – Marschal - Leiningen and Seppenburg.
- between Aspern and Wagram: the 9th Bat. may be confused with the Salzburger Jäger operating in the same territory.
- at Wagram: the "Salzburger" were with Brig. Eckhart, Div. Frimont, Armée of. Innerösterreich.
- after Wagram: 1 comp. was left in Tirol.

As for other campaigning Jäger: Arader, Carneville, Archduke John (Salzburger), Lobkowitz, Niederösterreicher, Prager, Schlegenbergische (Wiener), Siebenbürgische, Thurnsche, Triester, Wattrich (1st Bn. Legion Archduke Charles), see under Landwehr and Volunteers units.

Jäger Organisation between 1808 and 1815

Note that IR 64 (Tiroler Jäger Rgt.) was disbanded in 1808 and nine new divisions (then batallions) were raised, followed by three more in 1813 (see table).

JÄGER BATTALIONS 1808/1815

N°	Raised	Commanding officer	District	Garrisons
1	1808	1808 Oberstleutnant. C. Lutz 1813 Major F. von Plisnier 1814 Major J. von Penz	Bohemia	1809 Brüx 1814 Jablunka 1815 Salzburg
2	1808	1808 Major Freiherr C. Schneider von Arno 1813 Major Freiherr J. Reicht	Bohemia	1809 Freistadt 1810 Kloster Schlegel 1811 Mauthausen 1812 Linz 1815 Freistadt
3	1808	1808 Major Barone Daniele Baroni-Cavalcabò	Bohemia	1808 Tetschen 1809 Efferding 1812 Wels 1814 Kirchberg a.d. Mosel 1815 Efferding
4	1808	1808 Oberstleutnant. Conte M. Piombazzi 1812 Oberstleutnant. Chevalier C. von Becke	Bohemia	1809 Gmunden 1811 Busk 1812 Neutitschein 1815 Plan
5	1808	1808 Major Freiherr G. von Suden 1812 Major Count F. Hartopp 1812 Major Count J. Sickingen-Hohenburg	Moravia	1808 Butschowitz 1809 Tepl 1810 Plan 1811 Wieliczka 1815 Tetschen
6	1808	1808 Oberstleutnant E. Zaborsky de Zabora 1813 Major Freiherr L. von Mareschall	Moravia	1808 Mährisch-Neustadt 1810 Aussig 1811 Kalsching 1812 Gabel 1815 Nachod
7	1808	1808 Oberst Joseph von Steffanini 1809 Major Freiherr L. von Steinmetz 1810 Oberst J. von Steffanini 1812 Oberst Freiherr C. Veyder von Malberg 1814 Major W. Weikersreutter 1815 Major D. von Saintenoy	Salzburg, Upper and Lower Austria	1809 Mistelsbach 1809 Lietzen 1810 Leoben 1811 Krems 1814 Chiavenna 1815 Leoben
8	1808	1808 Oberstleutnant H. Mumb 1813 Major H. Fletté von Flettenfeld	Inner Austria	1808 Wels 1810 St Veit 1812 Leoben 1815 Masseveaux
9	1808	1808 Oberst Freiherr C. Göldlin von Tieffenau 1814 (interim)Hauptmann E. de Gobiery 1815 Major Freiherr F. Werdt von Teuffen	Inner Austria	1808 St Veit 1809 Villach 1810 Cilli 1814 Treviso 1815 Gorizia

1813 Battalions

N°	Raised	Commanding officer	District	Garrisons
10	1813	1813 Major Cavaliere V. Casassa di Valmonte	Inner Austria	1814 Cremona 1815 Roanne
11	1813	1813 Major Freiherr F. von Ensch	Inner Austria, Salzburg, Upper and Lower Austria	1814 Lombardy 1815 Alsace (France)
12	1813	1813 Major Freiherr E. Beelen de Bertholff	Galicia Moravia	1815 Mährisch-Schönberg

Notes:

[1] The Jäger Batallions (as the Tiroler Jäger Regiment) were more than "simple light troops". Until the end of the monarchy the Jäger units were more notable or respectable than the normal infantry regiments. They all were trained to fight in closed as well as in open formation. Additionally they had no simple muskets but rifles and much more shooting exercise than the infantry. Because of all that the recruitment selection was much more severe than the recruitment of infantry men. Courtesy of Leopold Kudma (Napoleon Series).

[2] Sittig Heinrich (lieutenant.), Geschichte des k. w. k. Feldjäger-bataillons nr. 1. 1808-1908, gebrüder Stiepel, 1908.

[3] This military rank had the following origin: with the birth of the infantry Regiments, Owners and field officers were formerly also proprietors of a company; while the "Capitäns" were appointed for all other companies of the regiment, the "Capitänlieutenanten" got the command of the first Company, the Owner's one; then there were not Lieutenants (and not yet "Ober" lieutenants) who could differentiate the higher officers. With the Captains they became the "chief people" or "Hauptleute", and the word Capitänlieutenant became, in the course of the time, a real military rank, while originally belonging only to a genering meaning of subaltern officer.

[4] This was, for example, the peacetime quarters for the companies of the 1st Jäger battalion: Staff and 1st company Taus, 2nd comp. Klentsch, 3rd comp. Medaken, 4th comp. Ronsperg, 5th comp. Heiligenkreuz, 6th comp. Holtau.

[5] In Austria there were 4 monetary systems. The main one had the Gulden (Reichsgulden) or forint (Fl. or Florin in latin; German: or Hungarian: forint) as currency of the Austrian Empire since 1754 (till 1892 when it was replaced by the Krone as part of the introduction of the gold standard). In Austria, the Gulden was initially divided into 60 Kreuzer (a kreuzer, Kr., was 4 pfennig), and in Hungary, the forint was divided into 100 hungarian Pfennige (or 60 krajczár). In Galicia there was the Polnischen (polish) Gulden, 80 of which made the Cöllnische Mark in fine silver; in the italian territories Austria had the Lire (each of 20 Soldi, each Soldo = 12 Denari). The home Exchange rates of 1812 were: 1 Gulden = 5 Lire (1 Lira = 12 Kreuzer). Joseph C. Bisinger, General-Statistik des österreichischen Kaiserthumes: ein Versuch, Verlag Geistinger, 1807.

[6] The other way for a foreigner (Ausländer) to serve the Austrian army was to enter the army during his (maybe holiday) stay in one of the Austrian countries. These two ways existed for a foreigner to enter the Austrian army. So Ausländer-Werbung (recruitment of foreigners) consisted of the "Konfinen-Werbung" (Konfinen recruitment) and of the recruitment of Ausländer within the Austrian empire. Courtesy of Leopold Kudma

[7] Light Divisions were units formed by Jäger, Volunteers and light cavalry, which had mainly vanguard or rearguard tasks.

[8] Company Hauptmann von Wechs, Brigade Am-Ende (then Radivojevich). May 25, clash at Peterwalde. In June Am-Ende was reached by the Brunswick volunteers (duke of Brunswick-Oels Corps) and fought a clash at Wilsdruff (June 12). The 5th company was attached to the Brunswick Corps under FML Kienmayer (combat of Gefrees on June 8).

[9] Freiherr Carl Schneider in 1799 was a Fähnrich of the Italian 4th Light infantry battalion Bach (Corps Klenau). When the "Viva Maria" insurrection outbroke in Tuscany (Arezzo and Cortona), the insurgents asked the Austrian Command to have an Officer, who could led the peasants in battle. Klenau proposed Schneider and FZM Kray gave his approval. On June 16 the young Officer reached Arezzo and began to organize his troops. He raised a "division" of 6000 trained rebels in a mass of 30000 armed peasants and was helped by the former florentine general InghiramI He occupied Florence, Siena and Livorno clearing all the French weak garrisons. In August he captured Perugia and then marched against the Roman territory. In November he was openly praised by general Fröhlich for his conduct (also Suvorov mentioned him as an example). The man who actually had led up to 45000 insurgents, 4000 of which completely equipped, 1200 trained cavalrymen and an artillery battalion, organized with captured guns, returned to his battalion at Sarzana. The Emperor awarded him with the promotion to Capitän-Leutnant and granted him the use of the **von Arno** suffix, in order to remember the main Tuscany's river (officially this from 1819). Later he was also awarded with the Commander Cross of the Tuscany's Order of St.Joseph.

[10] Promoted Lieutenant-Colonel on May 22, 1809.

[11] A light wagon or wooden handcart was a wooden, biaxial vehicle (4 wheeled) with train pole and with wooden poles cover sides. The standings provided for the 3rd battalion can be actually referred to all other Jäger battalions. Karl Kandelsdorfer, Geschichte des K.u.k. Feld-jäger-bataillons Nr. 3 dermal Feld-bataillon Nr. 13 der Tiroler Kaiser-jäger, E. Vergani & comp., 1899.

[12] Like a sutler or victualer, but not a civilian merchant, rather a military supplier who sold provisions to army in field, in camp or in quarters.

[13] Some sources quoted Marco (Markus) Ritter von Piombazzi from Arco (Trentino). Count from 1812.

[14] Oberstleutnant Scheibler of the Chevaulegers Vincent led a special corps of 600 men with order to harass the Bavarians along the Danube. In the 1809 campaign (like in 1813), in spite of the war shortness, they were created special Streifkörper or large columns (detachment) of fast moving units, for the guidance of the "small war" against the flanks and the rear line of communications of the enemies. The rapid striking Streifkorps, so, was formed almost completely by army detachment, not volunteers or territorial units.

[15] Baron Göldlin von Tiffenau led the stubborn defense of the pass Strub (May 11), with an half Jäger company, a company of the infantry n. 45 De Vaux and 4 companies of the Tiroler Landsturm, against 3000 (?) Bavarians supported by 4 guns of 12 pdrs. and howitzers. Göldlin received the MTO Knight Cross in 1810 for that episode.

▲ Austrian jäger 1809. From Ottenfeld artwork

AUSTRIAN ORDER OF BATTLE JAN. 1809

Campaign Army		
Gorpi	Divisioni	Brigate
Austria-Salisburgo (Liechtenstein)	1. Wiener (Rosenberg-Orsini) 2. Wiener (von Vincent) 3. Wiener Kavallerie (O Reilly) Wiener Platz (Maximilian Este) Niederoesterreich (Kottulinsky) Linz (Stipsicz)	Vienna - St Polten Vienna - Vienna - Jetzeldorf (technische truppen) Bianchi - von Riese Linz - SalzburgWels
Inner Austria (von Kerpen)	Styrian 1. Graz (Gyulai) Radkersburg (Knezevic)	Graz Platz Graz (Berelat - Bellegarde) - Klagenfurt Laibach - Triest
Moravia and Silesia (Ferdinand Carl)	Troppau (Sommariva) Olmutz (Waldsee) 1. Brunn (Kosarczow) 2. Brunn (Lusignan) Kremsier (Hessen-Homburg) Olmutz (Rouvroy)	Troppau (Bieber - Liechtenstein) Olmutz - Teschen Brunn (Prochaska) Brunn (kérékes) - Znaym (Grill) Kremsier - Hradish Kavallerie (technische truppen)
Galizia-Lodomeria (Bellegarde)	Crakow (Hohenzollern) Tarnow (Mondet) Lemberg (Merveldt)	Civalart - Rothbacker - von Spetk Tarnow (Neustadter) - Rzeszow (v. Mohr) Dinnersberg - Hertelendy
TOTALE	15 fanteria, 1 cavalleria	27 fanteria, 3 cavalleria
FORZE TERRITORIALI		
Moravia Silesia	Argentau	Teschen LW, Olmutz LW (2), Brunn LW (2), Troppau LW
Galizia (Hohenlohe-Ingelfingen)	Merveldt	Lemberg LW, Crackow LW, Tarnow LW, Sandomierz LW
Boemia (Riesch)	Von Richter Von Oberndorf Schoental Kinski Festung Josefstadt (v. Szénassy) Festung Koeniggraz (De Baut) Sterndahl	Schuettenhofen LW - Strakoniz LW Elbogen LW (2) Sandau LW - Auscha LW Jungbunzlau LW - Liebenau LW 2 2 Prag LW
TOTALE	9 fanteria	23 Landwehr

IN AUSTRIA AND SALZBURG
Field Commander: Gdk Prince Johann Liechtenstein

1st Vienna Division FML Prince Franz Rosenberg-Orsini
Vienna Brigade GM Ignaz Buol von Berenburg
Vienna - IR 2 Hiller – (1st and 2nd Battalions of 6 companies; 3rd Battalion of 4 companies; Grenadier Division)
Vienna – IR 33 vacant Sztáray - (1st and 2nd Battalions of 6 companies; 3rd Battalion of 4 companies; Grenadier Division)
St. Pölten Brigade GM Josef von Mayer
Krems – IR 3 Archduke Carl · (1st and 2nd Battalions of 6 companies; 3rd Battalion of 4 companies; Grenadier Division) St.Pölten – IR 50 Stain - (I and II Battalions of 6 companies; Grenadier Division)
Herzogenburg – K.K. 7th Feldjäger Battalion

2nd Vienna Division FML Baron Carl von Vincent
Vienna Brigade GM Count Nikolaus Weissenwolf
Vienna - IR 49 Kerpen – (1st and 2nd Battalions of 6 companies; 3rd Battalion of 4 companies; Grenadier Division)
Wiener Neustadt - IR 4 Hoch und Deutschmeister – (1st and 2nd Battalions of 6 companies; 3rd Battalion of 4 Company; Grenadier Division)

3rd Vienna Cavalry Division FML Earl Andreas O'Reilly
Vienna Brigade GM Count Josef Radetzky
Vienna – 1st Dragoons Erzherzog Johann – 6 squadrons **Vienna Brigade GM Baron Jozsef Meskó de Felső-Kubinyi** Jetzelsdorf – 8th Hussars Kienmayer – 6 squadrons

Platz Vienna Division FML Archduke Maximilian d'Este
Vienna – Bombardier Korps – 5 companies
Vienna – 2nd Artillery regiment Archduke Maximilian – 13 companies Vienna – Artillerie Handlanger – 2 companies
Bruck an der Leitha – Sappers and Miners – 3 companies Klosterneuburg – Pontoniere – 6 companies

Niederösterreichische Division FML Baron Friedrich Kottulinsky
Brigade GM Federico Bianchi
Mistelbach - IR 39 Duka – (1st and 2nd Battalions of 6 companies; 3rd Battalion of 4 companies; Grenadier Division) Retz - IR 60 Gyulai – (1st and 2nd Battalions of 6 companies; 3rd Battalion of 4 companies; Grenadier Division) **Brigade GM Baron Carl von Riese**
Hainburg - IR 32 Eszterházy – (1st and 2nd Battalions oc 6 companies; 3rd Battalion of 4 companies; Grenadier Division)

Linz Division FML Baron Jozsef von Stipsicz
Linz Brigade GM Count Otto Hohenfeld
Linz - IR 14 Klebek – (1st and 2nd Battalions of 6 companies; 3rd Battalion of 4 companies; Grenadier Division)
Enns - IR 59 Jordis – (1st and 2nd Battalions of 6 companies; 3rd Battalion of 4 companies; Grenadier Division)
Salzburg Brigade GM Baron Ignaz von Legisfeld
Salzburg - IR 45 De Vaux – (I and II Battalions on 6 companies; ½ III Battalions 2 companies; Grenadier Division)
Wels Brigade GM Carl Dollmayer von Provenchères
Wels – 3th Chevaulégers O'Reilly – 8 squadrons Wels – K.K. 8th Feldjäger Battalion.

IN INNER AUSTRIA
Field commander: FML Baron Wilhelm von Kerpen
Graz Platz Brigade GM Anton von Reisner
Graz – 2nd Artillery Regiment Archduke Maximilian –3 companies Graz – Artillerie Handlanger – 2 companies

Styrian 1st Graz Division FML Count Albert Gyulai
Graz Brigade GM chevalier Peter Marchal de Berelat
Judenburg - IR 45 De Vaux – (½ III Battalions 2 Companies see also Salzburg)
Leoben – IR 16 Lusignan - (1st and 2nd Battalions of 6 companies; 3rd Battalion of 4 Companies; Grenadier Division)

Styrian 2nd Graz Division FML Marquis Friedrich Bellegarde Graz
Brigade GM Count Hyeronymus Colloredo-Mansfeld
Graz – IR 61 St.Julien - (1st and 2nd Battalions of 6 companies; 3rd Battalion of 4 Companies; Grenadier Division) Graz – IR 27 Strassoldo - (1st and 2nd Battalions of 6 companies; 3rd Battalion of 4 Companies; Grenadier Division) **Klagenfurt Brigade GM Anton von Gajoli**
Klagenfurt - IR 26 Hohenlohe-Bartenstein – (1st and 2nd Battalions of 6 companies; 3rd Battalion of 4 Companies; Grenadier Division)
Görz (Gorizia) - IR 52 Archduke Franz Carl – (1st and 2nd Battalions of 6 companies; 3rd Battalion of 4 Companies; Grenadier Division)
St. Veit – K.K. 9th Feldjäger battalion

Radkersburg Division FML Baron Vinzenz Knezevich von St.Helena
Laibach Brigade GM Vitalis von Kleinmayrn
Laibach – IR 43 Simbschen – (1st and 2nd Battalions of 6 companies; 3rd Battalion of 4 Companies; Grenadier Division) Pettau – 9th Hussars Frimont – 8 squadrons
Triest Brigade GM Franz Fenner von Fenneberg
Trieste – IR 13 Reisky – (1st and 2nd Battalions of 6 companies; 3rd Battalion of 4 Companies; Grenadier Division)

IN MORAVIA AND SILESIA
Field commander: General der Kavallerie (GdK) Archduke Ferdinand Carl d'Este Troppau

Division FML marquis Hannibal Sommariva
Troppau Brigade GM Josef von Bieber
Odrau - IR 57 Joseph Colloredo – (half III Battalion or 2 Comp.)
Troppau – IR 20 Kaunitz - (I and II Battalions on 6 comp.; half III Battalion or 2 comp.; Grenadier division)
Troppau Brigade GM Fürst Moritz Liechtenstein
Troppau - 3rd Hussars ArchdukeFerdinand – 8 sqns.

Olmütz Division FML count Franz St.Julien-Waldsee
Olmütz Brigade GM Nikolaus von Kayser
Olmütz - IR 12 Manfredini – (I and II Battalions on 6 comp.; half III Battalion or 2 comp.; Grenadier division)
Olmütz - IR 23 Würzburg – (I and II Battalions on 6 comp.; Grenadier division)
Schönberg - IR 15 Zach – (half III Battalion or 2 comp.) Neustadt – 6th Feldjäger battalion
Teschen Brigade GM Georg Croll von Herzberg
Teschen - IR 56 Wenzel Colloredo – (I and II Battalions on 6 comp.; half III Battalion or 2 comp.; Grenadier division) Leipnik – IR 7 Schröder - (I and II Battalions on 6 comp.; half III Battalion or 2 comp.; Grenadier division)

1st Brünn Division FML Guido Lippa von Duba und Kosarczow
Brünn Brigade GM Johann von Prochaska
Prossnitz – IR 1 Kaiser Franz - (I and II Battalions on 6 comp.; half III Battalion or 2 comp.; Grenadier division)
Brünn – IR 29 Lindenau – (I and II Battalions on 6 comp.; half III Battalion or 2 comp.; Grenadier division)
Tischnowitz - IR 10 Anton Mittrowsky – (half III Battalion or 2 comp)

2nd Brünn Division FML marquis Franz Lusignan
Brünn Brigade GM Timothäus von Kérekes
Butschowitz – 5th Feldjäger Battalion Brünn - IR 38 Württemberg – (I and II Battalions on 6 comp.; Grenadier division)
Znaim Brigade GM Josef von Grill
Iglau - IR 8 Archduke Ludwig - (I and II Battalions on 6 comp.; half III Battalion or 2 comp.; Grenadier division) Znaim – IR 22 Coburg - (I and II Battalions on 6 comp.; half III Battalion or 2 comp.; Grenadier division)

Kremsier Division FML Friedrich Erbprinz zu Hessen-Homburg
Kremsier Brigade GM Josef Rheinwald von Waldegg
Kremsier - IR 40 vacant Josef Mittrowsky – (I and II Battalions on 6 comp.; half III Battalion or 2 comp.; Grenadier division)
Hradisch Cavalry Brigade GM Armand von Nordmann
Gaya – 3rd Uhlans Archduke Carl – 8 sqns. Ungarische Brod – 7th Hussars Liechtenstein – 8 sqns.

Olmütz Division FML baron Carl Rouvroy
Olmütz – 3rd artillery regiment Rouvroy – 13 comp. Olmütz – artillery Handlanger Battalion – 2 comp. Olmütz – Sappers and Miners – 2 comp.
Olmütz – Pioneers – 5 comp.

IN GALICIA-LODOMERIA
Field commander: GdK Graf Heinrich Bellegarde

Crakow Division FML Friedrich Franz prince zu Hohenzollern-Hechingen
Crakow Brigade GM count Carl Civalart
Solec - IR 50 Stain – (III battalion on 4 companies)
Sandomierz – IR 34 Davidovich - (I and II Battalions of 6 companies; III Battalion of 4 companies; Grenadier division) Pinczów – IR 7 Schröder – (half of III Battalion 2 companies) [2]
Neu-Slupia – IR 22 Coburg – (half of III Battalion 2 companies) Konsk - 4th Hussars Hessen Homburg – 8 squadrons
Crakow Brigade GM Franz Schulz von Rothbacker
Crakow - IR 9 Czartoryski – (I and II Battalions or 6 companies; Grenadier division) Kety - IR 57 Joseph Colloredo – (half of III Battalion or 2 companies)
Kalwarya - IR 15 Zach – (half of III Battalion or 2 companies)
Niegardów - IR 10 Anton Mittrowsky – (half of III Battalion or 2 companies)
Crakow Brigade GM Sebastian Solan Baron von Speth
Crakow - IR 55 Reuss Greitz – (I and II Battalions or 6 companies; Grenadier division) Crakow – 5th Cuirassier Sommariva – 6 squadrons

Tarnów Division FML Ferdinand von Mondet
Tarnów Brigade GM Johann von Neustädter
Bochnia - IR 30 De Ligne – (I and II Battalions or 6 companies; Grenadier division) Tarnów - IR 41 Kottulinsky – (I and II Battalions or 6 companies; Grenadier division) Neusandez - IR 8 Archduke Ludwig - (half of III Battalion or 2 companies)
Mielec - IR 12 Manfredini - (half of III Battalion or 2 companies)

Krosno - IR 40 vacant Josef Mittrowsky – (half of III Battalion or 2 companies) Dukla – IR 29 Lindenau - (half III battalion or 2 companies)
Myslenice - IR 56 Wenzel Colloredo – (half of III Battalion or 2 companies)
Rzeszów Brigade GM Baron Johann von Mohr
Lancut – IR 1 Kaiser Franz - (half III battalion or 2 companies) Jaroslau - IR 9 Czartoryski – (III battalion on 4 companies) Rzeszów – IR 20 Kaunitz - (half of III Battalion or 2 companies) Jaroslau – 1st Chevaulégers Kaiser Franz – 8 squadrons Rzeszów – 7th Cuirassiers Lothringen – 6 squadrons

Lemberg Division FML Earl Maximilian Merveldt
Lemberg Brigade GM Baron Peter von Dinnersberg Lemberg - IR 30 De Ligne – (III battalion on 4 companies) Lemberg - IR 63 Baillet – (III battalion on 4 companies) Lemberg - IR 24 Strauch – (III battalion on 4 companies) Tarnopol - IR 46 Chasteler – (III battalion on 4 companies)
Lemberg Brigade GM Gabriel (Gábor) von Hertelendy Zamość - IR 23 Würzburg – (III battalion on 4 companies) Lublin - IR 55 Reuss Greitz – (III battalion on 4 companies) Konsko Wola - IR 38 Württemberg – (III battalion on 4 companies) Siedlec – 1st Hussars Kaiser Franz – 8 squadrons
Crakow artillery
Crakow – 1st Artillery Regiment Schuhay – 2 companies Crakow – 3rd Artillery Regiment Rouvroy – 1 companies

JANUARY 1809 - TERRITORIAL FORCES

RESIDENT UNITS IN MORAVIA - SILESIA
after beginning of campaign and before commitment of the Landwehr Battalions

Territorial commander (interim): FZM count Argenteau
Vice-commander and Landwehrinspektor: FML baron Lelio Spannocchi

Teschen Territorial Landwehr Brigade GM Johann Pietsch von Wollishofen
Teschen – Depot Wenzel Colloredo – 1 company Silesian Borders – 1st Landwehr Battalion Prerau Silesian Borders – 1st Landwehr Battalion Teschen Jablunkau – 2nd Landwehr Battalion Teschen Friedeck – 2nd Landwehr Battalion Prerau
Olmütz Territorial Landwehr Brigade GM baron Franz von Bojakowsky-Knurow
Olmütz – Depot Manfredini – 1 company Olmütz – Depot Kaiser – 1 company Olmütz – Depot Zach – 1 company Olmütz – 3rd Landwehr Battalion Prerau Olmütz – 1st Landwehr Battalion Iglau Olmütz – 1st Landwehr Battalion Znaim Olmütz – 2nd Landwehr Battalion Znaim Olmütz – 3rd Landwehr Battalion Brünn
Olmütz Territorial Landwehr Brigade GM Baron Johann Joseph Wodniansky von Wildenfeld
Leipnik – Depot Schröder – 1 company Sternberg – Depot Kaunitz – 1 company Prerau – Depot Josef Colloredo – 1 company Olmütz – 1st Landwehr Battalion Olmütz Schönberg – 2nd Landwehr Battalion Olmütz Hohenstadt – 3rd Landwehr Battalion Olmütz Mährische Weisskirchen – 2nd Landwehr Battalion Hradisch
Hradisch Territorial Landwehr Brigade GM count Du Noyer Ungarische Hradisch – Depot Josef Mittrowsky – 1 company Gaya – Reserve Squadrons 3rd Uhlans Archduke Carl Ungarische Brod – Reserve Squadrons Cuirassiers Archduke Franz Strassnitz – 1st Landwehr Battalion Hradisch Ungarische Hradisch – 3rd Landwehr Battalion Hradisch
Brünn Territorial Landwehr Brigade GM baron Franz Jordan Pöck
Brünn citadel – Depot Lindenau – 1 company Brünn – Depot Anton Mittrowsky – 1 company Iglau – Depot Archduke Ludwig – 1 company Znaim – Depot Coburg – 1 company
Brünn Territorial Landwehr Brigade Oberst count Chorinsky
Brünn – 1st Landwehr Battalion Brünn Brünn – 2nd Landwehr Battalion Brünn Brünn – 4th Landwehr Battalion Brünn Iglau – 2nd Landwehr Battalion Iglau
Troppau Territorial Landwehr Brigade Oberst von Romberg
Odrau – Depot Company 5th Feldjäger Battalion Troppau – Depot Company 6th Feldjäger Battallionalion Troppau – Reserve Squadrons Archduke Ferdinand Hussars Troppau – 1st Landwehr Battalion Troppau Freudenthal – 2nd Landwehr Battalion Troppau Würbenthal - 3rd Landwehr Battalion Troppau Hof – 4th Landwehr Battalion Olmütz Kunzendorf – 5th Landwehr Battalion Olmütz At the Border were 4 Cordon companies.

RESIDENT UNITS IN GALICIA
Territorial commander (interim): FML Friedrich Karl Wilhelm Prince von Hohenlohe- Ingelfingen
Vice-commander ad Latus: FML Earl Maximilian Merveldt

Galician Territorial Division Earl Merveldt
Lemberg Brigade GM Anton Bicking von Sobinak
Lemberg - IR 30 De Ligne – (2 companies) Lemberg - IR 63 Baillet – (2 companies) Lemberg - IR 24 Strauch – (2 companies) Lemberg - IR 46 Chasteler – (2 companies) Lemberg - IR 58 Beaulieu – (2 companies) Lemberg - IR 41 Kottulinsky – (2 companies) Jaroslau - IR 9 Czartoryski – (2 companies) Sambor - IR 44 Bellegarde – (2 companies) Dukla – IR 29 Lindenau - (1 company) Zolkiew – 12th Palatinal Hussars– 1 squadron
Crakow Brigade GM Carl Starczynsky von Pittkau Neusandez - IR 8 Erzherzog Ludwig – (1 company) Tarnów - IR 12 Manfredini - (1 company)
Krosno - IR 40 vacant Josef Mittrowsky – (1 company) Myslenice - IR 56 Wenzel Colloredo – (1 company) Kety - IR 57 Joseph Colloredo – (1 company) Kalwarya - IR 15 Zach – (1 company)
Zator - IR 10 Anton Mittrowsky – (1 company) Crakow – 1st Chevaulégers Kaiser Franz – 1 squadron **Tarnów Brigade GM Bernhard von Grosser** Zamość - IR 23 Würzburg – (2 companies)
Zamość - IR 55 Reuss Greitz – (2 companies) Lublin - IR 38 Württemberg – (2 companies) **Sándomierz Brigade FML Ignaz von Eggermann** Lancut – IR 1 Kaiser Franz - (1 company)
Rzeszów – IR 20 Kaunitz - (1 company) Sándomierz – IR 7 Schröder – (1 company) Sándomierz - IR 50 Stain – (2 companies) Sándomierz – IR 22 Coburg – (1 company)
Total of Galician dGivision – 36 infantry companies or 7480 men – 2 cavalry squadrons or 125 men.

MILITARY TERRITORIAL DEFENSE AND AUSTRIAN RESIDENT UNITS IN BOHEMIA
at the beginning of campaign and before complete commitment of the Landwehr battalions
Territorial commander (ad interim): FZM Count Riesch
Vice-commander and Landwehrinspektor: FML Baron von Loudon

Territorial Division GM Johann von Richter
Schüttenhofen Landwehr Brigade oberst Rosenhayn
Janowitz – 1st Landwehr battalion Klattau Welhartitz – 2nd Landwehr battalion Klattau Schüttenhofen – 3rd Landwehr battalion Klattau Bergreichenstein – 3rd Landwehr battalion Prachin
Winterberg – 4th Landwehr battalion Prachin
Strakonitz Landwehr Brigade GM Johann von Richter Frauenberg – 1st Landwehr battalion Budweis Budweis – 2nd Landwehr battalion Budweis Höritz – 3th Landwehr battalion Budweis Prachatitz – 1st Landwehr battalion Prachin Strakonitz – 2nd Landwehr battalion Prachin
Wodnan – IR 54 Froon Depotdivision– 2 companies Pisek – IR 25 Zedzwitz Depotdivision– 2 companies Horazdiowitz – Reserve (Depot) squadron Uhlans Schwarzemberg

Territorial Division GM Johann Friedrich von Oberndorf
Elbogen Landwehr Brigade oberst von Ullrich territory – 1st Landwehr battalion Elbogen territory – 2nd Landwehr battalion Elbogen territory – 3rd Landwehr battalion Elbogen **Elbogen Landwehr Brigade GM von Oberndorf** territory – 1st Landwehr battalion Pilsen
territory – 2nd Landwehr battalion Pilsen territory – 3rd Landwehr battalion Pilsen Elbogen   IR 35 Erzherzog Johann Depotdivision– 2 companies

Territorial Division GM Johann von Schöntal
Sandau Landwehr Brigade Oberst Count Waldstein
Bautzen – 2nd Landwehr battalion Leitmeritz Tetschen – 3rd Landwehr battalion Leitmeritz
Böhmische Kamnitz – 5th Landwehr battalion Leitmeritz Böhmische Leipa – 1st Landwehr battalion Bunzlau Sandau – 4th Landwehr battalion Bunzlau
Auscha Landwehr Brigade GM Johann von Schöntal (later GM Baron Am-Ende)
Brozan – 1st Landwehr battalion Saaz Lobositz – 2nd Landwehr battalion Saaz Theresienstadt – 1st Landwehr battalion Rakonitzudin – 2nd Landwehr battalion Rakonitz Theresienstadt – 1st Landwehr battalion Leitmeritz Theresienstadt – 4th Landwehr battalion Leitmeritz Theresienstadt – 6th Landwehr battalion Bunzlau Theresienstadt – IR 36 Kolowrat Depotdivision– 2 companies Theresienstadt – IR 17 Reuss-Plauen Depotdivision – 2 companies Auscha – Depot companies 3rd Feldjäger battalion Theresienstadt – Reserve (Depot) squadron Klenau chevaulégers

Territorial Division GM Count Carl Kinsky
Jungbunzlau Landwehr Brigade Oberst Novak Weisswasser – IR 42 Erbach Depotdivision– 2 companies Jungbunzlau – IR 11 Rainer Depotdivision– 2 companies Bakow (then Brüx) – Depot companies 1st Feldjäger battalion Münchengrätz – Reserve (Depot) squadron Merveldt Uhlans Jungbunzlau – Reserve (Depot) squadron Riesch Dragoons
Liebenau Landwehr Brigade GM Count Carl Kinsky Reichenberg – 2nd Landwehr battalion Bunzlau Turnau – 3rd Landwehr battalion Bunzlau Liebenau – 5th Landwehr battalion Bunzlau Böhmische Aicha – 2nd Landwehr battalion Kaurzim Hühnerwasser – 3rd Landwehr battalion Časlau
Festungkommando Josefstadt GM Johann von Szénassy
Hohenelbe – 1st Landwehr battalion Bydzow Kopildno – 2nd Landwehr battalion Bydzow Jičin – 3rd Landwehr battalion Bydzow Josefstadt – 4th Landwehr battalion Bydzow Josefstadt – 1st Landwehr battalion Königgrätz Politz – 2nd Landwehr battalion Königgrätz Josefstadt – 3rd Landwehr battalion Königgrätz Geiersberg – 4th Landwehr battalion Königgrätz Königgrätz – 5th Landwehr battalion Königgrätz Josefstadt – IR 18 Stuart Depotdivision– 2 companies Josefstadt – IR 21 Rohan Depotdivision– 2 companies Josefstadt (Jaromirz) – Depot companies 2nd Feldjäger battalion Josefstadt – Reserve (Depot) squadron Blankenstein Hussars
Festungkommando Königgrätz GM Baron Franz Peter Ignaz De Baut
Polička – 1st Landwehr battalion Chrudim Chotzen – 2nd Landwehr battalion Chrudim Königgrätz – 3rd Landwehr battalion Chrudim Chrudim – 4th Landwehr battalion Chrudim Königgrätz – IR 28 Frelich Depotdivision– 2 companies Königgrätz (then Prachatitz) – Depot companies 4th Feldjäger battalion
Territorial Division FML Baron Karl Joseph von Sterndhal
Prague Landwehr Brigade GM Count Franz Kinsky
Prague – 1st Landwehr battalion Prague Prague – 2nd Landwehr battalion Prague Prague – 1st Landwehr battalion Beraun Prague – 2nd Landwehr battalion Beraun Prague – 1st Landwehr battalion Kaurzim Prague – 1st Landwehr battalion Časlau Prague – 2nd Landwehr battalion Časlau Prague – 1st Landwehr battalion Tabor
Prague – IR 47 Vogelsang Depotdivision– 2 companies
Alt-Bunzlau – Reserve (Depot) squadron Rosemberg chevaulégers Detached in the Border – 6 Kordon companies. [ii]
At Prague it was organized an open bureau (an enlistment table or Werbtisch), where volunteers could enroll under a fee of 15 fl. (Konventionsmünze). The border Circles were now occupied by highest Corps Officers: Bellegarde at Saaz (I Corps), Hohenzollern at Prague (III Corps), prince Rosenberg at Pisek (IV Corps) and the Archduke Louis at Budweis (VI Corps). The Field commander of the Bohemian army was the Feldzeugmeister (FZM) Count Carl Kolowrat-Krakowsy, who went in war as commander of the II Corps.

SPRING 1809 AUSTRIAN RESIDENT UNITS IN AUSTRIA - SALZBURG

Territorial commander (interim): FML Count Andreas O'Reilly
Vice-commander and Landwehrinspektor: FML Baron Anton von Mittrowsky
Salzburg Brigade GM Baron von Legisfeld Salzburg – 1st Landwehr Battalion Salzburg Salzburg – 2nd Landwehr Battalion Salzburg Salzburg –3rd Landwehr Battalion Salzburg Salzburg – 4th Landwehr Battalion Salzburg Salzburg – Depot De Vaux – 1 company
Schärding Brigade Oberst von Nesslinger
Strasswalchen – 1st Landwehr Battalion Hausrück viertel Strasswalchen – 2nd Landwehr Battalion Hausrück viertel Schärding – 3rd Landwehr Battalion Hausrück viertel Schärding – 1st Landwehr Battalion Innviertel Braunau – 2nd Landwehr Battalion Innviertel Salzburg – 3rd Landwehr Battalion Innviertel Braunau – 1st Landwehr Battalion Traunviertel Herzogenburg – Depot 7th Feldjäger – 1 company
Linz Brigade GM Count Sinzendorf (at Neufelden)
Linz platz Commander: GM Rüffer in Mühlviertel – 1st Landwehr Battalion Mühlviertel in Mühlviertel – 2nd Landwehr Battalion Mühlviertel in Mühlviertel –3rd Landwehr Battalion Mühlviertel in Mühlviertel – 4th Landwehr Battalion Mühlviertel Braunau – 2nd Landwehr Battalion Traunviertel Braunau – 3rd Landwehr Battalion Traunviertel Schärding – 4th Landwehr Battalion Traunviertel Schärding –4th Landwehr Battalion Hausrück viertel Wels – Depot 8th Feldjäger – 1 company Linz – Depot Division 14 Klebek – 2 companies Linz – Depot Division 59 Jordis – 2 companies Mauthausen –3rd Landwehr Battalion Ober Wienerwald Mauthausen – 4th Landwehr Battalion Ober Wienerwald Krems Brigade GM von Albert

Linz – 1st Landwehr Battalion Ober Mannhartsberg
Walpensdorf – 2nd Landwehr Battalion Ober Mannhartsberg Linz –3rd Landwehr Battalion Ober Mannhartsberg Hollenburg – 4th Landwehr Battalion Ober Mannhartsberg Linz– 5th Landwehr Battalion Ober Mannhartsberg Krems – Depot Division 3 Archduke Carl – 2 companies St.Pölten – Depot Division 49 Kerpen – 2 companies Wilhelmsburg – Depot 9th Feldjäger – 1 company

1st Vienna territorial Brigade GM Count Paar Grafendorf –1st Landwehr Battalion Ober Wienerwald Wilhelmsburg – 2nd Landwehr Battalion Ober Wienerwald Mechters – 1st Landwehr Battalion Unter Wienerwald Vienna – 2nd Landwehr Battalion Unter Wienerwald Böheimkirchen –3rd Landwehr Battalion Unter Wienerwald Spratzen – 4th Landwehr Battalion Unter Wienerwald Vienna– 5th Landwehr Battalion Unter Wienerwald Pihra– 6th Landwehr Battalion Unter Wienerwald Pottenbrunn – 1st Landwehr Battalion Unter Mannhartsberg St. Andrä – 2nd Landwehr Battalion Unter Mannhartsberg Gemeinlebarn –3rd Landwehr Battalion Unter Mannhartsberg Traismauer – 4th Landwehr Battalion Unter Mannhartsberg

2nd Vienna territorial Brigade GM Ambschel
Penzing – Reserve Squadron Albert Cuirassiers – 1 squadron
Vienna – Reserve Squadron ArchdukeFerdinand Cuirassiers – 1 squadron Vienna – Reserve Squadron Hohenzollern Cuirassiers – 1 squadron Vienna – Reserve Squadron O'Reilly Chevaulégers – 1 squadron Vienna – Reserve Squadron Archduke Johann Dragoons– 1 squadron Vienna – Reserve Squadron Württemberg Dragoons– 1 squadron Wiener Neustadt – Reserve Squadron Levenehr Dragoons– 1 squadron

3rd Vienna territorial Brigade GM Ambschel
Vienna – Depot Division 4 Deutschmeister – 2 companies Also 10 Kordon companies at the Borders

SPRING 1809 AUSTRIAN RESIDENT UNITS IN INNER AUSTRIA

Territorial commander (interim): FML Baron Wilhelm von Kerpen
Vice-commander and Landwehrinspektor: FML Baron Guido Ferdinand Lippa von Duba und Kosarczow

Graz territorial Division FML Baron Guido Ferdinand Lippa von Duba und Kosarczow

45146 men, 80 horses

Triest Brigade GM Count Alois von Gavassini
Görz – 1st Landwehr Battalion Görz Tolmein – 2nd Landwehr Battalion Görz Trieste –1st Landwehr Battalion Stadtmiliz Triest Trieste – 2nd Landwehr Battalion Territorial Miliz Triest Pisino – 1st Landwehr Battalion Adelsberg Lippa – 2nd Landwehr Battalion Adelsberg Adelsberg – 3rd Landwehr Battalion Adelsberg Loitsch – 4th Landwehr Battalion Adelsberg

Laibach Brigade GM Jozsef de Munkácsy
Laibach – 1st Landwehr Battalion Laibach Radmannsdorf – 2nd Landwehr Battalion Laibach Laibach – 3rd Landwehr Battalion Laibach Rudolfswerth (Neustädtl) – 1st Landwehr Battalion Rudolfswerth Gottschee – 2nd Landwehr Battalion Rudolfswerth Tschernembl – 3rd Landwehr Battalion Rudolfswerth Rudolfswerth – 4th Landwehr Battalion Rudolfswerth

Klagenfurt Brigade GM Franz Fenner von Fenneberg
Villach – 1st Landwehr Battalion Villach Sachsenburg – 2nd Landwehr Battalion Villach Klagenfurt – 1st Landwehr Battalion Klagenfurt Althofen – 2nd Landwehr Battalion Klagenfurt Lavamünd – 3rd Landwehr Battalion Klagenfurt

Marburg Brigade GM Ritter Peter von Lutz
Cilli – 1st Landwehr Battalion Cilli Peilenstein – 2nd Landwehr Battalion Cilli Marburg –1st Landwehr Battalion Marburg Pettau – 2nd Landwehr Battalion Marburg

Leoben Brigade Oberst Auracher
Mürzzuschlag – 1st Landwehr Battalion Bruck Leoben – 2nd Landwehr Battalion Bruck Judenburg –1st Landwehr Battalion Judenburg Rottenmann – 2nd Landwehr Battalion Judenburg

Graz Brigade GM Baron Ignaz Anton Sebottendorf von der Rose
Graz – 1st Landwehr Battalion Graz Eggenburg – 2nd Landwehr Battalion Graz Wilden –3rd Landwehr Battalion Graz Fürstenfeld – 4th Landwehr Battalion Graz Hartberg– 5th Landwehr Battalion Graz

Graz Reserve Brigade FML Baron Guido Ferdinand Lippa von Duba und Kosarczow
Graz – Depot Division 27 Strassoldo – 2 companies Graz – Depot Division 45 De Vaux – 2 companies Graz – IR 16 Lusignan – (1st and 2nd Battalions) Graz – Depot-squadron Frimont Hussars – 1 squadron Graz – Depot Division Grazer – 2 companies Bruck – Depot Division Brucker – 2 companies Judenburg – Depot Division Ju-

denburger – 2 companies Marburg – Depot Division Marburger – 2 companies Cilli – Depot Division Cillier – 2 companies Graz – Grenz Cordon – 3 companies

Laibach Reserve Brigade FML prince Franz Maria Johann Josef Hermann von Khevenhüller-Metsch
Laibach – Grenz Cordon – 6 companies Trieste – Depot Division 13 Reisky – 2 companies Laibach – Depot Division 43 Simbschen – 2 companies Laibach – Depot Division Laibacher – 2 companies Rudolfswerth – Depot Division Rudolfswerther – 2 companies Trieste – Depot Division Triester – 2 companies Görz – Depot Division Görzer – 2 companies Adelsberg – Depot Division Adelsberger – 2 companies

Klagenfurt Brigade GM Anton Vogl (Vogel)
Klagenfurt – Depot Division 26 Hohenlohe – 2 companies Klagenfurt – Depot Division Klagenfurter – 2 companies Villach – Depot Division Villacher – 2 companies Klagenfurt – Grenz Cordon – 3 companies

AUSTRIAN ADRIATIC SEA FLEET - TRIEST, APRIL 23, 1809

GeneralMajor Count Josef L'Espine
Fleet 1 – Vs. Dalmatia under command of the Oberstleutnant Nepomuk Maidich
Brig "Dolfino" Schooner "Indagatore" Trabaccolo (Trabakel) "Dromedario" Felucca "Mora" 12 Gunboats and Sloops
Fleet 2 – Vs. Venice under command of the Oberstleutnants Matthias Flanagan
Corvette „Armonia" (rented by private owners) Brig "Eolo" Brig "Pilade" sent on April 22 in an expedition to Sicily Brig "Oreste" Trabaccolo "Bravo" Trabaccolo "Cammello" Large tartane "Isabella" 8 Gunboats and Sloops

AUSTRIAN RESIDENT UNITS IN MORAVIA-SILESIA

after Landwehr committment
Territorial commander (interim): FMZ Count Argenteau
Vice-commander and Landwehrinspektor: FML baron Lelio Spannocchi

Moravian Territorial Division FML count Franz St. Julien Waldsee Troppau Territorial Landwehr Brigade GM von Pietsch
Odrau – Depot Company 5th Feldjäger Battalions Troppau – Depot Company 6th Feldjäger Battalion Teschen – Depot Wenzel Colloredo – 1 company Troppau – Reserve Squadrons ArchdukeFerdinand Hussars Silesian Borders – 1st Landwehr Battalion Teschen Jablunkau – 2nd Landwehr Battalion Teschen Troppau – 1st Landwehr Battalion Troppau Freudenthal – 2nd Landwehr Battalion Troppau Würbenthal - 3rd Landwehr Battalion Troppau

Olmütz Territorial Landwehr Brigade GM baron von Bojakowsky
Olmütz – Depot Manfredini – 1 company Olmütz – Depot Kaiser – 1 company Olmütz – Depot Zach – 1 company Olmütz – 1st Landwehr Battalion Olmütz Olmütz – 1st Moravian Volunteers Olmütz – 1st Landwehr Battalion Prerau Olmütz – 2nd Landwehr Battalion Prerau Olmütz – 3rd Landwehr Battalion Prerau

Olmütz Territorial Landwehr Brigade GM Baron von Wodniansky
Olmütz – Depot Schröder – 1 company Olmütz – Depot Kaunitz – 1 company Olmütz – Depot Josef Colloredo – 1 company Olmütz – 2nd Landwehr Battalion Olmütz Olmütz – 3rd Landwehr Battalion Olmütz Olmütz – 4th Landwehr Battalion Olmütz Olmütz – 3rd Landwehr Battalion Brünn

Hradisch Territorial Landwehr Brigade GM count Du Noyer Ungarische Hradisch – Depot Josef Mittrowsky – 1 company Gaya – Reserve Squadrons 3rd Uhlans ArchdukeCarl
Ungarische Brod – Reserve Squadrons Cuirassiers ArchdukeFranz Strassnitz – 1st Landwehr Battalion Hradisch Mährische Weisskirchen – 2nd Landwehr Battalion Hradisch Ungarische Hradisch – 3rd Landwehr Battalion Hradisch

Brünn Territorial Landwehr Brigade GM baron Franz Jordan Pöck
Brünn citadel   Depot Lindenau – 1 company Brünn – Depot Anton Mirtrowsky – 1 company Brünn – 2nd Moravian Volunteers

Brünn Territorial Landwehr Brigade Oberst Count Chorinsky
Brünn – 1st Landwehr Battalion Brünn Brünn – 2nd Landwehr Battalion Brünn Brünn – 4th Landwehr Battalion Brünn

Znaim Territorial Landwehr Brigade Oberst von Romberg
Iglau – Depot Archduke Ludwig – 1 company Znaim – Depot Coburg – 1 company Znaim – 1st Landwehr Battalion Znaim Znaim – 2nd Landwehr Battalion Znaim Iglau – 1st Landwehr Battalion Iglau Iglau – 2nd Landwehr Battalion Iglau

MAY 1809 AUSTRIAN RESIDENT UNITS IN AUSTRIA - SALZBURG

Territorial commander (interim): FML Count Andreas O'Reilly Vice-comm. and Landwehrinspektor: FML Baron Anton von Mittrowsky

38315 men, 440 horses

Landwehr Division FML Baron Anton von Mittrowsky Salzburg Brigade GM Baron von Legisfeld
Salzburg – 1st Landwehr Battalion Salzburg Salzburg – 2nd Landwehr Battalion Salzburg Salzburg –3rd Landwehr Battalion Salzburg Salzburg – 4th Landwehr Battalion Salzburg Salzburg – Depot De Vaux – 1 company

Ried Brigade Oberst Hermann von Nesslinger
territory – 1st Landwehr Battalion Hausrück viertel territory – 2nd Landwehr Battalion Hausrück viertel territory –3rd Landwehr Battalion Hausrück viertel territory – 1st Landwehr Battalion Innviertel territory – 2nd Landwehr Battalion Innviertel territory – 3rd Landwehr Battalion Innviertel territory – 1st Landwehr Battalion Traunviertel

Linz Brigade GM count Sinzendorf
Linz platz Commander: GM Rüffer territory – 1st Landwehr Battalion Mühlviertel territory – 2nd Landwehr Battalion Mühlviertel territory –3rd Landwehr Battalion Mühlviertel territory – 4th Landwehr Battalion Mühlviertel territory – 2nd Landwehr Battalion Traunviertel territory – 3rd Landwehr Battalion Traunviertel territory – 4th Landwehr Battalion Traunviertel - territory –4th Landwehr Battalion Hausrück viertel Wels – Depot 8th Feldjäger – 1 company Linz – DepotDivision 14 Klebek – 2 companies Linz – DepotDivision 59 Jordis – 2 companies Mauthausen –3rd Landwehr Battalion Ober Wienerwald Mauthausen – 4th Landwehr Battalion Ober Wienerwald

Krems Brigade GM von Ulbrecht
Linz – 1st Landwehr Battalion Ober Mannhartsberg Walpensdorf – 2nd Landwehr Battalion Ober Mannhartsberg Linz –3rd Landwehr Battalion Ober Mannhartsberg Hollenburg – 4th Landwehr Battalion Ober Mannhartsberg Linz– 5th Landwehr Battalion Ober Mannhartsberg Krems – DepotDivision 3 Archduke Carl – 2 companies St.Pölten – DepotDivision 49 Kerpen – 2 companies Wilhelmsburg – Depot 9th Feldjäger – 1 company Wilhelmsburg – Depot 7th Feldjäger – 1 company

1st Vienna territorial Brigade GM Count Paar
Grafendorf –1st Landwehr Battalion Ober Wienerwald Wilhelmsburg – 2nd Landwehr Battalion Ober Wienerwald Mechters – 1st Landwehr Battalion Unter Wienerwald Vienna – 2nd Landwehr Battalion Unter Wienerwald Böheimkirchen –3rd Landwehr Battalion Unter Wienerwald Spratzen – 4th Landwehr Battalion Unter Wienerwald Vienna– 5th Landwehr Battalion Unter Wienerwald Pihra– 6th Landwehr Battalion Unter Wienerwald Pottenbrunn – 1st Landwehr Battalion Unter Mannhartsberg St. Andrä – 2nd Landwehr Battalion Unter Mannhartsberg Gemeinlebarn –3rd Landwehr Battalion Unter Mannhartsberg Traismauer – 4th Landwehr Battalion Unter Mannhartsberg

2nd Vienna territorial Brigade GM Ambschel
Penzing – Reserve squadron Albert Cuirassiers – 1 squadron Vienna – Reserve squadron Archduke Ferdinand Cuirassiers – 1 squadron Vienna – Reserve squadron Hohenzollern Cuirassiers – 1 squadron Vienna – Reserve squadron O'Reilly Chevaulégers – 1 squadron Vienna – Reserve squadron Archduke Johann Dragoons– 1 squadron Vienna – Reserve squadron Württemberg Dragoons– 1 squadron Wiener Neustadt – Reserve squadron Levenehr Dragoons– 1 squadron

3rd Vienna territorial Brigade GM Ambschel
Vienna – Depot Division 4 Deutschmeister – 1 company

▲ Austrian jäger 1807-1815. From Ottenfeld artwork

TITOLI PUBBLICATI - ALREADY PUBLISHING

WWW.SOLDIERSHOP.COM   WWW.BOOKMOON.COM

SOLDIERS&WEAPONS 030

Made in the USA
Las Vegas, NV
23 March 2025

19997455R00071